D0425677

reading and reader development

the pleasure of reading

reading

and

reader development

the pleasure of reading

Judith Elkin
Briony Train
Debbie Denham

facet publishing

Published by
Facet Publishing
7 Ridgmount Street
London WC1E 7AE

Facet Publishing (formerly Library Association Publishing) is wholly owned by CILIP: the Chartered Institute of Library and Information Professionals.

First published 2003

British Library Cataloguing in Publication Data
A catalogue record for this book is available from the British Library.

ISBN 1-85604-467-X

Typeset in 9.5/13pt New Baskerville and Franklin Gothic Condensed
by Facet Publishing.
Printed and made in Great Britain by MPG Books Ltd, Bodmin, Cornwall.

Contents

Introduction

The death of reading has been predicted for many years. Each new technological revolution brings with it yet another doom-laden prediction about the demise of the book in anything other than an electronic or online version. This book attempts to redress the balance by exploring the role of books and reading in today's society, offering a comprehensive exploration of readers and reading for pleasure. It provides timely evidence of the value of reading in personal, cultural and social development, and presents case studies and reading trends involving both the reading adult and the reading child.

For the first time, the opportunity is taken to consider the theory of reading within the context of current reading initiatives and reader development practice. No monograph currently exists that combines new definitions of reader development theory with research and practice-based initiatives worldwide. Texts promoting reading as a leisure activity have tended to focus on reaching an exclusively child-based or adult-based target audience. However, the authors recognize that adults and children are equally affected by reading for pleasure, both as individual readers and as members of groups. The subjects of this book are therefore all members of society, whatever their age, social background or special need.

The book combines the authors' considerable academic and practice-based knowledge and expertise in the broadly defined area of reading for pleasure. In line with their interest in the application of theory to practice, it builds on both prior and new research on reading and reader development, while aiming to be accessible and, above all, relevant to both national and international practitioners, presenting highly transferable models of good practice.

A strategic approach was undertaken by the authors to ensure that practice and theory were fully integrated. This involved interviewing key individuals either face to face, by phone or by e-mail and seeking written contributions or case studies from a range of significant players in the field of reading and reader development in the UK. Thus individual chapters include original contributions, inter alia, from Liz Attenborough, Daniel Brown, Genevieve Clarke, Jonathan Douglas, Tom Forrest, Miranda McKearney, Gary McKeone, Beverley Mathias, Rachel Van Riel, Rosemary Stones, Astrid Todnem; authors, Jonathan Coe, Farrukh Dhondy, Mary Hoffman, Beverley Naidoo; publishers, Mishti Chatterji, Guy Pringle, Verna Wilkins; librarians,

Catherine Blanshard, Helen Brazier, Linda Corrigan, Jane Faux, Dinah Gough, Grace Kempster, John Lake, Geoff Mills, John Readman, June Turner, John Vincent, Sue Wilkinson, Doreen Williams; academics, Gayner Eyre, Jenny Hartley, Robert Hidderley, Marian Koren, Glen Mynott, Pauline Rafferty, Bob Usherwood, Margaret Wallis. This wealth of contributors from the UK was balanced, through a comprehensive literature survey, with significant reference to other writers, particularly in the USA and Europe. In addition, Chapters 4 and 6 take a deliberately international approach to reading and reader development. For most developing countries, reader development, even reading for pleasure, as can be seen in Chapter 6, is a very new concept.

The authors found, as they wrote the book, that in many areas the early pioneers of working with books and promoting reading, again particularly in the UK, USA and Australia – certainly before the late 1980s – related to children and their reading needs. If there is an imbalance in the book, it is as a result of far more being available in the literature about the educational and literacy needs of the child than about those of other sections of the population. It is fair to say that much of what is included here about children and their reading and initiatives associated with the child is readily transferable to adults or to special groups.

Inevitably, individual chapters have different voices, reflecting the particular approaches and expertise of the three authors and the voices of individuals contributing to chapters.

Chapter 1 presents a discursive overview of the reader, looking at why and where people read and what motivates individuals to read, whether children or adults. It explores the joys and pleasures of reading for the individual from the perspective of many writers and commentators, acknowledging that reading is, on the whole, a very private, intimate and unique experience. It also analyses the benefits of reading, deliberately bringing together a wide variety of views and perspectives on reading in different societies and cultures. The role of story in everyday life, and the growth of reader development and how libraries are supporting initiatives, are introduced.

Chapter 2 looks at the dramatic growth in reader development in recent years, with adult readers in particular. This growth is considered both in terms of its approach to changing library service delivery, and in the context of its social benefits. Definitions of the term reader development as opposed to reading development are discussed. Themes frequently used in definitions of reader development are then presented, such as social inclusion, cultural change and the readers' advisory interview (readers' advisory), and a number of reader development projects described in order to exemplify the various facets of these definitions. The recent increase in reader development activity has meant that public library authorities throughout the UK have become involved in a wide range of project-based promotional initiatives. This chapter considers the impact of these on current practice and investigates to what extent sustainable cultural change has occurred in service provision, presenting transferable models of good practice.

Chapter 3 looks at the growth of reading research in the fields of literacy and reader development that has taken place as a direct consequence of recent UK government initiatives. A large amount of government and partnership funding has been allocated both to raising literacy standards, via the implementation of the National Literacy Strategy, and to promoting reading as a leisure activity, via the National Year of Reading, the National Reading Campaign and through the DCMS/Wolfson Public Libraries Challenge Fund. The growth of recent collaborative initiatives such as World Book Day and National Poetry Day provides a basis for the discussion of partnership working. The importance of advocacy is considered through the work of The Reading Agency and the London Libraries Development Agency.

Chapter 4 addresses the issue of how reading for pleasure is perceived internationally. Evidence is taken in part from the IFLA (International Federation of Library Associations) funded international scoping survey of reader-centred service provision in public libraries. Data collected illustrates staff perceptions of the impact of reader-centred work on their service and investigates those promotional activities organized in libraries – and elsewhere – to promote reading. The four key areas of the survey were reading policy, partnerships to promote reading, reading activities, and staff skills and training needs. Additional contributions, in the form of brief experiential accounts, are made by representatives from countries with a particular view of this subject. This chapter also focuses on reading research from different countries, assessing different approaches to, and perspectives on, reading.

Chapter 5 comprises a summary of the cultural experience of reading and its effect on people's lives. It highlights the value of reading and reader development within a multicultural society and explores issues concerning multiculturalism, racism and language from the perspectives of writers, librarians, publishers and a range of individuals involved with celebrating cultural diversity through reading.

Chapter 6 turns to the value of reading and reader development for people with special needs, interpreting special needs from many viewpoints, as identified both by individual readers and librarians. Reading therapy and bibliotherapy are considered as part of this agenda, as well as the growing recognition in developing countries that literacy and reading can empower individuals and emerging societies, after years of poverty and neglect.

Chapter 7 investigates the tensions between book reading and technology and explores how technology can support readers and enhance access to, and enjoyment of, a wide range of books.

Chapter 8 examines the use and potential misuse of quantitative and qualitative research methodologies employed to investigate the value and impact of reading, and discusses the increased recognition of the efficacy of qualitative data to conduct this investigation. Examples of data obtained from the evaluation of, for example, the National Year of Reading (1998–9), DCMS/Wolfson reader-development funded initiatives (2000–1, 2001–2) and Branching Out (1998–2001) are used. The difficulties and impact of the dissemination of research to practice are also considered.

Chapter 9 provides an overview of the major issues presented in the book and offers a summary of good practice in reader development initiatives. Suggestions are made as to the future of reader development and reading for pleasure.

For all three authors, the book emanates from a life-long passion for reading. Judith Elkin writes:

> Books were an important part of my childhood and I remember, still with a shiver, the pleasure of reading under the bedclothes with a torch, after a strict lights-out policy from my parents, as well as the joy of getting lost in the magic of books in all kinds of situations and environments. This followed through to my early wish to become a librarian and my early baptism in inner city libraries in Birmingham. An early challenge was to pioneer a programme of storyhours for children (fairly unusual in the late 1960s); how enormous and unexpected was the thrill I got from being able to excite (and control, most of the time) large groups of anything up to 150 children of all ages. Introducing children, as well as parents, carers, teachers and grandparents to the joys of reading, the pleasures of sharing books with children and finding the 'right book for the right child at the right time' became a passion, accompanied by a mission to try to ensure that no child missed out on the potential benefits of reading. Whether my own daughters benefited from their exposure to books has to be their story but they still think that any contemporary who missed out on the pleasures of Elmer, the patchwork elephant, and any number of other well-loved characters, had a deprived childhood!
>
> I was lucky, over the years, to work very closely with authors, illustrators, publishers and booksellers and enjoy many early partnerships within the book world. Inevitably, I finally moved away from working with children themselves but was able to motivate others, librarians, students, parents and teachers, to share the thrill of reading with children. This remained a personal passion, in terms of research, writing and teaching. I have been pleased to share this passion with fellow authors, Briony Train and Debbie Denham.

Finally, the authors would like to thank all those individuals who contributed so much to this book, by their written submissions or their willingness to be interviewed face to face or by telephone. Individual names have been highlighted above but in addition, the authors would like to thank members of the IFLA Reading Section working group for their help and support, in particular Thomas Quigley, Gertrude Kayaga Mulindwa and Shirley Fitzgibbon; and also students at the University of Central England and colleagues in the UK and around the world who have contributed to discussions and workshops on the values of reading, in particular colleagues who attended conferences in Egypt, France, Kenya, Portugal, Spain and Thailand. Final thanks go to Uno Nilsson for allowing us to use his poem at the beginning of Chapter 4.

Judith Elkin, Briony Train, Debbie Denham

Note: Numbers in parentheses refer to page numbers of quoted texts throughout.

1
The reader

Judith Elkin

Introduction

Even in these days of the internet and technology beyond our wildest dreams, the book remains the medium of choice for millions of people for leisure reading, relaxation, escapism and many other individual and intimate purposes explored in this book. This chapter focuses on the individual reader and explores, through their own words, the joys and pleasures of reading from the perspective of many writers and readers. It looks at why and where people read and what motivates them, at different times and in different moods, to read.

Why do people read?

A number of eloquent writers have considered why reading is important to them, expressing their feelings in ways with which many readers will empathize. Gold describes the benefits of reading in his testimonial to reading, *Read for Your Life* (Gold, 1990), as:

> one of the central, unwearying pleasures of my life (xv) . . . When we practice reading as an art and a discipline, we are not wasting time and being frivolous and irresponsible. . . . When we still the outside world and turn to our inner minds, we are exercising our imagination, and getting in touch with our feelings, increasing our information, coping with the world through simulated situations. We come back from reading refreshed, restored, recharged (34) . . . Reading is not necessary to our survival, if by survival we mean eating and staying warm. It is necessary to our larger survival, however, to an enriched, aware life in which we exercise some measure of control over our well-being, our creativity and our connection to everything around us (100).

Francis Spufford, in his inspirational *The Child that Books Built* (Spufford, 2002a) is passionate about reading fiction, declaring himself an addict:

> A great part of the power of fiction rests on its ability to indicate, to point out truths once we allow it to work as an arena for people like ourselves, who happen to be imaginary. Our reverence for books, too, has really not much to do with them requiring deeper concentration than Mortal Kombat. It is the directions they can point us in that we value – and then the way those interact deep down in our reading minds with the directions our own temperaments are tentatively taking . . . when a fiction does trip a profound recognition . . . the reward is more than an inert item of knowledge. The book becomes part of the history of our self-understanding. The stories that mean most to us join the process by which we come to be securely our own (7).

Brewis, Gericke and Kruger (1994, 3) sum up the range of motives for reading as: 'pleasure, relief of tension, communication and to enhance societal consciousness. Further motives are to acquire education and information about life, to escape quotidian drudgery and stress, and to seek assistance in resolving personal problems'. Reading fiction for pleasure is described by Nell (1988, 7) as a form of play and free activity outside ordinary life, which has the power, to 'change consciousness, turning sadness to laughter and anxious introspection to the relaxed contemplation of some other time and place'. Coetzee (1983) thinks that reading for pleasure is essential for psychological and mental health as a way of relieving stress and that people read to compensate for loneliness and satisfy a need for communication, believing that fiction reading can provide pleasure at different levels from intellectual satisfaction to a simple vicarious experience, from entertainment to a complete treatment of problems.

The joy of reading

In his thought-provoking *A History of Reading* (1996), Alberto Manguel explores the joy of reading. He suggests: 'We read to understand, or to begin to understand. We cannot do but read. Reading, almost as much as breathing, is our essential function' (7). He cites Kafka's belief that books should:

> bite and sting us. If the book we are reading doesn't shake us awake like a blow on the skull, why bother reading it in the first place? What we need are books that hit us like a painful misfortune, like the death of someone we loved more than we love ourselves, that make us feel as though we had been banished to the woods, far from any human presence, like a suicide. A book must be the axe for the frozen sea within us.
>
> (Manguel, 1996, 93)

Kafka's approach, while getting support from many readers, is quite tough. In contrast, author P. D. James (1992, 1–2) takes a much gentler approach:

> We have what is arguably the most beautiful, the most versatile and the richest language in the world and a literature which is generally recognized as among the world's greatest. . . . To enjoy reading, to love books, is to have a source of joy, satisfaction and pleasure throughout the whole of life from childhood to old age, and a sure shield against its inevitable disappointments and griefs. In the words of Anthony Trollope: 'Book love, my friends, is your passport to the greatest, the purest and the most perfect pleasures that God has prepared for His creatures'.

Author Jonathan Coe (2002) is clear about his defence of the novel:

> an art form of inestimable value. . . . The novelist, by creating character, focuses on individuals. But then, through the generation of sympathy for these imagined people, through the pricking of narrative curiosity in the reader, a kind of alchemy takes place, and a miracle happens: the particular becomes general. Becomes universal. . . . And the readers of a novel, too, are made to enter into a great community of feeling which at its best can cross all boundaries of nationality, ethnicity, time and place. To create and sustain this community is the novelist's greatest task: it is at once a heavy responsibility and an almost unimaginable privilege and pleasure.

Chambers, Spufford and Manguel all talk about 'transformational' writing:

> literature which, if read creatively, reader and author making the story together, had the effect of transforming us as readers and as people . . . literary reading is the single most important cultural and educational activity we all – adults and children – engage in. . . . Literary reading begins where the reader is and goes from there. Unless you find yourself in books you have a hard time finding anybody else. . . . (Chambers, 1985, 15–16) Transformational books enrich in some degree our image of the world and its being; they help illuminate me, and others for me, and the society I live in, as well as the societies other people live in. . . . The transforming books are multi-layered, multi-thematic, linguistically conscious, dense (19).

> We can remember readings that acted like transformations. There were times when a particular book, like a seed crystal, dropped into our minds when they were exactly ready for it, like a supersaturated solution and suddenly we changed. Suddenly a thousand crystals of perception of our own formed, the original insight of the story ordering whole arrays of discoveries inside us, into winking accuracy (Spufford, 2002a, 9). . . . The dominant sensation of reading was excited delight. . . . They freed us from the limitations of having just one limited life with one point of view; they let us see beyond the horizon of our own circumstances. . . . The books you read as a child brought you sights you hadn't seen for yourself, scents you hadn't smelled, sounds you hadn't heard. They introduced you to people you hadn't met, and helped you to sample ways of being

> that would never have occurred to you. . . . And the result was . . . somebody who was enriched by the knowledge that their own particular life only occupied one little space in a much bigger world of possibilities (10).

> It is the reader who reads the sense; it is the reader who grants or recognizes in an object, place or event a certain possible readability; it is the reader who must attribute meaning to a system of signs, and then decipher it (Manguel, 1996, 7). . . . The act of reading establishes an intimate, physical relationship in which all the senses have a part: the eyes drawing the words from the page, the ears echoing the sounds being read, the nose inhaling the familiar scent of paper, glue, ink, cardboard or leather, the touch caressing the rough or soft page, the smooth or hard binding (244) . . . the meaning of a text is enlarged by the reader's capabilities and desires. Faced with a text, the reader can transform the words into a message that deciphers for him or her a question historically unrelated to the text itself or to its author. This transmigration of meaning can enlarge or impoverish the text itself; invariably it imbues the text with the circumstances of the reader. Through ignorance, through faith, through intelligence, through trickery and cunning, through illumination, the reader rewrites the text with the same words of the original but under another heading, re-creating it, as it were, in the very act of bringing it into being (211).

Reading is personal

The special and intimate bond that is formed between writer and reader is recognized by writer Alan Bennett (1996, 5): 'Books do have their time . . . something in the book speaks to part of you that is just waiting to be spoken to. You and the book are ripe for each other. It is in this sense that you don't only read a book: the best books read you.'

Margaret Meek similarly acknowledges this bond:

> not all the electronic media in the world will replace what happens when a reader meets a writer. Reading is far more than the retrieval of information from a collection of printed records. It is the active encounter of one mind and one imagination with another. Talk happens; the words fly, remembered or not. Writing remains; we read at our own pace, which is the rate of our thinking. Real reading cannot be done without thought. As it is a kind of 'inner speech', it is bound to have a marked effect on the growth of the mind of the reader. (1982a, 10–11)

> Silent as he is to the onlooker, the author speaks to his reader as clearly as if he were present. The relationship between them is made and sustained by a mutual agreement that the one should tell and the other should interpret the telling in a way that seems like listening. (Meek, Warlow and Barton, 1977, 7)

> Behind the visible words of every written text there lurks the writer's context, his or her life in the world and in the mind, in actions and in language. The words of the text are laden with the meanings of their time and place, augmented by the writer's reading as well as by the assumptions of the culture. To the reading of any text the reader similarly brings her or his context, and his or her language with different assumptions and other reading experiences. The conflux of reader and writer seems to make the giving and receiving of a simple, incontrovertible message impossible. . . . No text or book 'stands by itself', much as it seems to do so. It needs a reader to bring it alive (1991, 35).

Author A. S. Byatt (1992, 15) recognizes that reading:

> entails a private relationship between two people, reader and writer. Spoken language can take short cuts, take cues from the respondent's face or situation. Written language is addressed to someone you don't know and you can't see and so you have to be very clear. It makes an imaginable world, a sustained argument, a passionate plea, out of a person's inner life, and offers it to another separate person to experience and think about . . . reading lets us into someone else's privacy while we retain our own. It is in this sense that I can say that I know George Eliot better than I know my husband. I have shared her inner life. It has changed mine, as have those of Iris Murdoch, Kafka, Dostoevsky and Doris Lessing. . . . The nature of consecutive words on the page means that at any time one can stand back, look again, think, re-imagine. The relationship between feeling, thinking and imagining are not the same in any other art form. . . . Reading is a means of encountering the world outside in a safe way in the world-in-the-head, which can give both experience and understanding.

Gold (1990) recounts his own experience with clients in therapy:

> readers take what is personally applicable from what they read – what they select is what they most relate to and remember . . . fiction uses image, metaphor, character, situation and temporal sequence, there is a layered, complex network of meaning and information. The reader is able to select and reorganize this to make it relevant, even to make it understandable, to her own experiences, which is stored in the form of story in her mind. Readers *make meaning* in what they read (35). . . . Avid novel readers go back and forth continually and forage for psychic or spiritual supplies like squirrels getting ready for the winter. In this way they use fiction as a continuous resource, a supply base for life on the front line (45).

Author Philip Pullman (2002) talks about 'the silence of the written word – tentative, provisional, hesitant – private words, secret words communicating in silence with the private world of the reader'.

Rachel Van Riel and Olive Fowler (1996), in their very practical and down-to-earth primer which gives sensible advice on developing as an individual reader and becoming a creative reader, talk about reading personality:

> when you read you get angry, you get upset, you fall in love, you laugh out loud! You don't just sit there and let it all sweep over you. You are involved in a creative partnership with the author. Your part in the book is as important as the writer's because without your contribution the author can't make theirs (14).

They describe readers looking for different things in their reading: 'the thrill seeker; the stressed out reader; the avid reader; the indulgent reader' (15).

Gold (1990) pays tribute to: 'all those writers of prose and poetry who have enriched my life. Often against overwhelming odds, political, financial, social, these women and men have persisted in telling the truth as they see fit, in the most entertaining way possible' (xiii).

Lost in a book

Readers often talk about being 'lost in a book', a feeling of being so engrossed in an activity that nothing else matters: 'A truly enjoyable experience leads to an altered sense of time duration, a sense of control over one's own action and the emergence of a stronger sense of self' (Csiksentmihalvi, 1990, 132). Manguel (1996, 296) recognizes this state as being 'buried in books, isolated from the world of facts and flesh, feeling superior to those unfamiliar with the words preserved between dusty covers'.

Spufford (2002a, 1) describes his mother's reaction to his reading as a child:

> 'I can always tell when you're reading somewhere in the house. There's a special silence, a *reading* silence'. I never heard it, this extra depth of hush that somehow travelled through walls and ceilings to announce that my seven-year-old self had become as absent as a present person can be. The silence went both ways. As my concentration on the story in my hands took hold, all sounds faded away. . . . The silence that fell on the noises of people and traffic and dogs allowed an inner door to open to the book's data, its script of sound.

Anita Desai, who as a child in India was known in her family as a Lese Ratte or 'reading rat', a bookworm, remembers how, when she discovered *Wuthering Heights* at the age of nine, her own world of:

> an old Delhi bungalow, its verandas and plastered walls and ceiling fans, its garden of papaya and guava trees full of shrieking parakeets, the gritty dust that settled on the pages of a book before one could turn them, all receded. What became real, dazzlingly real, through the power and magic of Emily Bronte's pen, were the Yorkshire moors, the storm-

> driven heath, the torments of its anguished inhabitants, who roamed therein in rain and sleet, crying out from the depths of their broken hearts and hearing only ghosts reply.
>
> (Desai, 1990)

Meek (1991, 39–40) reinforces a sense of being elsewhere when reading a novel:

> I am where the action is, where the sufferings are, of the people or events that the writer has made me care about, in nineteenth-century Russia, in a house in Suffolk or on the high seas, or in a quite different other world. I am on holiday from myself, yet when I finish I know myself better. . . . Readers re-create experience, extend it, think about it, resist it even, as a distinctive form of desire. . . . I learn to make meanings, to analyse meanings. I can do all this at my own pace, re-reading, skipping, turning to the end, pausing for thought when I like. I can go in deep, as it were, when my interests are most engaged. . . . Reading makes me excited about ideas as much as about events and people. . . . Reading can be both a kind of day-dreaming and very hard work.

The act of reading

Manguel (1996, 303) captures wonderfully well the emotions associated with the act of reading:

> Depending on the time and the place, our mood and our memory, our experience and our desire, the enjoyment of reading, at its best, tightens rather than liberates the tensions of our mind, drawing them taut to make them sing, making us more, not less, aware of their presence. . . . We know that we are reading even while suspending disbelief; we know why we read even when we don't know how, holding in our mind at the same time, as it were, the illusionary text and the act of reading. We read to find the end, for the story's sake. We read not to reach it, for the sake of the reading itself. We read searchingly, like trackers. Oblivious of our surroundings, we read distractedly, skipping pages. We read contemptuously, admiringly, negligently, angrily, passionately, enviously, longingly. We read in gusts of sudden pleasure, without knowing what brought the pleasure along. . . . We read in slow, long motions, as if drifting in space, weightless. We read full of prejudice, malignantly. We read generously, making excuses for the text, filling gaps, mending faults. And sometimes, when the stars are kind, we read with an intake of breath, with a shudder, as if someone or something had 'walked over our grave', as if a memory had suddenly been rescued from a deep place within us – the recognition of something we never knew was there, or of something we vaguely felt as a flicker or a shadow, whose ghostly form rises and passes back into us before we can see what it is, leaving us older and wiser.

This magical experience of reading is also emphasized by both Spufford and Gold:

> a child is sitting reading. Between the black lines of print and eye, a channel is opening up [into] which information is pouring; more and faster than in any phone call, or any micro-coded burst of data fired across the net either, if you consider that these signals are not a sequence of numbers, not variations on a limited set of digital possibilities, but item after item of news from the analogue world of perception, each infinitely inflectable in tone and intent. . . . This heterogeneous traffic leaves no outward trace. You cannot tell what is going on by looking at it; the child just sits there, with her book or his. It cannot be overheard, makes no incomprehensible chittering like the sounds of a modern modem working on a telephone line. The subtlest microphone lowered into the line of transmission will detect nothing, retrieve nothing, from that incalculable flow of image.
> (Spufford, 2002a, 22)

> If you read a story that really involves you, your body will tell you that you are living through the experience. You will recognize feelings that have physical signs – increased heart rate, sweaty palms, or calm, relaxed breathing and so on, depending on your mood. These affects are the same as you would feel in similar real-life experiences – fear, anger, interest, joy, shame, or sadness. Amazingly, you can actually 'live' experience without moving anything but your eyes across a page. (Gold, 1990, 29)

The magic of reading identified by Spufford and Gold above is beautifully described through Bastian Nalthazar Bux's passion for books in Michael Ende's *The Neverending Story*:

> If you have never spent whole afternoons with burning ears and rumpled hair, forgetting the world around you over a book, forgetting cold and hunger – if you have never read secretly under the bedclothes with a flashlight, because your father or mother or some other well-meaning person has switched off the lamp on the plausible ground that it was time to sleep because you had to get up so early. If you have never wept bitter tears because a wonderful story has come to an end and you must take your leave of the characters with whom you have shared so many adventures, whom you have loved and admired, for whom you have hoped and feared, and without whose company life seems empty and meaningless – If such things have not been part of your experience, you probably won't understand what Bastian did next. . . . Staring at the title of the book, he turned hot and cold, cold and hot. Here was just what he had dreamed of, what he had longed for ever since the passion for books had taken hold of him. A story that never ended! The book of books!! (Ende, 1984, 10)

Manguel (1996, 19) writes movingly about his early experience of reading aloud to blind poet and writer Jorge Luis Borges in his home in Buenos Aires, and how this was instrumental in shaping his own reading:

> Reading out loud to the blind man was a curious experience because, even though I felt, with some effort, in control of the tone and pace of the reading, it was nevertheless Borges, the listener, who became the master of the text. I was the driver, but the landscape, the unfurling space, belonged to the one being driven, for whom there was no other responsibility than that of apprehending the countryside outside the windows. Borges chose the book, Borges stopped me or asked me to continue, Borges interrupted to comment, Borges allowed the words to come to him. I was invisible. . . . I quickly learned that reading is cumulative and proceeds by geometrical progression: each new reading builds upon whatever the reader has read before . . . reading aloud to him texts that I had read before on my own modified those earlier solitary readings, widened and suffused my memory of them, made me perceive what I had not perceived at the time but seemed to recall now, triggered by his response.

Reading spaces

People have different and very individual reading places where they choose to indulge their reading: in bed, up a tree, in the bath, in a favourite armchair. People read on buses, trains, planes, in airport lounges, on railway stations, in doctor's surgeries, as well as in libraries, in schools, in hospitals and at home. For many people, reading places are chosen with care and may dictate the appropriate reading material for that particular situation or environment.

Manguel (1996) expresses his pleasure of reading in bed, as a child:

> I don't think I can remember a greater comprehensive joy than that of coming to the last few pages and setting the book down, so that the end would not take place until at least tomorrow, and sinking back into my pillow with the sense of having actually stopped time (50). . . . Reading in bed is a self-centred act, immobile, free from ordinary social conventions, invisible to the world, and one that, because it takes place between the sheets, in the realm of lust and sinful idleness, has something of the thrill of things forbidden (53).

Alan Sillitoe (1996) feels that: 'the best time for reading a good stylish story is in fact when one is on a train traveling alone. With strangers round about, and unfamiliar scenery passing by the window . . . the endearing and convoluted life coming out of the pages possesses its own peculiar and imprinting effects.'

While Marcel Proust (1996) prefers the toilet: 'the little room destined for a more special and more vulgar use was a place for all my occupations which required an inviolable solitude: reading, reverie, tears and sensual pleasure!'

Marguerite Duras (1996) feels more comfortable reading in artificial light: 'I seldom read on beaches or in gardens. You can't read by two lights at once, the light of day and the light of the book. You should read by electric light, the room in shadow, and only the page lit up!'

Reading makes a difference

Sabine and Sabine (1983) interviewed 1400 Americans to ask them what book made the greatest difference in their lives. The differences expressed range from 'they make you feel better' to 'it literally saved my life'. The authors claim there is a hunger for books, because so many people are looking for something to make a difference in their lives. They cite an adult who remembers being small for his age. He lived in a tough area where 'neighborhood rowdies' regularly threatened to 'beat him up'. But books helped him; as a result of visiting his local library to listen to stories: 'What happened next is that I became the storyteller of the neighborhood, and very simply this kept me from being beaten up. They all knew me, and nobody would touch the storyteller' (43). One interviewee chose *The Hobbit*, 'because it showed me you can overcome your handicaps and be whatever you want to be' (43). Another interviewee contrasted her experience living in China in the 1970s, where people were not free to read what they pleased, with the situation in the USA: 'That's a very precious freedom, the liberty we have here that most people take for granted' (121).

Reading is power

Books can offer huge opportunities and can be a particular tool for development of the human being in developing countries. Literature should be empowering, allowing people to change, opening new roads, new ways to help people find ways to progress. Books need to be placed in the right context, to allow people to be listened to, to share ideas with others who cannot easily articulate their own ideas. However, in many totalitarian or former totalitarian states there remains considerable concern about the association of books with the power base. The book is not inherently good; books, reading and publishing can be tools of oppression.

Manguel (1996, 21) acknowledges that being a reader may not always be easy, recognizing that totalitarian governments have always feared reading and readers continue to be bullied in playgrounds, classrooms, offices and prisons around the world:

> The community of readers has an ambiguous reputation that comes from its acquired authority and perceived power. Something in the relationship between a reader and a book is recognized as wide and fruitful, but it is also seen as disdainfully exclusive and excluding, perhaps because the image of an individual curled up in a corner, seemingly oblivious of the grumblings of the world, suggests impenetrable privacy and a selfish eye and singular secretive action.

He muses on the freedom that learning offered for slaves: 'not an immediate passport to freedom but rather a way of gaining access to one of the powerful instruments of their oppressors: the book' (281). Recognizing that the slave-owners (like dictators, tyrants, absolute monarchs and other illicit holders of power) were strong believers in the power of the written word:

> They knew, far better than some readers, that reading is a strength that requires barely a few words to become overwhelming (281). . . . Authoritarian readers who prevent others from learning to read, fanatical readers who decide what can and cannot be read, stoical readers who refuse to read for pleasure and demand only the retelling of facts that they themselves hold to be true: all these attempt to limit the reader's vast and diverse powers. But censors can also work in different ways, without need of fire or courts of law. They can reinterpret books to render them serviceable only to themselves, for the sake of justifying their autocratic rights. . . . Thus, not all the reader's powers are enlightening. The same act that can bring a text into being, draw out its revelations, multiply its meaning, mirror in it the past, the present and the possibilities of the future, can also destroy or attempt to destroy the living page. Every reader makes up readings, which is not the same as lying; but every reader can also lie, willfully declaring the text subservient to a doctrine, to an arbitrary law, to a private advantage, to the rights of slave-owners or the authority of tyrants (288).

Aidan Chambers (1985, 5) muses on the power of the reader:

> The prison authorities know that the worst you can do to people is not so much cut them off physically from each other, but cut them off from attempting to communicate their inner lives to each other – to throw them totally on to their own selves. While we can tell each other what is going on inside us and be told what is going on inside other people we remain human, sane, hopeful, creative. In short, we remain alive. Once storying stops, we are dead.

Values of reading

Despite its potential for misuse highlighted in the previous section, reading offers endless pleasure. Through books, readers can be transported into another time, another place, another planet, into numerous situations vastly different from their own. Through shared experiences, shared emotions and feelings, readers can begin to get a better understanding of others, as well as themselves. Through stories, readers repeat their experiences and feelings to help them formulate their own ideas; they experience new feelings and begin to see their lives in perspective. Reading can give access to more experience than anyone can encompass in a single lifetime. Himmelweit (1958, 322) claims that stories can offer a vein of experience richer than that obtainable through any other medium and Stratta (1973, 43) argues that literature extends experience, offering a 'complex kaleidoscope for our contemplation', in a way which is not possible with film or television, since reading allows for greater reflection about the complexity of relationships and events.

As both an adults' and children's librarian in the 1960s and 1970s and as an academic from the mid-1980s onwards, the author has worked with many groups of librarians, teachers, parents, children and students, of education, English and librarianship, both in the UK and abroad. Working from the premise that books are one of the most valuable possessions anyone can have, she taxed groups at numerous workshops and seminars to reflect on the value and meaning of reading to themselves as individuals and to adults and children. Below is an amalgam of their ideas.

Reading:

- generates ideas and stimulates creativity: readers think creatively as they bring the reader's text alive through their imagination
- stimulates the imagination and aids intellectual development
- helps develop a critical and thinking mind
- aids personal growth and emotional development
- helps us to shape, store and reflect on our past and our future, by experiencing the life of other periods
- gives a better understanding of human nature and insight into life; offers role models
- offers cultural and ethnic awareness and understanding of moral codes/ethics/values
- offers social awareness of different regions, communities and peer groups, and understanding of the complexities of relationships
- enables the reader to see things from other angles, to appreciate and understand other people's problems, aiding tolerance and understanding
- gives an opportunity to relive and re-experience the adventures and ideas of others
- gives insights into the reader's own personality and problems; means of self-discovery
- helps people learn and practise literacy skills and develops concentration and reflection
- makes people feel good and has health benefits: stress relieving, relaxation, mental balance
- widens horizons
- offers escapism
- develops worthwhile tastes and permanent interest in good literature
- fosters independence
- informs and educates.

For the child, whose imagination and understanding of things around them is increasing at an exponential rate, yet is potentially dominated by television, videos, computers and other electronic media, reading is particularly important:

- as a language and audio stimulus. Learning to read depends to a large extent on the child's experience of language. Storytelling and reading help the child by expanding vocabulary; by providing new sentence patterns and improving spelling, grammar and writing skills; by creating an opportunity to learn to listen as distinct from merely hearing.
- as enrichment to the imagination. Good stories can enrich the imagination, develop compassion, humour and understanding; arouse curiosity and the ability to question.
- as a visual stimulus. Picture books provide a valuable aid to encourage perception and discrimination. Apart from the purely aesthetic experience, the concentration involved in the activity of looking at pictures aids the child in coming to terms with the text and the structure of the book.
- in widening horizons. Children's limited experiences expand as they are presented with new experiences in story form and answers to problems and fears. Emotional and intellectual needs need to be recognized and satisfied if the whole person is to thrive and children are to be equipped to organize their world effectively and be sensitive to the world in which they live. Stories evoke response, recognition, identification, stimulation; they educate the emotions (fear, greed, love, good and evil are the basic ingredients of most stories); they educate the imagination by stretching it to other dimensions.
- as a therapeutic effect. It is important to have understood the meaning of violence, of love, of friendship, of compassion through books; how reassuring for children to be able to identify themselves with a central character and know how to deal with certain situations; how comforting for children who can build up a secure background of characters and situations they have known and lived through intimately; how much better prepared they are for the realities of life.
- for information. Reading introduces wider knowledge, offering children the opportunity to think, to reflect, to ask questions, to develop comprehension, stimulating curiosity, unfreezing the imagination, aiding natural learning and the educational process.
- for social development. Reading can create a social sense, involving the whole family in learning together and developing life-long reading habits. Sharing is the best incentive to learning to read and continuing to read, the joy of books shared with another person, whether parents, teachers, siblings, friends, grandparents. Reading can introduce children to human relationships and acceptable behaviour/codes.

- for physical development. Reading can be part of confidence building, aiding development of physical/manual skills, hand/eye co-ordination and motor skills.

Specifically, with respect to teenagers:

- Reading may compensate for the difficulties of growing up and complex ways of living: the story can have the psychological value of showing children that someone else has been there before them; they enable teenagers to move forward in experience to consider what lies ahead, to contemplate experiences as it were 'by proxy' (Leeson, 1977, 45) before encountering them directly. Story heightens the reader's awareness, shaping the raw material of life and so organizing even that which is sad or painful into satisfying experience. In particular, reading offers identity, subversion, being part of the crowd, comfort, opportunity to be alone, intellectual credibility.

How do readers select books?

Ross (2001) studied the book selection strategies of heavy readers in the USA and found that readers draw on several interrelated considerations when choosing a book to read for pleasure. A reader's selection strategy develops through their entire reading experiences and is a personalized process: 'It's a very personal choice and nobody can make it but me. . . . Choosing books is wonderful (6). . . . Some of it is retrospective because you deliberate on what you have read, it's current because you're experiencing and also it's anticipatory because you know what you want to read' (10).

Ross found the most important factor in the selection process was mood, with the reader considering how they are feeling and what else is going on in their lives: 'Some days you don't want a book that reaches too deep into you and other days you do' (13). Readers are more likely to pick short, easy reads and old favourites when they are feeling stressed as a way of seeking safety, reassurance and confirmation. However, they will risk more demanding and unfamiliar material when they are feeling calmer. As well as the reader's current mood, one reader believes that you need to be emotionally ready for a book, saying: 'There are some books it's not your time to read, or it's not their time to be read by you. Sometimes a book just has nothing to say to you and that's probably because you have to have had some prior experience' (12).

Readers often rely on their knowledge of authors and tend to stick with known and trusted authors: 'It's like finding a gold mine and following a vein when you find a good author' (14). Readers also act on recommendations from friends and family. As well as looking for books by known authors, some readers make a conscious effort to try something new and unknown. One reader liked to run her finger along the books and stop at a random point, while some pick a book from a different letter each time as an experiment. Experienced readers get clues about what type of book it is and whether they are going to enjoy it from the appearance, title and blurb on the book cover: 'So the book is auditioning for me. . . . It's only got that one chance to succeed' (14).

Writer Annie Proulx talks about picking library books as a child according to the colour of their covers: 'I was very partial to beige' (Campbell, 2003).

Selecting good books is particularly important for less committed readers, as a poor choice of book can deter them from reading. People are also more likely to enjoy reading if they have the freedom to choose which books they read and the choice not to finish a book if they are not enjoying it.

Ross and Chelton (2001) list five key elements in the book selection process:

- The reading experience wanted: familiarity vs novelty, safety vs risk, easy vs challenging, upbeat/positive vs hard-hitting/ironic/critical, reassuring vs stimulating/frightening/amazing, confirming values and beliefs vs challenging them.
- Sources about new books: browsing in bookstores or libraries, monitoring displays and 'just returned' shelves; recommendations from friends, co-workers, family; reviews or ads in popular media; productions (TV, movie etc.) of author's work; jacket blurbs; lists of prizes from libraries, literary critics or other readers.
- Elements of a book: subject, treatment, characters depicted, setting, ending, physical size of the book.
- Clues on the book itself: author, genre, cover, title, sample page, publisher.
- Cost in time or money to access the book: intellectual access (knowledge of content or literary conventions), physical access (time and work required to get it), length of time or commitment required by the book.

Sharing reading

Reading is often a solitary occupation but sharing has inestimable value, too. For example, Butler (1998) is of the firm belief that:

> there is no parents' aid which can compare with the book in its capacity to establish and maintain a relationship with a child. Its effects extend far beyond the covers of the actual book, and invade every aspect of life. Parents and children who share books come to share the same frame of reference. Incidents in everyday life constantly remind one or the other – or both simultaneously – of a situation, a character, an action, from a jointly enjoyed book, with all the generation of warmth and well-being that is attendant upon such sharing (xii).

> Giving parents the idea of 'the book as a tool' will do more for the dual purpose of establishing the parent–child relationship and ensuring the child's adequate language development, than any amount of advice on talking to children. . . . Shades of meaning which may be quite unavailable to the child of limited language experience are startlingly present in the understanding – and increasingly the speech – of the 'well-read-to' toddler (6). . . . For relationships, minds have to engage. Ideas are essential, and books constitute a superlative source of ideas. Books can be bridges between children and parents and children and the world (243–4).

Bedtime stories are still acknowledged as an important part of childhood development and sharing pleasures: 'Reading aloud makes the intimate bond between parent and child into a conduit for discovery, for joint exploration of the world beyond the family' (Spufford, 2002b).

Jim Trelease (1982, 22) emphasizes the pleasure of shared reading:

> We have searched for wayward brothers and sisters, evaded wolves, lost friends and learned how to make new ones. We have laughed, cried, shaken with fright, and shivered with delight. And best of all, we did it together. Along the way we discovered something about the universality of human experience – that we, too, have many of the hopes and fears of the people we read about. The cost of such a wondrous experience is well within your means. . . . It costs you time and interest, if you are willing to invest both, you can pick up a book, turn to a child, and begin today. I promise you, you will never want the experience to end.

People also share their pleasure in books through book groups where they discuss their opinions about books. Hartley (2001) describes reading groups as 'active and interactive' and says: 'The premium is on empathy, the core reading group value: the empathy between reader and character, author and character and between all the readers in the room' (205). Reading groups are further explored in Chapters 2 and 3.

Story

Story itself remains important; we continue to rely on story to sort out the world.

> we dream in narrative, daydream in narrative, remember, anticipate, hope, despair, believe, doubt, plan, revise, criticize, construct, gossip, learn, hate, and love by narrative. In order really to live, we make up stories about ourselves and others, about the personal as well as the social past and future. (Hardy, 1977, 13)

> behind the news bulletin, the strip cartoon, the sports report. Ask a friend about his holiday, how he moved house, what happened to his car, wife, sweetheart, dog and the result will be narrative. We sort out our sense impressions into storying.
>
> (Meek, Warlow and Barton, 1977, 7–8)

> We so readily construct stories out of past experience that it is difficult to perceive that anything has been constructed at all. (Britton, 1977, 8)

Meek extols the merits of story:

> In the playground children learn stories that are secrets, narrative initiation rites of the new tribe, that seem, but only seem, to disappear. This is the time to discover storying as gossip and scandal, to overturn the established mode of orderly telling, to introduce incoherence and chaos, crisis and social drama (Meek, 1982b, 9).

> Storytelling is a universal habit, a part of our common humanity . . . all cultures have some form of narrative. Stories are part of our conversation, our recollections, our plans, our hopes, our fears. Young and old, we all tell stories as soon as we begin to explain or describe events and actions, feelings and motives. (Meek, 1991, 103)

> in human remembering the past stays alive, so story-telling not only supplies children with memories they cannot yet have, it also gives them 'virtual' memory, the idea of remembering what they have heard others tell. . . . Story-telling lies at the back of all literacy, powerful in its effect and distinguished by its cultural differences.
>
> (Meek, 1991, 65)

Chambers and Gold echo this:

> In every language, in every part of the world, Story is the fundamental grammar of all thought and of all communication. By telling ourselves what happened, to whom, and why we not only discover ourselves and the world, but we change and create ourselves and the world too. . . . Story is not only about the who and the what and the why. It is not only about character, action and motivation. . . . It is quite as importantly about the how. As our finest critical readers have so often shown, how a story is made tells us quite as much about the world as a writer understands it as anything in the story's content.
>
> (Chambers, 1982, 15)

> We are all storymakers. We use story to organize and control. Without the management and order of story, the chaos and confusion of disturbing experience controls us by confusing us. Human beings strive for order, control and peace, but we can never be static. We must change, age, learn more, grow and adapt. So we are always in a cycle of

> creative struggle, changing and striving to manage our changing and to integrate what we learn into our own story. This is what we do when we 'story' it. (Gold, 1990, 45)

This was certainly made clear to the author when she was at a conference in Moscow during the 1991 coup. There were tanks on the streets, the Kremlin was sealed off and there was a complete news blackout. The only source of information for the first 24 hours was hearsay and rumour. Everyone lived on stories; from colleagues, from people on the streets. Stories helped to make sense of what was an extremely emotional and frightening situation. Stories helped everyone to reflect on their own experiences. Stories helped to share understanding with other colleagues, family and friends.

Story has also been acknowledged as a powerful tool for organizational change. According to the former programme director for Knowledge Management at the World Bank, Steve Denning (2000), persuasion is worth 28% of Gross National Product (GNP); if two-thirds of persuasion is narrative then in the context of the UK economy, storytelling is worth $1.8 trillion! Denning's masterclasses focus on the use of storytelling for effectively communicating knowledge and associated learning within organizations and include sessions on narrative as advanced knowledge repository; narrative as a means of cultural integration and cross-cultural understanding.

The use of storytelling as a form of reflective learning about teaching skills has recently been developed in New Zealand, by Maxine Alterio, at Otago Polytechnic, Dunedin: 'Storytelling is a very powerful form of communication. If it is used as a professional development tool, formalized storytelling has the capacity to explore, inform and advance teaching practice' (Currie, 1999).

Fairy tales

Elaine Moss (1980, 74) refers to Bruno Bettelheim's seminal *The Uses of Enchantment* (1976) as a 'significant statement on the life-enriching force of story in childhood, because folk and fairy tale are universal and for all time'. Bettelheim suggests that:

> Fairy tales reassure because they demonstrate that others have the same kind of fantasies; children possess an inner world of fantasy which is irrational, subjective, sensual, violent and often frightening. Fairy tales can bring order to the child's inner life by offering symbolic solutions to his difficulties . . . they both reflect the child's inner life and convey a sense of order. . . . For a story truly to hold the child's attention, it must entertain and arouse his curiosity. But to enrich his life, it must stimulate his imagination; help him to develop his intellect and to clarify his emotions; be attuned to his anxieties and aspirations; give full recognition to his difficulties, while at the same time suggesting solutions to the problems which perturb him . . . giving full credence to the seriousness of the child's predicaments, while simultaneously promoting confidence in himself and in his future (5).

> . . . these tales, in a much deeper way than any other reading material, start where the child really is in his psychological and emotional being. They speak about his severe inner pressures in a way that the child unconsciously understands and – without belittling the most serious inner struggles which growing up entails – offer examples of both temporary and permanent solutions to pressing difficulties . . . The fairy tale . . . confronts the child squarely with the basic human predicaments (56).

Meek (1982b, 8) emphasizes the global value of fairy tales which: 'initiate us and our children into the wisdom of not only our local culture – important though that is – but also into a universal culture unity of motifs, forms and characters. They are our most helpful means of becoming truly multicultural, at home in the wider world as well as in a particular corner of it'. This is reinforced by storyteller Grace Hallworth (1985):

> We cannot take steps in life or literature without narrating . . . we cannot stir without telling stories . . . of dreams, of love affairs, trials and tribulations of the wife, the husband, the child . . . science and technology uses the anecdotal method of storytelling. Sharing is central to strategies of encouraging international understanding and developing heightened sensitivities to other cultures, as well as our own culture. . . . We need to build a bridge between the culture of literature and the culture of life . . . in many cultures, grandmothers provide this source. . . . All children should have their horizons given psychological and physical breadth – exploration and habitation of worlds in space. It is part of the cultural mosaic from which we gain; folklore shows how we are the same and uniquely different; it reflects the universal human predicament . . . if you take a person's folklore and dialect, you begin to enter into/to see another culture.

Language and literacy

Meek (1991, 54) notes that one of the distinguishing features of habitual readers and writers is their curiosity about language: 'They enjoy it. They use it with feeling and flair when they talk, tell jokes, invent word games and do crossword puzzles. They are, in a sense, in control of language, as a skilled player manages a football, a versatile violinist interprets a score or a racing driver handles a car'.

> Although literacy is at the heart of our social cohesion, the way society works, it is also a strong factor in individual and social differences. There are boundaries of literacy which are hard to define. Yet, in a sense that is generally understood, literacy, like language itself, is a map of any society. It separates people, differentiates them. Not everyone has the same range of literate expertise or confidence. (Meek, 1991, 49)

> What children willingly read, the books they choose, define literacy, and literature, for them. Their growth in literacy depends on their freedom to choose, to value, to exploit and to reject different texts, different kinds of literature in response to their purposes and intentions. (Meek, 1991, 64)

Poet David Dabydeen (1992, 68) is concerned that the English language should develop and be enriched by the communities of writers and readers within society:

> If you look at the writers who have emerged from the immigrant communities, Ben Okri or Salman Rushdie or Timothy Mo, Buchi Emecheta, Naipaul, Ichiguro – what distinguishes these writers, is not a desire to displace or fire the canons but to enrich and renew English literature from within by creolising the language or by other methods of formal experiment and innovation. After all, Rushdie's genius is the ability to splice Latin American magical realism with the Indian sagas with that kind of Joycean method of narration to produce a new syncretic form of expressing stories . . . . it's creating a new art form for all of us. . . . The issue in Britain today is not about illiteracy. It's about the illiteracy of the imagination, in other words our inability to read other texts . . . how you get over a sense of the otherness of Asians and the otherness of their texts seems to demand a lot more effort.

Encouraging reading

Not all people, however, come easily to reading, for a variety of reasons, and many may need help. Manguel (1996, 11) cites James Hillman's belief that those who have read stories or had stories read to them in childhood: 'are in better shape and have a better prognosis than those to whom story must be introduced . . . coming early with life it is already a perspective on life . . . these first readings become something lived in and lived through, a way in which the soul finds itself in life'.

Butler (1998, 8) is convinced that it is the early years that have the most influence on the child's and subsequently adult's reading:

> There is nothing magic about the way contact with books in early years produces early readers. One would surely expect it to. A baby is learning about the way language arises from the page each time her parent opens a book, from earliest days. She is linking the human voice to the print at a very early age. Given repeated opportunity, she notices how the adult attends to the black marks, how he can't go on reading if the page is turned too soon. . . . Skills come apparently unbidden as the toddler advances into three- and four-year-old independence. Print is friendly and familiar for this child. She is already unconsciously finding landmarks, noting regular features, predicting patterns. . . . Unbidden? Not a bit of it! This child has had her reading skills handed to her on a golden platter.

Meek (1991, 33) acknowledges that early reading builds life-long reading, as part of a developmental process towards creating 'expert reader' and 'powerful literates':

> Good readers are more than just successful print-scanners and retrievers of information – they find in books the depth and breadth of human experience. . . . Think of all that you would never have experienced if you had not learned to read – readers are at home in the life of the mind; they live with ideas as well as events and facts; they understand a wide range of feelings by entering into those of other people. . . . Powerful literates are those who read a lot, and know their way round the world of print. . . . Literate adults make their reading work for them. They use books as tools, as sources of information and means of checking. They choose with confidence what they want or need to read. . . . All expert readers understand, practically, consciously, how reading works. It is not simply intelligence . . . or even social class that makes efficient readers, although these things undoubtedly help. It is knowing what reading is like, including what it feels like, and what it makes possible.

Chambers (1985, 15–16) highlights the importance of a wide range of books, mediated by a literate adult, as being central to helping children to become expert readers: 'to browse among them frequently, to hear them read aloud, and being given time to read them for oneself . . . the mediation of literature to children by a literate, sympathetic adult is the single most important factor in the creation of a desire among children to read, and to read adventurously'.

Spufford (2002a) relates how he was turned on to reading:

> When I caught the mumps, I couldn't read; when I went back to school, I could. The first page of *The Hobbit* was a thicket of symbols, to be decoded one at a time and joined hesitantly together . . . (69). So the reading flowed, when I was six, with the yellow hardback copy of *The Hobbit* in my hands; and the pictures came. I went to the door of the hobbit hole with Bilbo as he let in more, and more, and more dwarves attracted by the sign Gandalf had scratched there in the glossy green paint. I jogged with him on his pony out of the Shire, away from the raspberry jam and crumpets, and towards dragons (65).

Bettina Hurlimann (1967) writing in the 1960s, is much quoted for her view that:

> in this restless age of technology, when the emphasis is always on records of attainment and productivity, there is some danger of forgetting that a child does not require too much in the way of books. . . . What he does need are the right books at the right time so that he may find in literature a true point of balance in an often disordered world. It is for us as parents or teachers, librarians or publishers, to recognize this need and to know how best, how most imaginatively, to fulfil it (xviii).

Chambers' (1969, 117) views on the quality of a mediator in this process, whether teacher or librarian, were expressed over 30 years ago but still carry considerable weight:

> The effectiveness of any teacher in the encouragement of the reading habit varies in proportion to the teacher's depth of knowledge of children's books and literature generally. . . . The teacher who reads avidly himself, the teacher who knows and reads children's books, invariably fosters a similar interest in a high percentage of his pupils. . . . The teaching profession is a profession of reluctant readers. They are rarely seen to read a novel, purr over it with pleasure, dwell on it with interest, talk about it with enthusiasm or anger; worse, they are never even seen carrying one. . . . They are heard hacking a set book to pieces.

Echoes of the past are picked up in Chapter 3's look at the recent Literacy Strategy in the UK, which many commentators feel has further distracted teachers and detracted from reading for pleasure. Chambers continues (129):

> Librarians are reluctant about books in quite a different way from most other mortals. . . . They are often very well-read people: it is among the children's public librarians one finds the most informed knowledge of children's books. . . . The reluctance of far too many librarians lies in their refusal to move out with any energetic zeal into the world at large and encourage people to come in.

Reading and libraries

Some of this lack of 'energetic zeal' identified by Chambers is still applicable in 2003, in terms of a failure by librarians to extol the crucial and unique role that libraries can play in supporting and developing readers. Miranda McKearney has accused the library profession of 'lack of clarity about libraries' core purpose which has led them to try to be all things to all people and to spread themselves too thinly' (McKeone and McKearney, 2002).

Catherine Blanshard, City Librarian of Leeds, is a strong advocate of librarians as champions of reading, believing that reader development work is fundamental to cultural and community development. She sees reading as 'subversive, invasive, life-changing and having the power to unlock creativity'. She believes that sustainability of reader development initiatives in libraries comes from library staff, with book knowledge, confidence, communication skills and new skills, for example that of facilitating reading groups (Blanshard, 2001).

In an attempt to counteract lack of public and government awareness, the UK Library and Information Commission (1996) articulated its vision of the value of library and information services in economic, education and social policy development, in *2020 Vision*. This was followed by two further policy statements on libraries and lifelong learning and libraries and social inclusion (1998, 2000). With respect to reading and access to reading, they promoted the idea that:

Libraries:

- provide a socially inclusive cultural and creative environment for everyone, regardless of age, gender, background, ability, ethnic origin or wealth
- offer an accessible, neutral learning space
- are a place of sanctuary, a secure risk-free social place that is welcoming to all
- are non-judgemental, non-competitive, non-accrediting places
- have a long-term, sustainable impact on a child's quality of life into adulthood
- empower the individual to engender a sense of community for their users.

The newly formed Reading Agency is a strong advocate for libraries. Their advocacy materials recognize that:

Libraries are the UK's most significant providers of the reading experience:

- There are 121 million books in the public library service.
- Public libraries lend 430 million books a year.
- 107 million are children's books, 221 million are adult fiction.

Libraries have a unique role in the nation's reading life. They

- provide reading in a shared, civic space which emphasizes community trust and respect.
- provide reading free – as well as equalizing access, thus encouraging adventurousness and experimentation
- emphasize in their ethos voluntary engagement and empowerment of the individual
- validate all forms of reading
- provide reading materials in different formats – comics, magazines, audiovisual, large print, through ICT
- take reading to people outside the library who can't get to the building – prisoners, the sick, the housebound
- create and develop chances for people who may be experiencing social, technical or psychological barriers to reading
- create lively, welcoming spaces suitable for readers
- provide trained staff, able to talk to readers about their reading choices
- create accessible, interesting displays and access points to reading choices

- provide a wide range of stock, targeted at different areas of the community
- create opportunities for people to share their reading experiences – reader to reader and reader to library
- encourage experimentation and adventurousness
- involve the community in shaping the service to readers.

Children's reading and libraries

A Place for Children

Research in *A Place for Children* found that libraries contributed to the child's reading development in terms of:

- the quality of life in a civilized society
- offering children a first right of citizenship through library membership
- being a comfortable, welcoming, safe place where staff were helpful and supportive
- being a neutral ground for those disaffected from school
- family support: family reading groups, family literacy groups, advice to parents, home-educated children
- promoting literacy: supporting reader development and encouraging love of books and reading: 'you only have to look around to see the need of a library. . . . There is no home environment of books, there is low educational aspiration . . . there is no bookshop and no book-buying tradition. Here they have access to a free source of information. . . . We build on the strong oral tradition that still exists. The children have good listening skills and we connect with these roots by myths, legends and poetry'.
- providing a welcoming environment: 'Library as a warm place, a safe place where children learn a sense of ownership'.
- social inclusion: 'a social space in a pretty desolate area: roaming dogs, broken windows, peeling paint characterize the landscape . . . security to meet their friends on neutral, well regulated territory'.
- developing social skills: 'to make them feel part of the community and this tied in well with citizenship education; providing self-development and education on children's own terms; providing independence, giving children confidence to do things on their own'.
- developing ICT skills: complementing education offered in schools . . . 'a chance [to get] out of the cycle of poverty' (Elkin & Kinnell, 2000).

Start with the Child

The recently published and visionary report, *Start with the Child* (CILIP, 2002), echoes much of this:

> Libraries are a hugely important part of children's and young people's lives because they bring books and children together; they provide reading opportunities free of charge, and so they encourage experimentation and learning. They represent a non-judgmental place for children to feel safe and empowered to make their own choices. The library ethos emphasises individual rights, voluntary involvement and exposure to minority interests and challenging ideas, through print based or other media. Reading and libraries are crucial to achieving our national ambitions for community cohesion, social inclusion, lifelong learning, active citizenship, creativity and healthy and happy lives for our children (9).

Framework for the Future

The Department for Culture, Media and Sport has recently launched, after extensive consultation, its long-term strategic vision for public libraries in England: *Framework for the Future: libraries, learning and information in the next decade*. One of the key strengths identified is 'books, learning and reading': 'reading is ever more important in modern life. The rise of the Internet has not displaced reading since most web pages are text based. People cannot be active or informed citizens unless they can read. Reading is a pre-requisite for almost all cultural and social activities' (Great Britain, DCMS, 2003, 7–8).

Conclusion

This chapter has focused on the reader and the pleasure and joy the individual can gain from reading. Belief in the importance and value of reading for individuals of all ages, abilities and backgrounds has given rise to many initiatives which aim to support the reader and reader development activities that are explored throughout the rest of this book.

It has looked at the life-enhancing opportunities to be gained from reading and taken the stance that no individual should miss out on such pleasures: readers of all ages, abilities and backgrounds should be empowered to enjoy, to share and to expand their reading; pre-readers should be caught during babyhood to ensure they become readers for life; people should be helped to understand that reading is a very personal experience and to be confident in their own interpretation of a text, a story, a poem; individuals should be confident and sufficiently relaxed with a book or picture to be emotionally moved, excited or frightened by it; parents and carers should be helped to share books, stories and rhymes with children as a pleasurable, constructive, bonding, learning opportunity.

Reading is significant in current government policy terms, as Tessa Jowell, Secretary of State for Culture, Media and Sport, says: 'Public libraries' work with young readers makes a unique and powerful contribution to community cohesion, active citizenship, lifelong learning and happy lives for our children' (2002). Reading and work with readers also supports and contributes to social inclusion, education standards and life skills, creativity and creative industries, community cohesion, the economy, Best Value, health, support for family life, emotional literacy and access. Many of these issues are explored in later chapters.

References and further reading

Bell, H. (2001) The Pleasures and Pitfalls of Reading Groups, *Logos*, **12** (4), 203–9.

Bennett, A. (1996) Foreword. In Van Riel, R. and Fowler, O. (eds), *Opening the Book: finding a good read*, Yorkshire, Opening the Book, first published by Bradford Libraries.

Bettelheim, B. (1976) *The Uses of Enchantment: the meaning and importance of fairy tales*, London, Thames and Hudson.

Blanshard, C. (2001) Panel discussion at the Library and Information Show, National Exhibition Centre, Birmingham.

Book Marketing Ltd and The Reading Partnership (2000) *Reading the Situation: book reading, buying and borrowing in Britain*, London, Book Marketing Ltd and The Reading Partnership.

Brewis, W. L. E., Gericke, E. M. and Kruger, J. A. (1994) Reading Needs and Motives of Adult Users of Fiction, *Mousaion*, **12** (2), 3–18.

Britton, J. (1977) In Meek, M., Warlow, A. and Barton, G. (eds), *The Cool Web: the pattern of children's reading*, London, The Bodley Head.

Butler, D. (1998) *Babies Need Books: sharing the joy of books with children from birth to six*, rev. edn, London, The Bodley Head.

Byatt, A. S. (1992) In Van Riel, R. (ed.) (1992) *Reading the Future: a place for literature in public libraries. A report of the seminar held in York, 2 and 3 March 1992, organized by the Arts Council of Great Britain in association with the Library Association and the Regional Arts Boards of England*, London, The Arts Council and Library Association Publishing.

Campbell, D. (2003) Wild in the Country: profile of Annie Proulx, *The Guardian*, G2, (13 January), 4–5.

Chambers, A. (1969) *The Reluctant Reader*, Oxford, Pergamon.

Chambers, A. (1982) The Child's Changing Story. In *Story in the Child's Changing World: papers and proceedings of the 18th Congress of the International Board on Books for Young People, Churchill College, Cambridge 1982*, 15–26.

Chambers, A. (1985) *Booktalk: occasional writing on literature and children*, London, The Bodley Head.

Chambers, N. (ed.) (1980) *The Signal Approach to Children's Books: a collection*, London, Kestrel.

CILIP (2002) *Start with the Child: report of the CILIP Working Group on library provision for children and young people*, London, CILIP.

Coe, J. (2002) Acceptance speech on being awarded an Honorary Doctorate by the University of Central England in Birmingham, UK, March 2002.

Coetzee, J. M. (1983) In Brewis, W. L. E., Gericke, E. M. and Kruger, J. A. (eds) (1994) Reading Needs and Motives of Adult Users of Fiction, *Mousaion*, **12** (2), 3–18.

Collinson, R. (1976) A Sense of Audience. In Fox, G. et al. (eds), *Writers, Critics and Children*, London, Heinemann Educational Press.

Csiksentmihalvi, M. (1990) In Towey, C. A. (2001) Flow: the benefits of pleasure reading and tapping readers' interests, *Acquisitions Librarian*, **25**, 131–40.

Currie, J. (1999) Tell Your Side of the Story, *The Times Higher Educational Supplement*, (16 April), 30–1.

Dabydeen, D. (1992) In Van Riel, R. (ed.), *Reading the Future: a place for literature in public libraries. A report of the seminar held in York 2 and 3 March 1992, organized by the Arts Council of Great Britain in association with the Library Association and the Regional Arts Boards of England*, London, The Arts Council and Library Association Publishing.

Denning, S. (2000) *The Springboard: how storytelling ignites action in knowledge-era organizations*, London, Butterworth-Heinemann.

Desai, A. (1990) A Reading Rat on the Moors. In Manguel, A. (ed.), *Soho Square III*, London, Bloomsbury.

Duras, M. (1996) In Manguel, A., *A History of Reading*, London, Viking, 152.

Egoff, S., Stubbs, G. T. and Ashley, L. F. (eds) (1969) *Only Connect: readings on children's literature*, Toronto, Oxford University Press.

Elkin, J. and Kinnell, M. (2000) *A Place for Children: public libraries as a major force in children's reading*, British Library Research and Innovation Report 117, London, Library Association Publishing.

Ende, M. (1984) *The Neverending Story*, translated by Ralph Manheim, London, Penguin Books.

Fisher, M. (1961) *Intent upon Reading*, Leicester, Brockhampton,

Fox, G. et al. (1976) *Writers, Critics and Children*, London, Heinemann Educational Press.

Gold, Joseph (1990) *Read for Your Life: literature as a life support system*, Ontario, Fitzhenry & Whiteside.

Great Britain. Department for Culture, Media and Sport (2003) *Framework for the Future: libraries, learning and information in the next decade*, London, Department for Culture, Media and Sport.

Hallworth, G. (1985) Public speech at UNESCO/IFLA conference: The Library, a centre for promoting international understanding, Salamanca, Spain, June, 1985, unpublished.

Hardy, B. (1977) Narrative as a Primary Act of Mind. In Meek, M., Warlow, A. and Barton, G. (eds) *The Cool Web: the pattern of children's reading*, London, The Bodley Head.

Hartley, J. (2001) In Bell, H. The Pleasures and Pitfalls of Reading Groups, *Logos*, **12** (4), 203–9.

Himmelweit, H. T. et al. (1958) *Television and the Child*, Oxford, Oxford University Press.

Hurlimann, B. (1967) *Three Centuries of Children's Books in Europe*, translated and edited by B. Alderson, London, Oxford University Press.

Iser, W. (1978) *The Act of Reading*, London, Routledge and Kegan Paul.

James, P. D. (1992) In Van Riel, R. (ed.) *Reading the Future: a place for literature in public libraries. A report of the seminar held in York, 2 and 3 March 1992, organized by the Arts Council of Great Britain in association with the Library Association and the Regional Arts Boards of England*, London, The Arts Council and Library Association Publishing.

Jowell, T. (2002) *Launch of The Reading Agency at the British Library, September 26, 2002*, Press release.

Leeson, R. (1977) A Reluctant Literature. In Foster, J. L. (ed.), *Reluctant to Read?*, London, Ward Lock.

Library and Information Commission (1996) *2020 Vision*, London, Library and Information Commission.

Library and Information Commission (1998) *Libraries: the lifeforce for learning*, London, Library and Information Commission.

Library and Information Commission (2000) *Libraries: the essence of inclusion*, London, Library and Information Commission.

McKeone, G. and McKearney, M. (2002) Hard to Ignore: The Reading Agency, *Public Library Journal*, **17** (4), 105–7.

Manguel, A. (1996) *A History of Reading*, London, Viking.

Meek, M. (1982a) *Learning to Read*, London, The Bodley Head.

Meek, M. (1982b) The Role of Story in the Child's Changing World. In *Story in the Child's Changing World: papers and proceedings of the 18th Congress of the International Board on Books for Young People, Churchill College, Cambridge, 1982.*

Meek, M. (1991) *On Being Literate*, London, The Bodley Head.

Meek, M., Warlow, A. and Barton, G. (eds) (1977) *The Cool Web: the pattern of children's reading*, London, The Bodley Head.

Moss, E. (1980) Seventies in British Children's Books. In Chambers, N. (ed.), *The Signal Approach to Children's Books: a collection*, London, Kestrel.

Nell, V. (1988) In Brewis, W. L. E., Gericke, E. M. and Kruger, J. A. (eds) (1994) Reading Needs and Motives of Adult Users of Fiction, *Mousaion*, **12** (2), 3–18.

Proust, M. (1996) In Manguel, A., *A History of Reading*, London, Viking, 152.

Pullman, P. (2002) Accepting the Eleanor Farjeon Award, London, September 2002.

Ross, C. S. (2001) Making Choices: what readers say about choosing books to read for pleasure, *Acquisitions Librarian*, **25**, 5–21.

Ross, C. S. and Chelton, M. K. (2001) Readers' Advisory: matching mood and material,

Library Journal, **126** (2), 52–5.

Sabine, G. and Sabine, P. (1983) *Books that Made the Difference: what people told us*, Connecticut, USA, The Shoe String Press.

Sillitoe, A. (1996) In Manguel, A., *A History of Reading*, London, Viking, 151.

Spufford, F. (2002a) *The Child that Books Built: a memoir of childhood and reading*, London, Faber.

Spufford, F. (2002b) Pillow Talk: are you snuggled up?, *The Guardian*, G2, (13 March), 8–9.

Stratta, L., Dixon, J. and Wilkinson, A. (1973) *Patterns of Language*, London, Heinemann.

Trelease, J. (1982) *The Read Aloud Handbook*, London, Penguin.

Van Riel, R. (ed.) (1992) *Reading the Future: a place for literature in public libraries. A report of the seminar held in York, 2 and 3 March 1992, organized by the Arts Council of Great Britain in association with the Library Association and the Regional Arts Boards of England*, London, The Arts Council and Library Association Publishing.

Van Riel, R. and Fowler, O. (1996) *Opening the Book: finding a good read*, Yorkshire, Opening the Book, first published by Bradford Libraries.

2
Reader development

Briony Train

Introduction

Reader development, with adult readers in particular, has experienced a dramatic growth in relatively recent years. This chapter explores this growth, in terms of its impact on library service delivery and policy, and in the context of its more social benefits. Themes frequently used in definitions of reader development are considered, such as intervention, cultural change, reader-centred and social inclusion. A number of frequently cross-sectoral initiatives are presented in order to exemplify the various facets of these definitions. The chapter ends with a consideration of the future of reader development.

Intervention in the act of reading

Public libraries were developed in the mid-19th century to promote and encourage the act of reading. Despite considerable changes in appearance as a result of the introduction at the end of the 20th century of Information Technology and electronic access to information, the original aim has been maintained. Proponents of the public library service believe that reading has an intrinsic value to all citizens, not only in a formal educational setting, but as a means of informing and enhancing the lives of all who choose to use it.

The public library is non-judgemental: the materials selected by the fiction reader have always been regarded as equally important as those by the academic. An equity of access, therefore, to a service used by a broad cross-section of populations, irrespective of age, gender, race or class.

However, what happens when a person entering a public library requires information from the library staff? Is the fiction browser looking for 'a good read' offered the same degree of advice and information as the student looking for an academic text on a particular subject? The author is not suggesting that public library staff do not perceive all readers' needs as equal, rather that adult fiction librarians have previously tended not to intervene in their clients' search for fiction, have perhaps felt that any such intervention would remove the neutrality of the service provided. Was it their role to tell people what they should be reading? Was it ethical to promote reading, essentially to direct people who should be self-directed? Former children's librarian Grace Kempster spoke of the views of her colleagues, 'who sometimes felt that we should not be trying to guide people in their reading at all' (Kempster, 2002b).

It was these kinds of concerns that ensured that adult fiction library staff provided an essentially passive service to the fiction reader: information was readily available if the demand was articulated, but otherwise, library users were expected to select and locate their own reading matter, without promotion or encouragement. Any form of intervention in this selection process would have been regarded by some as curtailing the freedom of choice: 'Librarians have tended to take a neutral stance, giving information rather than advice on reading' (Kinnell and Shepherd, 1998, 103).

Intervention in young people's reading

For the children's librarian, the story is very different: somehow it has always been more acceptable to intervene in the reading lives of young people. The young are automatically involved in the formal education process, and are subsequently more accustomed than adults to others offering them information and advice. As Kempster suggested to the author, 'They [adult fiction librarians] talked a lot about book selection and publishers and numbers of copies – but we talked about the excitements and impacts of the stories encountered' (Kempster, 2002b).

Children's librarians have for many years organized programmes of activities to promote reading as an enjoyable experience, in an attempt to foster 'the reading habit', to ensure that the avid young readers of today will become the avid older readers of tomorrow. In the book trade, the active promotion of reading to young people is perceived as equally vital. At the Reading the Future conference in 1992, an event that considered the role of literature in public libraries, Tim Waterstone, the founder of the Waterstone's bookshop chain, made the following statement: 'The future of the book trade largely lies in the hands of educationalists . . . and I just hope that they are up to the challenge and the responsibility they have to put literacy back on the map and in the consciences of our children' (25).

Unsurprisingly, this disparity in the approach to fiction service delivery and the promotion of reading to adults and young people has not gone unnoticed by library professionals. Kempster described an experience she had while working as a children's librarian for Bexley libraries in 1985:

> We organized a marquee celebration for the twenty-first birthday of the authority and had in one half books, drawings, story blankets and dressed-up characters for children, along with author visits and events and also a huge 'cake' made from display panels

> . . . this half of the tent just throbbed with families. . . . In sad contrast, the adult 'half' of the marquee was poorly attended: book displays on tables . . . some sparsely attended author events. It made me feel sad: why hadn't our colleagues used the skill, excitement and inventiveness to engage people? Did they not realize that people [adults] . . . were simply more reticent and complex and diverse about their reading [than young people] . . . ?
>
> (Kempster, 2002b)

The need for cultural change

During the late 1980s and into the 1990s there was an increasing professional awareness that public libraries in Britain were not engaging adult readers as much as they could – and should. Borrowing statistics were declining as a result of external pressures such as budgetary restrictions, local government reorganizations and the 'gradually improving prosperity of the population', and as a result the library's very existence was in question: 'The changing needs and values of the public library's owners have pushed it this way and that until it's really quite hard . . . to see what it's actually for' (Matarasso, 2000, 35).

As part of the Reading the Future conference, a seminar was conducted that investigated the education and training needs of library staff in promoting contemporary writing (Van Riel, 1992b). Delegates from both public and private arts organizations underlined 'the need for large scale change in library culture', and suggested that 'The pressures of accountability and structures have overwhelmed the qualities which should be looked for in library staff. These are [the] perceptions of their role as active, [their] ability to communicate well, [their] love of books, [their] love of people' (45).

Also at this time there was a growing recognition within and outside the library profession that reading, the essential business of the public library, was being overshadowed by the need to fight these external pressures. Suggestions were made that libraries had lost confidence in their fiction sections, and were no longer interacting with their readers: 'The complicated taboos and snobberies which surround attitudes to reading fiction have reinforced the reluctance of public library staff to enter the danger zone of developing policies in this area. Provision has been largely passive and user demand the main criterion' (Van Riel, 1993, 81).

A change in library culture was called for, and a need expressed to meet the needs of the many library users who are not sure what they are looking for, to prioritize fiction reading as essential library public library work:

> This making a priority of non-fiction over fiction runs right from senior management . . . to the library assistant at the counter. In response to queries, library staff will confidently recommend books on do-it-yourself or travel. Asked for 'a good read' they hesitate and tend to fall back on their personal tastes. Is this a professional response?

> Why do we not have systems which enable staff to recommend fiction they have not read with the confidence they recommend non-fiction they have not read? When you consider that 75% of adult issues are fiction, this lack of support and attention is extraordinary.
>
> (Van Riel, 1993, 81)

Towards reader development

It is not the purpose of this chapter to present a chronology of reader development; nor would it be feasible, as sadly, in recent years, a good deal of time has arguably been wasted debating the origins and ownership of the concept of reader development. Why, children's librarians have argued, has reader development been hailed by the rest of society as such a great new idea? We've been doing it for years! The children's library service has undoubtedly promoted and encouraged reading for pleasure for many years, using a wide range of activities and programmes, and highly trained, specialist staff. As the Aslib (1995) review of the public library service in England and Wales reported: 'By making books available to all who want them, together with specialist staff to make them accessible through advice and assistance in the choice and use of them, libraries are uniquely placed to make a significant contribution to the encouragement of reading amongst children and young people.'

However, it would be unreasonable not to take into account the significant recent increase of reader development activities for both adults and young people that has taken place not only in libraries but in all educational and social centres. Perhaps it would be more helpful to view this increase not as a threat to the funding and status of children's librarianship, but as a means of bridging the gap between adult and young people's reading. Why not be delighted that this vital work is no longer left to the same group of people to carry out, but is now the concern and interest of many?

The cultural change referred to above began to occur largely because of the pioneering reader development work conducted not within the library profession itself, but by the private, *independent* reading promotion agencies Opening the Book and Well Worth Reading (the latter now part of The Reading Agency (discussed in detail in Chapter 3)). Although neither one works exclusively with one age group, it is frequently the case that Opening the Book works with adult readers, and The Reading Agency with younger readers. These agencies have been described as 'catalysts for change' (McKearney, Wilson-Fletcher and Readman, 2001, 116), using reader development techniques to offer support to library staff who are in turn able to support their readers.

Definitions of the term

In 2001 it was suggested that the term 'reader development' was 'a buzz phrase in the library world' (The Bookseller, 2001, 26), 'part of the everyday vocabulary of public libraries' (Forrest, 2001, 168). Yet what did professionals understand by the term? Reader development has often been confused with reading development, but the two are very different. Whereas reading development focuses on the acquisition of reading skills, reader development focuses on the reading experience itself.

The underlying principles of this concept were defined in 1992 as raising the status of reading as a creative act, increasing people's confidence in their reading, and finding ways of bringing isolated readers together (Van Riel, 1992a, 4). Today, Opening the Book and The Reading Agency provide very similar definitions of reader development. Opening the Book states that it is an 'active intervention to open up reading choices, to increase people's confidence and enjoyment of what they read, and to offer reader-to-reader activity' (Van Riel, 1998). The Reading Agency refers to 'work that intervenes to expand people's reading horizons, often by connecting people to each other to share reading experiences' (McKearney, Wilson-Fletcher and Readman, 2001, 116).

From these definitions it would appear that the concept of reader development emphasizes the importance of intervention, of increased choices and of shared activity between readers: reader-centred promotion that recognizes the creative role of the reader as well as the artistic role of the writer. Would the practitioners agree that this is a fair description of their work with readers?

> putting the reader at the centre of the process is the key determinant. Putting people first in other words.
> (Library staff)

> I much prefer [the term] 'reader engagement' – finding ways, however subtle or explicit, to help someone trip over a new experience, visit a new concept or world, debate a view, challenge their own and others' thinking, or just escape from their worries.
> (Senior Library Manager)

> To me reader development is a movement. It is creating opportunities for discovery and difference and with readers in the lead. It involves risk taking, trust, respect for difference and [is] about open doors – neither books nor readers being categorized for life. Reader development is powerful – it can change lives, attitudes. It is definitely about seeing our reading lives co-existing with our lived ones: disappointments, discoveries and respecting differences all included.
> (Kempster, 2002b)

The reader-centred approach

Each of these perspectives underlines the fact that the reader is at the centre of all reader development activity, is given the freedom to discover, to challenge, to escape, to take risks. Reader development has the potential to create the environment, to give the opportunity and to present the range of elements that can entice the reader, and draw him or her to the reading experience. It is not prescriptive, and although the role of the librarian in reader development is to 'intervene', this is not to suggest that he or she manipulates the reader in any way, rather that their personal intervention could make the fiction collection more relevant and more accessible to an interested reader. Visiting a public library can be an overwhelming experience because of the sheer scale of what's available:

> Faced with the huge quantity of books in a library or bookshop, finding the right book for you can become a time-consuming and frustrating task. A few people are searching for a particular book or author; a lot more recognize a familiar author or title while browsing; many of us pick something completely unknown from the look of the cover. With so much to choose from, how do you make a decision about what to take home with you?
>
> (Van Riel and Fowler, 1996, 23)

The reader-centred approach of reader development helps readers to answer this question, not by dictating or prescribing, but by enabling them to make a more managed, more informed choice. Access is increased, and even without direct human intervention, the reading environment offers a service that is more tailored to the individual.

As reader development aims to encourage wider reading and reading for pleasure, it follows that participation must be voluntary, and absolutely removed from the formal education system. Although it promotes 'great works of literature' as much as the most popular genre fiction, its aims are not to instruct or 'improve' the reader in any way. As Van Riel (2002) commented:

> Some people feel awkward or ashamed about how much pleasure they get from reading. Creative reading was about liberating people who loved reading to feel OK about it – 'readers come out' was the message. And what then began to happen was that those messages about how reading connects to people's lives were so powerful and so complicated, as opposed to the very simple message of 'read a book and you'll do better in life', 'read a book and be a more moral person', 'read a book and you'll get a job', that they released new energies. Opening the Book was about promoting reading in ways which weren't just saying 'this is good for you'. So although some of those techniques could be used within an educational sector, their power came from being outside of that.

Reader development is driven by the individual and by choices made by the individual. It follows, therefore, that the public library, accessible to all and non-judgmental, is the ideal environment in which to conduct such activity.

Reader development: a solitary or shared activity?

> Reading is a very individual activity and a very communal one. The act of reading is done individually and sharing it makes it communal. One of the joys of reading is sharing the thoughts and feelings a book has provoked in you with others. (Kendrick, 2001, 85).

Although the obvious focus of reader development is the reader, taking into account his or her particular interests, this individual nature of reading is often overlooked when discussing reader development. However, as Van Riel told the author:

> there is a huge amount of reader development going on that people are doing entirely by themselves . . . the act of reading, that's where this starts, isn't it? The act of reading in itself . . . [is] people willingly choosing to put themselves in a position where they're going to be influenced by someone else . . . through the printed word. And some people then want the opportunity to talk to others face to face, and others don't.
>
> (Van Riel, 2002)

Unless being read aloud to, the reader reads a text alone and, outside the educational framework, will begin to interpret the text alone. From the readers' point of view and in the professional practice of intervention, the majority of reader development is concerned with the individual reader, and the choices of the individual. Krashen (1993) emphasizes the crucial role of 'free voluntary reading', which 'means putting down a book that you don't like and choosing another one instead'. 'When I go to the library, I'm completely engrossed in what I'm doing . . . it's a very personal choice and nobody can make it but me. . . . I don't know what I'm going to find and I don't want to be anticipated' (40-year-old interviewee, in Ross, 2001, 6–7).

How would reader development help the above reader? Is there a place for intervention in their reading life? Studies have suggested that there is a role for both passive and active means of promoting fiction to readers, means that can be tailored according to the reading interests of the individual (Towey, 2001). As Van Riel and Fowler suggest, 'promotion is the key to helping the majority of borrowers who don't know what they want find something they are willing to try' (Stewart, 1996, 1.02):

The passive approach takes into account that some people prefer to be left alone in their choice of reading materials, 'enjoying the solitary and serendipitous pursuit of browsing' (Towey, 2001, 135). This does not mean that they would not necessarily appreciate the intervention of the library staff, who can use promotion to make 'unspoken' suggestions using such ideas as pre-selected displays, groups or highlighted selections of texts, presentations of staff or reader comments about a particular book. Readers then have the freedom to accept or reject a title on display. The term 'display' is often interpreted to mean a large-scale presentation of titles, using expensive and purpose-built promotional materials. Equally valuable, however, are the simpler acts of turning books 'face-out' to display eye-catching covers, using tables and small shelving units to do the same, or even displaying paperback titles on a 'spinner', away from the usual A–Z sequence.

The active approach is one which encourages the individual to interact with another, to share his or her reading experience. This may be a one-to-one conversation with a librarian (often described as 'readers' advisory') or a group discussion with other readers or even perhaps the author of a chosen book.

Readers' advisory

The one-to-one conversation with the librarian, initiated either by the member of staff or more likely by the reader, is frequently referred to as the readers' advisory interview. Readers' advisory is a term which originated in the USA in the 1920s, and has been defined as 'a patron-oriented library service for adult fiction readers', a service in which 'knowledgeable, non-judgmental staff help fiction readers with their reading needs' (Saricks and Brown, 1997, 1).

The primary difference between the original reader's advisory as developed in the 1920s and that which is in practice today is the attitude towards the reader. The original advisors perceived themselves to be educators, leading the reader in a particular direction that they felt would be beneficial to them. Today's role is different: 'Readers' advisors today see themselves as links between fiction readers and books, just as reference librarians are the connection between users and non fiction materials' (Saricks and Brown, 1997, 9).

During the readers' advisory interview, the reader describes his or her reading tastes or interests to the librarian, and what he or she is in the mood to read at that particular time. In the course of what is essentially a conversation rather than an interview, the librarian could first ask the reader to tell him or her about a book they previously read and enjoyed, or even if they have read anything lately that they disliked. Listening to the response to either of these questions should provide detailed information about the person's reading tastes, although Saricks and Brown (1997) suggest that further discussion could take place regarding the special characteristics of the books enjoyed or disliked, for example the nature of the plot and characters (69–71).

Following the conversation, readers will hopefully walk away armed with a number of suggestions of ways in which they can explore their reading interests. Furthermore, none of the titles, authors or genres mentioned in the conversation will be anything more than a suggestion – the reader is free to reject any or all of them:

> The measure of success for the readers' advisory interview is not whether the reader takes and reads the books the readers' advisor offers. Rather, the exchange is a success when readers perceive, based on the service they receive, that the library is a place where they can talk about books and obtain suggestions and resources to meet their reading needs.
> (Saricks and Brown, 1997, 57)

Some advocates of reading promotion feel that the above term 'suggestion' is of particular significance. Although it may be reasonable to 'recommend' titles to friends and family, based on our personal reading experiences and our knowledge of their interests, it would be inappropriate for members of staff to recommend titles to readers in a library: they could instead suggest a range of books that may be of interest, based on the readers' comments regarding their tastes and current mood.

> When we make this distinction, when we *suggest* rather than *recommend*, we change the focus of our readers' advisory and of our patron interactions. It is far less threatening to talk with a reader and suggest a range of books than to take the responsibility for recommending something we think is appropriate. Patrons are also more comfortable returning with comments, especially negative comments, about books we have suggested than about those that come recommended. (Saricks and Brown, 1997, 58)

Van Riel and Fowler agree that recommending books to library users can be 'a dangerous business', and that 'recommendation' is 'a loaded term'. They use the analogy of buying clothes to illustrate that people should not feel that they have 'failed' if they choose not to accept the suggestion of another – or if their suggestion is not taken: 'If you go to buy a new outfit, you can take three items into the changing room; the assistant hopes to sell you one but she doesn't feel implicated by your choice. You try on a lot of outfits before you find the one that's right for you. It is just the same with books' (Stewart, 1996, 1.03).

The question of quality

While examining the interaction between librarians and readers, it is appropriate to consider the issue of quality. There are no fixed 'quality standards' by which to assess the value of a book: if 50 readers were to read the same novel, there would be 50 different interpretations to bring to a discussion. As has previously been mentioned, the reader is at the centre of the reading experience, and one reader's view of the text is no less valid than another's.

If each member of the above group of 50 readers were asked if the book they had been given to read was 'well written', it is equally likely that there would be a further 50 different responses. What is the exact meaning of the phrase 'well written'? All readers could list books that they consider to be well written, if such books meet their own *personal* standards for a satisfying reading experience. They may prefer a novel with detailed characterization, a highly descriptive use of language, a fast pace, and any title that failed to contain such elements would be inadequate.

There are, of course, many hundreds of thousands of new books published every year, and it would be foolish to suggest that all are of an equal literary quality. Prizes such as the Booker, Pulitzer or Whitbread are awarded to those novels that a panel of judges feel to be particularly worthy of merit, and they have their place in informing the reader of the type of book that is 'critically acclaimed'. However, is a person a lesser reader if he or she fails to appreciate such an acclaimed novel? Is a critically acclaimed novel necessarily 'a good book' to the reader who prefers a different writing style?

Van Riel suggests that it is helpful to move from the quality of the book to the quality of the reading experience:

> Debates about standards tend to focus on the quality of the writer or the book . . . look instead at the quality of the reading experience. We all know that it is possible to have a fantastic reading experience with a book that is not generally considered to be great. It is also possible to have a poor reading experience with a book that has been accepted as brilliant.
> (Stewart, 1996, 1.48–9)

Because of the subjective nature of quality assessment in reading material, it is not the role of the readers' advisor to make a quality judgement on behalf of the reader, unless the reader has specifically asked for information concerning, for example, recent award-winning titles. Even if the reader asks for 'an easy read', it is first important to establish how he or she would define such a level of quality, 'to be aware that there are levels and variations at both ends of this quality spectrum' (Saricks and Brown, 1997, 59).

The reading group

> When Oprah Winfrey started her book group it seemed that she started a whole new craze. People all over the country were reading what she told them, and book groups started popping up all over the place. This resurgence in reading just shows that people were starved for the joys of reading, and needed someone to tell them it's OK to read and enjoy it; that's what Oprah did, gave reading the stamp of approval. People thought

> this book group idea was a new phenomenon, but it's not, it's just a new awakening, a new phase. It's not the new fad of the '90s. Book groups have been going on for years in different forms. Traditionally, book groups tend to be women, and I think this is because book groups provided community, provided a place of self-education, a chance to escape from the family for a time for some intelligent conversation.
>
> (Kendrick, 2001, 87)

Although readers have discussed their reading experiences with others since the advent of mass-market publishing, the book discussion group, or reading group, has grown dramatically in recent years, to the extent that we can go into almost any public library in the UK and be directed to a group that is either organized by the library staff or by interested individuals. Essex County Council, for example, supports more than 200 such groups!

Reading groups take place in libraries, bookshops, pubs, restaurants, the workplace, people's homes, residential homes, even via the internet. There is no fixed format for the reading group, either in terms of the frequency of meetings or the content of the discussion. Members may read the same book (or books) prior to a meeting, or may choose to bring an individual selection to the group. Some groups will be extremely informal, others will require more preparation or input from their members. Some will be open to all readers, others will target a particular age group or readers of a specific genre. Some will have a list of regular attendees, others will attract people who come to discuss one particular book. Some have a clear leader who decides the titles to be discussed, others will offer all members the opportunity to lead the discussion on their chosen title.

The reported benefits of participation in a reading group vary considerably. One librarian who had begun her own group gave the following response:

> For myself, it's the reading and sharing that goes on. I read books I've always wanted to but never got around to, and I read books I never would have on my own. The discussion is the second part of it. I like the sharing, the little insights, not only to the book but to the people themselves. I have fun with the group. One member is in three groups, she says she can't imagine reading a book and not discussing it. For her the groups give her a chance to catch up on all the reading she never had the time for when she was raising a family. Now she'll read anything, but she feels she misses something if she can't discuss it.
>
> (Kendrick, 2001, 87)

A member of the Clacton Booktalk group acknowledges the effect of participation on her reading choices:

> I doubt if I would have chosen any of the books [read by the Booktalk group] off the shelf for myself. Some I have loved, some have left me indifferent, some I have hated

> and a very few have proved to be almost unreadable but all of them, without fail, have produced lively discussions full of insight and humour. If I read something I enjoy I pester my friends and family to read it, then I have the joy of being able to talk about it all over again. While writing my reviews I find myself wondering what other members of the group might be thinking but there is always someone who surprises me – such an interesting collection of people brought together through a common love of reading.
>
> (Turner, 2002)

The obvious advantage of these groups is that they offer readers an opportunity to share their reading thoughts and experiences with others. In this way reading, often a solitary activity, becomes participatory.

Just as the reader is not obliged to read every book recommended by the library staff, neither should he or she feel that participation in a reading group in some way validates his or her reading. Many people will choose not to participate in such activities, believing that no external stimulus is necessary in order to enjoy the act of reading:

> I have . . . [a] friend who is an avid reader. . . . Though she loves reading she is not in a book group . . . she said sharing a book is like sharing your soul and you're giving someone a chance to stomp on it. Being in a group requires some trust. I find them too personal and I don't want to share the experience with others. I want to keep it safe, and there is a fear the group won't have the same feelings that I did and it would be a blow against me. (Kendrick, 2001, 88)

The reading experience: a summary

Reader development offers people a range of choices by which they can enhance their reading experiences. To provide these choices the public library is not required to spend vast amounts of money; reader development methods are inexpensive, and can be used to exploit all existing stock and back stock, to issue new stock to more people.

The project culture

The growth in reader development activity means that public libraries throughout the UK have become involved in a wide range of project-based promotional events and programmes. Over the periods 2000–1 and 2001–2 this growth had become sufficiently widespread for the Government, via its Department for Culture, Media and Sport (DCMS), to allocate two years' of its Public Libraries Challenge Fund specifically to reader development projects. This fund, created by the DCMS in 1997–8 to 'enhance the facilities and services provided by public libraries', resulted in a total investment of £4 million in projects that aimed to enhance 'libraries' traditional strength in promoting reading as a skill and pleasure' (Great Britain, DCMS, 2001a).

The overall impact of the DCMS/Wolfson funding was undeniably great, in terms of its support of the development of a wide range of projects for both adults and young people, many of which involved the creation of partnerships with other sectors. As the evaluators of the first year of the programme reported: 'The evidence showed that the Programme was resoundingly successful in stimulating short-term reader development initiatives and a great deal of extremely exciting innovative activity took place as a direct result of the award' (Wallis, Moore and Marshall, 2002, abstract).

However, it is necessary to acknowledge the potential dangers of operating within a project culture: 'There is a great danger, particularly because it has been funded largely from external, time-limited project budgets, that reader development is regarded as a fringe activity; something to engage in when a bit of money comes along or you need a quirky but worthy event to get some press coverage' (Forrest, 2001, 169).

Project timescale

The timescale of all funded projects is limited by the length of the funded period, and it will inevitably be difficult to maintain the momentum when additional resources are no longer available. The DCMS/Wolfson awards were given for one year, and the evaluation of the first year of funding (2000–1) illustrated that this was generally regarded as insufficient: 'Final reports expressed . . . frustration that a year is too short for the majority of projects of this nature. Further, many projects require more than a year to develop the momentum necessary to make them sustainable. This is particularly the case when projects require the active participation of other partners' (Wallis, Moore and Marshall, 2002, 16).

The second year of funding showed similar results. The evaluation of the Caring with Books in the West Midlands initiative (2001–2) revealed concerns over the project timescale, both in terms of the length and structure of the funded period (Train, 2002, 57):

> It has been very difficult: the money was suddenly there, and there was very little lead-in, by the time you're making in-roads it's nearly over. You're looking for a longer period: what takes the time is setting up the networks, making contacts. Time is running out! (Library staff)

> The timescale, that puts such a pressure on them [the library staff]. I think there's a quality issue when you put a hard timescale on like that, the timescale actually becomes the driving force rather than the project itself, and that's a big mistake, I think. (Project partner)

A second example is The Vital Link, an initiative linking adult literacy and libraries. Project managers suggested that overall management difficulties had been exacerbated by the limited time available in which to complete the project:

> It's a very tight time scheme in terms of the promotion, with very severe deadlines. . . . It's too short a time: everyone acknowledges that Wolfson is too short. It doesn't happen overnight, nothing can, when you're going for socially excluded people. It should be two to three years, to get the systems sorted out. (Train, et al, 2002, 118)

The evaluation reports of all the above projects recommended longer timescales for future funded reader development projects, possibly to include a preliminary research and partnership development phase, and a second phase during which to deliver the project (Train, 2002, 71; Train, Usherwood and Brooks, 2002, 132; Wallis, Moore and Marshall, 2002, 16).

Project planning

The second potential danger of the project culture, as underlined in the earlier comment by Forrest (2001, 169), is that work is often conducted with little long-term planning. Public library staff are always understandably pleased to receive additional funds, and project work is the obvious way in which to receive such support. However, such work is extremely resource intensive, and when funding ends it is difficult to continue at the same level of intensity, to maintain the impact.

To illustrate this point, the following comments are taken from data collected by the author for the evaluation of four DCMS/Wolfson projects, 2000–1 and 2001–2:

- Incredibly valuable work is being done with very little money.
- There are not enough staff available to do the project work.
- Hard work is often done by a small number of enthusiastic staff.
- Libraries are well known for their short-term projects . . . which then stop.

Perhaps the most significant benefit of working on a time-limited project is that it provides the public library with the opportunity to trial new ways of working and new methods of service delivery, before introducing them to the organization as a whole. Financial constraints that affect core services would otherwise leave little opportunity for experimentation. For such trials to work, however, the funding application process should be sufficiently rigorous that each project is based on an original idea that tests a hypothesis or an alternative mode of delivery, and is then evaluated in terms of its potential outcome on the overall service. Similarly rigorous should be the strategic direction of the project: what does the project intend to investigate? Will the funding period be sufficiently long to complete such an investigation? What measures will be taken to ensure that the work is continued after the funded period?

In order to ensure that such measures are taken, project managers should ensure that each project is considered in the light of the following:

- *mainstreaming* – i.e. making project work a part of everyday library work, with sufficient time, staff, resources, and commitment
- *sustainability* – i.e. ensuring that projects do not end after nine months or a year, but are continued in the daily work of the library.

A failure to consider these two issues will result in a failure to incorporate library-based project work, however excellent for a time, into core service provision.

Collaborative working with other sectors

For the second of the two years of DCMS/Wolfson reader development funding (2001–2), the DCMS (2001) stipulated: 'All applications must be in partnerships – we will not accept bids from single authorities or organizations acting alone. . . We are particularly keen to encourage partnerships between libraries and other learning organizations, and libraries and the private sector.'

This requirement emphasizes the growing expectation that public libraries develop partnerships with other agencies, in the first instance with other public libraries, but on a wider scale with external partners from both the public and private sectors. Wallis, Moore and Marshall (2002, 27) suggest that this expectation is due to the 'government's commitment to modernisation'. Some partnerships will take the form of commercial sponsorship, others will involve a mutual sharing of expertise and/or resources. Both are equally valid, but it is important to recognize that they are different in their objectives.

A commercial sponsorship could, for example, provide the library service with financial support and the opportunity to participate in a promotional campaign including the use of high-quality promotional materials and media advertising. This may attract members of the public and subsequently raise the overall profile of the service. In return, the sponsor would benefit from the advertising campaign, with publicity opportunities for its organization that may involve the materials, buildings and people of the library service. The potential danger of such a venture is that one party could benefit more than another: for example, if a library service agrees to promote the shortlisted titles for a particular literary prize, it may benefit to some extent from being mentioned in the advertising campaign, but with only a limited number of titles involved in the promotion, could it reasonably expect an increase in issue statistics? Has the reading public been offered something new as a result of the promotion? Benefits in terms of reader development would certainly be difficult to find in such a venture.

Perhaps more relevant to reader development are the many consortia-based projects that have taken place in recent years, in which resources and expertise are shared or jointly developed in order to bring reader development to particular groups or organizations. Projects on this scale require considerable co-ordination, with the development of committees, working groups, even boards. Yet it follows that as the size of the project increases, the potential for it to enhance the profile of the stakeholders is also greater.

DCMS/Wolfson Public Libraries Challenge Fund for reader development

The evaluation of the overall impact of the first year of DCMS/Wolfson funding suggested that as a result of partnerships with other local government departments and community-based services, 'the profile of the library service has been raised and its ability to support the Council's work . . . has been recognized across the Council' (Wallis, Moore and Marshall, 2002, 29).

Evaluation findings from two second-year projects, The Vital Link and Caring with Books in the West Midlands, revealed that project partners from other sectors (adult basic skills education and Social Services respectively) had begun to appreciate the value to their organizations of working with the public library service:

> What we're going to do now is find a way of carrying on the partnership in a way that would benefit both of us . . . from now on I'll be in [name] library every Monday morning with [name of librarian], because we're going to make a real positive drive to get a creative group going. (The Vital Link – basic skills tutor)

> We weren't aware of all the library services before. We have to continue that relationship: the library is very important to the carers, libraries go hand in glove with the work we do, because of the educational link.
>
> (Caring with Books in the West Midlands – Social Services representative)

Branching Out

Branching Out was a three-year initiative (1998–2001) from the Society of Chief Librarians, managed by Opening the Book and supported by the National Lottery through the Arts Council of England. With representatives from 33 partner authorities throughout England, the project raised the status of reader development within and beyond each of the 150 public library authorities through a series of regional networks and national partnerships. Since the completion of the first three years, additional funding has been awarded to Opening the Book to extend the work of Branching Out to Wales and Scotland, and to further develop the project website (see also Chapter 8).

Historically, the compatibility of library services and the commercial sector has been questioned, and the potential for partnerships has perhaps tended to be unexplored. The evaluation of the first year of DCMS/Wolfson funding gave the following report of Books & Business, a collaboration between the London Libraries Development Agency and the company Arts & Business: 'On the business side . . . scepticism remains about the ability of libraries to deliver against business objectives. Business managers "have begun to understand theoretically what library partnerships have the potential to achieve, but they still doubt the ability of librarians to deliver and execute the partnerships effectively"' (Wallis, Moore and Marshall, 2002, 28). Wallis, Moore and Marshall conclude that 'there is still much to learn on both sides'. (For more on the London Libraries Development Agency see Chapter 3.)

One of the commercial partners to Branching Out was Book Communications, a reading promotion agency in the private sector, an organization that worked with a team of Branching Out librarians to develop a world literature promotion. Jonathan Davidson of Book Communications summarized his perception of the partnership as follows: 'the whole process ran smoothly and, in our opinion, was a model example of how to work with partners . . . working with the Branching Out librarians was equally rewarding. They taught us a lot and were always well briefed, positive and most importantly reliable' (Train and Elkin, 2001).

Further evidence of the success of this partnership is the fact that a second Branching Out project was developed with Book Communications, a promotion called Future Tense which aimed to ease readers into the science fiction genre.

A second commercial partner to Branching Out was HarperCollins publishing house. Guy Pringle (2002), former marketing manager, describes the growth of the partnership and the increasing awareness of the relevance of reader development to its work:

> In the late 1990s, one of my responsibilities at HarperCollins was marketing the company's publishing to the library sector. At the time, HarperCollins' perspective of this market was – and for many publishers still is – that it was moribund, unexciting and unlikely to change.
>
> However, a chance conversation at Books for Students led to contact with Rachel Van Riel and, subsequently, HarperCollins' involvement with Branching Out . . . Initially, Terrie Riley (HarperCollins' Library Sales Manager) and I saw this as an opportunity to present HarperCollins' publishing plans direct to librarians rather than through the conventional channels of library suppliers.
>
> . . . HarperCollins became the publishing partner providing information on forthcoming

> paperback fiction by new and relatively unknown authors. The initiative was supported by HarperCollins' promotional materials and dumpbins and proved sufficiently successful for the publisher to widen it into its first Book of the Month scheme . . . having reached nearly 30 library authorities in England, HarperCollins is now actively promoting Book of the Month more widely.
>
> On behalf of HarperCollins, we also involved ourselves in the first, and subsequent Readers' Days in Bradford which proved influential in our decision to liaise more closely with librarians, now we realized what reader development meant and just how much of it was going on . . . The intention in each case was to initiate a dialogue between HarperCollins and a wide range of library authorities in order to make them aware of the company's publishing at first hand.
>
> . . . As a further result of HarperCollins' involvement in Branching Out, it also became the publishing partner in several other Wolfson funding bids.

As demonstrated here, reader development can be relevant to the work of non-library organizations, and as in the above example, an initial joint venture can lead to long-term, sustainable partnerships that are beneficial to both parties.

A second example of an effective partnership between the publishing and library sectors via the intermediary of reader development is the *newBOOKSmag* 'Book of the year' survey – and subsequent prize. *newBOOKSmag*, created by Guy Pringle, formerly of HarperCollins, is a magazine for readers and reading groups that is now widely used in public libraries in the UK. The most recent *newBOOKSmag* initiative is the search for 'the book of the year', as voted for by readers of the magazine. Its creator explains the potential impact of this initiative on the publishing industry:

> Publishers pump thousands of new books into the market place each year. Their only yardstick of success or failure is sales figures and anecdotal feedback. The statistics that will result from our 'Book of the year' survey will add another dimension to that assessment: what readers really enjoy reading and, by definition, want to read more of. The data could prove highly influential in guiding publishers to publishing more of what readers really want. (Pringle, 2002)

Further evidence of the growing impact of reader development on the bookselling and publishing sectors is that The Bookseller, the trade publication of the bookselling industry, included the following in its first edition of 2001:

> *Reader development* is a buzz phrase in the library world; but, unlike most buzz phrases, it has a real meaning. Library promotions are geared towards encouraging readers to make new discoveries: 'If you like so-and-so, why not try such-and-such?'; 'Here are some excellent thrillers/works of black literature/historical narratives' and so on. Publishers' and booksellers' promotions are mostly geared towards selling frontlist titles; many

> backlist promotions are of the 'three for two' variety designed to appeal to bargain hunters. These promotions are not, to use another buzz term, 'empowering' readers to make their own explorations; they are selling to customers what the book industry wants to promote. Publishers and booksellers need to encourage readers for the long term.
>
> (The Bookseller, 2001, 26)

Partnerships between the public library service and external agencies can be difficult, particularly when objectives and working methods may vary considerably. However, there is evidence to suggest that they can be both effective and beneficial, developing original initiatives that have the potential to be sustained in the longer term. Public libraries have a pivotal role to play in the promotion of reading and reading materials, and should ensure that all potential partners are aware of this. Subsequent partnerships could then be mutually beneficial, sustainable and, above all, equal. 'Readers are the greatest resource libraries have. Reader development establishes an expanding mass of confident, empowered readers which benefits not only libraries but also writers, publishers, booksellers and everyone involved in literature. Reader development offers a role to public libraries which puts them at the centre of the world of literature' (Stewart, 1996, 1.20).

Social inclusion

Towards the end of the previous century, there was a growing realization in the public library sector that its user profile had changed considerably: 'As a universal and free service, the public library has gradually come to be used more by those who would not depend on it if it weren't there than by those who really need it' (Matarasso, 2000, 35).

At the same time, one of the priorities of the new Government was to combat the growing problem of social exclusion. This is defined by the government Social Exclusion Unit as 'a shorthand label for what can happen when individuals or areas suffer from a combination of linked problems such as unemployment, poor skills, low incomes, poor housing, high crime environments, bad health and family breakdown' (Lang and Wilkinson, 2000). Since the beginning of the Labour administration in 1997, the focus of government policies has shifted away from exclusion towards inclusion.

In accordance with the Government policy that 'social inclusion should be mainstreamed as a policy priority for library and information services' (DCMS, 2001b, 4.1), working towards social inclusion subsequently became one of the key priorities of all public libraries. The current Annual Library Plan for Worcestershire Libraries and Information Service, for example, states: 'Social inclusion is a fundamental policy of the library service in Worcestershire. Social inclusion is a factor in all policy decisions with the underlying aim being to improve access and services for all, particularly those people who are disadvantaged in some way' (Worcestershire Libraries and Information Service, 2001).

A widescale attempt to develop a more inclusive service was a key focus of the DCMS/Wolfson Public Libraries Challenge Fund (2000–1, 2001–2). This was awarded to reader development projects that specifically aimed to reach socially excluded groups, for example:

- the homeless
- those with poor literacy skills
- members of ethnic minority communities
- the physically and mentally disabled
- the visually impaired
- the elderly
- carers and looked-after children.

Evaluations of projects from both years have suggested that reader development can be an effective means of promoting reading to new audiences who have not previously used the library or read a certain type of book, and can support the development of new library services specifically for such audiences.

> *Inside Books*, a project to promote reader development in prisons, set up a reading group with male vulnerable prisoners, who have to be segregated for their own safety. These men are, in their own words, 'desperate to get hold of books' and the reading group 'has proved a lifeline to the real world'. (Wallis, Moore and Marshall, 2002, 12)

> The three projects that focused on ethnic minority groups . . . the *Bangladeshi Link*, *Black Inc.* and the *Turkish Community Readers' Project* all met or exceeded their targets and raised the profile and use of the library service with the targeted minority community.
> (Wallis, Moore and Marshall, 2002, 19)

Although there have been many successes in terms of reader development initiatives reaching marginalized groups, the difficulty of doing so is widely acknowledged. For example, the 2000–1 DCMS/Wolfson project 'Premiership reading challenge', a football-based reader development project targeted at men, boys and looked-after children, effectively reached fathers and their sons, but failed to reach looked-after children. The project manager reported that 'Reader development work with specific target groups needs to be more focused on those groups – we cannot necessarily expect such groups to join in alongside other library users, when there is no tradition or advantage for them to do so' (Wallis, Moore and Marshall, 2002, 20).

Other DCMS/Wolfson initiatives that aimed to reach different excluded groups had similar difficulties:

- *First Steps, Northumberland*: 'There were difficulties reaching the most needy families – parents with limited literacy skills lacked the confidence to participate'
- *Oldham, Something Lovely*: '[Local residents regarded the public library as] an alien, perhaps even hostile, environment with little or no relevance to their lives'
- *East Riding, Word on the Street*: 'young people felt unwelcome in libraries' (Wallis, Moore and Marshall, 2002, 21).

An alternative approach?

> Starting from the reader and not the book raises all sorts of questions about the differing needs of readers and the way those needs can be met. It is what makes reader development such a powerful force for change. (Turner, 2002).

Reader development has been considered so far as a means of reaching particular groups, groups that have been in some way 'marginalized' from society. There is evidence to suggest that such initiatives have been effective in many ways, introducing people to public library resources and the pleasure of reading. However, it is also clear that this form of outreach work is problematic: how do you encourage new audiences to try new services that they have previously felt unwelcome to use and have regarded as irrelevant to their lives? And should this be the main focus of the public library, a service to whom the established clientele is of equal importance?

The idea of the public library service is entirely socially inclusive, as it offers free access to reading and learning materials and information for all members of the public, regarding all people as individuals with equal rights to its resources. This idea acknowledges the inequalities that exist in society, and 'is dedicated to reducing the gap between a theoretical right to know and our actual ability to know' (Matarasso, 2000, 35).

In the same way, reader development begins with the individual, and fails to acknowledge any difference between one reader and another. It regards each person and his or her choice of reading as equally important, and makes no value judgements.

In its targeting of particular groups, the current practice of social inclusion could be interpreted as having an underlying assumption that those people who are 'included' are correct in what they do, and that others – who are different in some way – should be given access to another way of life in order to improve their own. 'Those people who are supposed to be having social inclusion done to them, they know when the people talking to them see a gap between 'them' (the needy) and 'us' (the providers). The real inclusion is to be included without that gap, and that's the reader-centred practice that we're doing' (Van Riel, 2002).

With reader development, therefore, the approach is 'reader-centred', its starting point is the reader as an individual with individual needs, not as a member of an excluded group:

> I think that the energy and dynamism of reader development came . . . [from] an understanding and an assertion that the fundamental act of reading was the same for all kinds of people. What they use it to do may vary hugely, but the practice of reading and what was going on there psychologically, socially and culturally . . . was something which could be shared. . . . That reader, that potential reader, is the same kind of human being as the people who are trying to provide the service. And the energy of reader development was to assert that fundamental connection . . . we recognize that the way in which somebody else reads is not fundamentally different from the way in which I read . . . that's a much healthier way to see it . . . and therefore there's no gap to bridge.
>
> (Van Riel, 2002)

A considerable proportion of the public library budget is today allocated to outreach work, to reaching those who, for many reasons, are not currently using the service. Many library staff are required to visit community groups or individuals either to bring the service to them, or to encourage them to go to the library building itself. Forrest (2002) suggests that this is not necessarily the role of library personnel:

> Libraries need to realize that when they are trying to reach the most disadvantaged groups, or individuals, who are excluded from the library service for all sorts of economic, social or cultural reasons, that they can never go there on their own. In fact librarians are often fairly ill equipped to reach the most disadvantaged or excluded people. Libraries are public institutions with all the strengths and benefits of a democratic cultural space – but the very fact of being a public institution can also be a barrier for some people. Nevertheless, they are the only sustainable way of delivering the service and we should give more attention to managing them better. The purpose of outreach and social inclusion work is to attract people in to the library but too many outreach programmes do not complete that loop. At the same time librarians feel the need to develop skills which are not germane to their role. Librarians need to articulate the benefits of what it is that they have to offer people and then work with the right agencies who can communicate that to the targeted audience. Then they need to make sure that when the targeted people do come in, that the library is vibrant and relevant, and inspiring to those people.

The public library service should reach out to the non-users, not necessarily by delivering more resources and services to them, but by giving them a greater access to such services, and above all a wider choice. Promotions would perhaps be more effective if the services they offered were integrated into the mainstream service, reducing the stigma of 'being different'.

Mind's Eye

Two examples of promotions that have been devised to be integrated into the core service in this way are Mind's Eye (2000–1) and the First Choice promotion of The Vital Link (2001–2).

The Mind's Eye project (managed by Opening the Book Ltd) was awarded to the Public Libraries Group of the former Library Association, as part of the first year of the DCMS/Wolfson Public Libraries Challenge Fund for reader development. It aimed to promote narrative non-fiction in particular to adult male readers under 50 – an age group that is widely recognized to be under-using the public library service for other than reference materials. However, the two book promotions that were devised during the project – 'Reflect' and 'Decide' – were integrated to the library service as a whole, and did not prioritize the reading needs of one reader over another. It moved the books away from the 'serried ranks of spine-on books in an A to Z sequence' (Van Riel, 2001, 30), towards a whole-library presence.

Pilot authorities participating in the Mind's Eye project reported that they had been encouraged to rethink not only the content but also the presentation of their stock promotions. For example, library staff planned procedural changes in terms of the location of their promotional activities:

> It clarified the purpose of non-fiction promotion and also gave me the enthusiasm to think up promotional ideas of my own.
>
> In general terms our expectations are to extend reader development practices throughout the library, which is why our main thrust has been in focusing upon the non-fiction/reference floor of the Central library. The ideas we are using in that are a totally new approach for us . . . using location creatively, breaking down stereotypes . . . and barriers to borrowing non-fiction.
>
> I believe that continuity of approach is most important if we wish to change the public perception of libraries. (Train, 2001, 19–20)

First Choice

The overall purpose of the First Choice exercise, developed as part of the Vital Link initiative, was to develop a promotion of appropriate titles to be enjoyed by all emergent readers. Titles were specifically selected from 'mainstream' lists, thereby widening the choice of reading materials available to those with reading difficulties, while at the same time making them equally available to any library user. A basic skills tutor made the following response to the collection: 'They're very adult, and they're certainly not in any way patronising . . . all that is excellent . . . you're dealing with quite sophisticated people . . . it's quite hard to have something that is adult and sophisticated, but still simple enough language to be accessible . . . this has got to be a move in the right direction!' (Train, 2002, 115).

The inclusive public library service can use reader development methods to focus its attention not on a specific group, but on the individual, offering to but not prescribing for each member of society:

> the independence, the space and the trust. And it's the structure of libraries, rules, regulations, often that stand in the way of those things. And if you're talking about reaching a group . . . libraries do have to do more than just make themselves open, to open the doors . . . they have to reach out. So in that sense, yes, they have to be more socially inclusive . . . [to be] available to those people, to make sure that they're getting all the same chances as everybody else. But because of what it is, because of what the library is, because of what reader development is, what you give them is the space to have the choice about whether to be included or not . . . because I have the right to be different! I have the right to access all of those books, but I don't have to read them in the same way as you. (Forrest, 2002)

The impact of reader development on service provision and policy

> The real issue facing the profession is how to maintain the creativity, the power and the passion while delivering policy statements and performance reports. Of course, they are not mutually exclusive, we need to know why we are doing things, and to gain budget we need to show the impact . . . The principle reason many of us are so passionate about engaging people with words is because of the impact it has . . . In reality, it is this impact that is important. To ensure support for this work we, of course, need to translate this impact to service output and national strategy. (Blanshard, 2002)

The field of reader development has dramatically increased in recognition in recent years. At a time when book funds are increasingly limited, reader development initiatives have arguably brought individuals together into stronger working groups.

Work conducted in partnership with agencies such as Opening the Book and The Reading Agency (discussed in detail in Chapter 3) has affected the quality and range of titles purchased by library services, and the way in which such materials are displayed and promoted. Other core reader development activities have similarly affected long-established stock policies:

> Libraries involved with reader development will already have registered the impact on their stock policy. Reading groups, for example, challenge our established, or budget-led decisions on numbers of titles stocked and the way in which we move the stocks between libraries. Buying in stock promotions affects the way in which our policy is determined for displays, exhibition and promotions. (Lake, 2002)

An ongoing reader development programme ensures that work conducted 'on the ground' is more visible, and reveals the benefits of reader development to both staff and end-users:

> The whole concept [of reader development] has had a huge impact on Gateshead. It has changed the way we select our stock, we buy fewer hardbacks now and have a much wider range of fiction. Staff have become more confident to display titles which at one time they would have hidden in case they caused offence and most important of all, we now have a tradition of reader-based events across the borough. . . . Authors, too, seem to be more prepared to come and give talks and to listen to readers' groups discussing their work. Use of high quality nationally produced promotional material has enhanced the appearance and raised the profile of our displays. (Cameron, 2002)

The role of all staff in policy development

Whereas changes in organizational culture are often driven from a strategic level only, it is significant that all library staff have a role to play in reader development, and can influence its impact on their workplace. For example, after three years of participation in the Branching Out initiative, senior managers and frontline library staff were able to provide equal evidence of the considerable impact of participation on their library service:

- increased staff knowledge of contemporary literature
- increased staff awareness of readers and their reading needs
- acquisition of (transferable) skills with which to design training programmes
- acquisition of tools with which to attract larger reading audiences to libraries
- demonstration of sustainable models of partnerships, e.g. between libraries and commercial partners
- increased collaboration and co-operation between staff across an authority
- sustained development or creation of regional networks for reader development work
- new focus on stock selection and book promotion as integrated processes
- development and provision of centralized stock selection processes
- increased use of ICT as a reader development tool
- development/revision of reader development policies, e.g. Annual Library Plans, policy documents.

Frontline staff engaged in reader development activities are regarded as 'good to do business with' (Kempster, 2002b). They are frequently instrumental in the development of partnerships with other cultural services, and can raise the profile of library staff and the overall public library service.

Reader development and technology

It could be argued that one reason for the impact of reader development on library service developments is that it has served to dispel fears that the increase of information technology will result in the demise of the book. Electronic reader development initiatives such as whichbook.net (formerly Book Forager) and Ask Chris (developed by Essex Libraries) have helped to convince both staff and users that ICT offers an alternative – and not a replacement – reading experience (see also Chapter 7).

As Saricks (2001, 120) states, 'Those of us who love books are not trying to win a battle against technology. We take advantage of that technology in serving patrons with reading interests . . . In the best of all worlds – and libraries – books and technology will continue to supplement each other.'

To regard the two as complementary would seem, therefore, to be the most effective strategy that today's public library manager could adopt: 'The future public library workforce will find reader development to be an ideal tool in squaring the circle of demand and resourcing . . . developing reader development virtual services and products will become a new area that could be both lucrative and high impact' (Kempster, 2002b).

The future of reader development

In recent years, particularly since the late 1990s, a considerable amount of public and private funding has been allocated to reader development initiatives managed within the public library service. The largest single fund to date has been the DCMS/Wolfson Public Libraries Challenge Fund for reader development (approximately £4 million awarded during the periods 2000–1, 2001–2), and when it ended fear was understandably expressed as to the future of reader development: 'Reader development is still quite young and vulnerable especially in environments that just have not "got it" in terms of the underlying and fundamental nature of reader development. So I think the jury is out on what will happen without the lure of a budget' (Kempster, 2002b).

The DCMS fund and similar awards strongly supported reader development work, giving public library services an ideal opportunity to trial and develop new and alternative elements of their overall service, to promote reading in innovative ways.

When the original funding period is over, it can be extremely difficult to sustain projects, promotions, websites, readers' groups, without additional resources – both human and financial. However, perhaps the time following a funded period should automatically be dedicated to applying the lessons of the pilot phase, to finding a way to incorporate the effective elements of the project to mainstream service provision? In doing so, public library managers can use the evidence collected during the pilot phase to allocate internal, existing funds to deliver and sustain an enhanced core service: 'Public library authorities know the agenda: this is what our readers want and it is up to us to maintain these services, to re-direct funds or create partnerships with bookshops, publishers and writers to provide the reader development services for the future' (Lake, 2002).

Writing in the *Independent* newspaper in 2001, Ken Worpole made the following statement: 'A few years ago Britain's public library service had the look of a tanker sailing slowly but inexorably into institutional oblivion. Crucially, it had lost its vital relationship with the culture of reading and an engagement with contemporary literature. Librarians had, in every sense, lost the plot'. Fortunately, however, he reported that he had subsequently noted 'a dramatic change in the public library's relationship with reading', and that 'the tanker has been turned round' (McKearney, Wilson-Fletcher and Readman, 2001, 116).

At the same time, McKearney et al (2001, 116) commented on the ever-increasing profile of the public library service in its promotion of reading: 'Not only are libraries now directing major resources into working with readers, they're getting much more confident about bagging the territory of being the UK's most significant provider of the reading experience.'

Further evidence of the increasingly widespread acceptance of the role of public libraries in promoting reading can be found at a national level. The Audit Commission Best Value inspection process in the UK specifically requires library services to focus on reader development, and its recent report 'Building better library services' (Great Britain. Audit Commission, 2002) refers to reader development as one of the key recent changes to the library service.

In the public library sector today 'the needs of readers are being seen as one of libraries' managerial priorities' (McKearney, 1999, 106). Reader development has become a high-profile activity, and its value and impact are being recognized by other agencies, both within the public sector and in the commercial world. Its recent dramatic growth was partially but not entirely due to the additional funding allocated specifically to reader development projects: the commitment of public library staff played an equal role.

Where library services have taken the initiative and incorporated successful elements of promotions or projects into the core service, and where staff at all levels are included in the process, sustainability is more likely to be ensured.

> 'Bearing in mind the fortitude needed for reader development to get thus far, I am optimistic that . . . it will go forward. This is because passion wins through and the reading animateurs I meet are not doing this because it's a job or a fashion: this is deep and strikes at the core values they hold as librarians'. (Kempster, 2002b)

References and further reading

Aslib (1995) *Review of the Public Library Service in England and Wales for the Department of National Heritage*, London, Aslib.

Blanshard, C. (2002) Personal communication with the author.

The Bookseller (2001) Three resolutions for the book trade in 2001, *The Bookseller*, (5 January, 2001), 26.

Cameron, D. (2002) *Reading and Reader Development: the pleasure of reading*, text written for the author, July.

Forrest, T. (2001) Who's Afraid of Those Declining Issues?, *Library Association Record*, **103** (3), 168–9.

Forrest, T. (2002) Interview with the author.

Great Britain. Audit Commission (2002) *Building Better Library Services: learning from audit, inspection and research*, London, Audit Commission. Also available at ww2.audit-commission.gov.uk/publications/lfair_libraries.shtml. [Accessed 13.03.03]

Great Britain. Department for Culture, Media and Sport (2001a) *DCMS/Wolfson Public Libraries Challenge Fund: overview*. Available at www.culture.gov.uk/PDF/Wolfsonoverview.PDF. [Accessed 13.03.03]

Great Britain. Department for Culture, Media and Sport (2001b) *Libraries for All: public libraries and social exclusion*, London, DCMS.

Kempster, G. (2002a) *So What? The power of action centred research to change perceptions*, Library and Information Research Group annual lecture, London, 27 March.

Kempster, G. (2002b) Personal communication with the author.

Kendrick, S. (2001) A Librarian's Thoughts on Reading. In Katz, B. (ed.), *Readers, Reading and Librarians*, New York, Haworth Information Press, 81–9.

Kinnell, M. and Shepherd, J. (1998) *Promoting Reading to Adults in UK Public Libraries*, British Library Research and Innovation Report 72, London, Taylor Graham.

Krashen, S. D. (1993) *The Power of Reading: insights from the research*, Englewood, CO, Libraries Unlimited.

Lake, J. (2002) Personal communication with the author.

Lang, C. and Wilkinson, S. (2000) *Social Inclusion Fact Sheet*, London, Museums and Galleries Commission.

McKearney, M. (1999) Spreading the Word, *Public Library Journal*, **14** (4), 106–10.

McKearney, M., Wilson-Fletcher, H. and Readman, J. (2001) Revolution by the Book, *Public Library Journal*, **16** (4), 116–9.

Matarasso, F. (2000) An Equal Chance to Know, *Public Library Journal*, **15** (2), 35–8.

Pringle, G. (2002) Personal communication with the author.

Ross, C. S. (2001) Making Choices: what readers say about choosing books to read for pleasure. In Katz, B. (ed.), *Readers, Reading and Librarians*, New York, Haworth Information Press, 5–21.

Saricks, J. (2001) Reading the Future of the Public Library. In Katz, B. (ed.), *Readers, Reading and Librarians*, New York, Haworth Information Press, 113–21.

Saricks, J. G. and Brown, N. (1997) *Readers' Advisory Service in the Public Library*, Chicago and London, American Library Association.

Stewart, I. (ed.) (1996) *Shelf Talk: promoting literature in libraries*, London, The Arts Council of England

Towey, C. A. (2001) Flow: the benefits of pleasure reading and tapping readers' interests. In Katz, B. (ed.), *Readers, Reading and Librarians*, New York, Haworth Information Press, 131–40.

Train, B. (2001) *Mind's Eye: evaluation report*, Birmingham, University of Central England. Available at www.cie.uce.ac.uk/cirt/projects/past/minds_eye.htm. [Accessed 13.03.03]

Train, B. (2002) *Caring with Books in the West Midlands: evaluation report*, Birmingham, University of Central England. Available at www.cie.uce.ac.uk/cirt/projects/past/cwb.htm. [Accessed 13.03.03]

Train, B. and Elkin, J. (2001) *Branching Out: overview of evaluation findings*, Birmingham, University of Central England. Available at www.cie.uce.ac.uk/cirt/projects/past/branching.htm. [Accessed 13.03.03]

Train, B., Usherwood, B. and Brooks, G. (2002) *The Vital Link: an evaluation report*, Sheffield, University of Sheffield.

Turner, J. (2002) Personal communication with the author.

Van Riel, R. (1992a) *Report to Arts Council Literature Department on Creative Reading Training in Libraries*, London, The Arts Council of England.

Van Riel, R. (ed.) (1992b) *Reading the Future: a place for literature in public libraries*, London, The Arts Council and Library Association Publishing.

Van Riel, R. (1993) The Case for Fiction, *Public Library Journal*, **8** (3), 81–4.

Van Riel, R. (1998) *Creating the Readership for Literature in Translation*, presentation to international conference at University of East Anglia, British Centre for Literary Translation, unpublished.

Van Riel, R. (2001) An eyeful for the curious, *The Bookseller*, (2 March 2001), 30–1.

Van Riel, R. (2002) Interview with the author.

Van Riel, R. and Fowler, O. (1996) *Opening the Book: finding a good read*, Yorkshire, Opening the Book, first published by Bradford Libraries.

Wallis, M., Moore, N. and Marshall, A. (2002) *Reading our Future: evaluation of the DCMS/Wolfson Public Libraries Challenge Fund 2000–2001*, Library and Information Commission Research Report 134, London, Resource: The Council for Museums, Archives and Libraries.

Waterstone, T. (1992) What's Happening to Books? In Van Riel, R. (ed.), *Reading the Future: a place for literature in public libraries*, London, Library Association Publishing, 24–30.

Worcestershire Libraries and Information Service (2001) *Annual Library Plan 2001.* Available at www.worcestershire.gov.uk/home/lib-plan-2001-introduction.pdf. [Accessed 13.03.03]

3
Reading: a UK national focus

Debbie Denham

Introduction

There has been a cultural shift in the perception of reading over recent years resulting in a reading renaissance that has permeated both the education and leisure sectors in the UK. This has been supported by a number of central government initiatives and a large amount of government funding that has been allocated to raising literacy standards. This chapter will focus on UK government-driven initiatives such as the National Literacy Strategy, the National Year of Reading and the National Reading Campaign. It also includes a discussion of the role of voluntary agencies such as the National Literacy Trust and other book-related institutions such as Booktrust and The Reading Agency. The growth of recent collaborative initiatives such as World Book Day and National Poetry Day provides a basis for the discussion of partnership working in the field of reader development.

Developing readers

The term 'reader development' has been defined earlier in this book, but it is worth reiterating the key intention of placing the reader and the reading experience at the centre of any initiative. In order to achieve this, much of the work undertaken beneath the umbrella of reader development is based on the promotion of books and of reading in general. The concept of reader development is a natural extension of reader-oriented literary theory, or reader-response theory, as discussed by academics such as Rosenblatt (1978), Fish (1980) and Iser (1978). The focus of this approach to literature is the triangular relationship between 'reader, text and the interaction between the two' (Appleyard, 1994, 6) although often one element of this triangle is emphasized above the others. In a move away from writer- and text-centred approaches to literature, Iser introduced the concept of the reader as co-author. He saw the text as a series of marks of little, if any, significance in their own right which needed 'the creative imagination of the reader . . . to fill in the gaps in the framework and so complete the work of the writer' (Walsh, 1993, 16). The natural succession to this argument is that 'each completion of the narrative is created in the active interaction between the individual reader and the unique text' (Walsh, 1993, 16). Reader development is not so much concerned with what happens and how it happens but with the outcome in the fact that there is an engagement, an interaction, between the reader and the text that in some way benefits the reader.

Although reader development work 'intervenes to expand people's reading horizons' (McKearney, Wilson-Fletcher and Readman, 2001), it is concerned with 'getting people to read more satisfying, not necessarily "better" books' (Goodall, 1991, 157). As outlined in Chapter 1 there is an underlying, implicit belief that reading is good for the individual and that necessarily wider reading will increase those benefits. It could be said that reader development is concerned with popularizing reading, moving away from the concept of a literary canon towards wider enjoyment and a focus on the reading experience as an end in itself.

Reading renaissance

The UK has experienced a growth in interest in reading over recent years. This has manifested itself in the media and in libraries, publishing and bookselling. There is growing interest in book prizes, for example recent television coverage of the Booker Prize has not only presented the awards ceremony but has also followed the deliberations of the panel members. The children's magazine programme 'Blue Peter' has for the last few years followed the progress of the Carnegie and Greenaway medals, the major awards for children's books, with television coverage for the shortlist and the prizewinners. This has also been supplemented by a huge growth in Carnegie shadowing events, with school children around the country reading and making their own assessments of the shortlisted books. The advent of prizes such as the Smarties Prize, awarded each year to 'a work of fiction or poetry for children written in English by a UK citizen, or an author resident in the UK' (Booktrust, n.d.), indicates a growing attention to the views of children and what they perceive to be the best books of the year. The Guardian Children's Book Award also invites readers to vote for their favourite titles. It is awarded 'to an outstanding work of fiction (not picture books) for children written by a British or Commonwealth author, first published in the UK during the preceding calendar year' (Booktrust, n.d.). The winner is chosen by a panel of authors and the review editor for *The Guardian*'s children's books section.

The growing emphasis on the importance of the reader has also resulted in generic national and international events such as National Poetry Day, World Book Day and the much longer running Children's Book Week. These events promote reading rather than focus on individual titles, authors or the output of individual publishers. This is done in the belief that reading is a vital part of everyday life and a general promotion of reading will provide benefits for all in the book supply chain from authors and publishers to libraries and the readers themselves.

National Poetry Day

Thursday 9 October 2003 will see the tenth anniversary of National Poetry Day. The BBC has been a major supporter of this event, which aims to raise awareness of poetry in schools, libraries, bookshops and the community at large. The National Poetry Day website contains a range of useful resources to support the promotion and sharing of poetry (National Poetry Day, 2002).

World Book Day

World Book Day (6 March) is a unique opportunity for people around the world to celebrate books and reading (World Book Day, 2002). As in previous years, every schoolchild in full-time education in the UK will receive a £1 World Book Day token that can be redeemed through sponsorship of Books Tokens Ltd and publishers and booksellers. Alongside celebrations in schools and communities, public libraries in the UK are hosting the first ever World Book Day Online Festival 2003, using the People's Network to broaden access to activities through the internet. The highlight of the day is to be a live web cast from Peckham Library by author Terry Pratchett and there are other live web chats for readers and writers (World Book Day Festival, 2003). The Festival has been made possible through a partnership between World Book Day, Resource: the Council for Museums, Archives and Libraries, CILIP and The Reading Agency.

Reading groups

The recent exponential growth of the reading group was explored in Chapter 2. The origins of the reading group can be traced back to the oral tradition of storytelling, where reading was an inclusive and shared experience that cut across age and societal boundaries. The coffee house of the 17th century offered places for men to meet to discuss politics, finance and their reading, and this opportunity was extended to the working man and his family with the advent of the public library service in the mid-19th century. As suggested in the previous chapter, reading groups are diverse in nature and in geography. However despite their diversity they have in common the sharing of the reading experience. This has been a major change in the perception of reading over recent years, this view of reading as a social as well as a solitary activity, something to be shared in an open forum rather than purely internalized.

Dr Jenny Hartley, Principal Lecturer, Roehampton University, Surrey, who has undertaken extensive research into reading groups, discusses her recent findings:

> Reading groups are the success story of our times. I first started hearing about them in the late 1990s, when they were attracting media attention. Many UK groups date from this time, but 21% of the 350 groups who filled in our questionnaires have been going

for ten years or more, and some for many years longer. The oldest extant group started in 1764. No one knows how many reading groups there are; estimates run as high as 50,000 for the UK and 500,000 for the US. And while every reading group is different, there are some significant national variations; in America, for example, paid leaders are more common.

Perhaps the most remarked upon feature of reading groups is the predominance of women. Sixty-nine per cent of the groups in our survey are all-female; 4% are all-male. In terms of age, about two thirds of the groups in our survey had members in their forties or over, but in at least 12% of the groups there was a wide age span, from for instance late twenties to over ninety. In 88% of the groups more than half the members had some form of higher education, and in 67% of the groups more than half the members were in paid work.

The reasons why people join and enjoy reading groups fall into two main categories, often of equal weighting and summarized succinctly by one correspondent as 'the books, the people'. In terms of reading, many correspondents describe starting or joining groups because they felt they were not reading enough or that their reading was getting 'stale'. They saw the group as a useful spur or challenge. Some feel the need for guidance through the 'jungle of books' in the bookshop, as one Austrian correspondent put it. Reading groups can take their members into new and challenging areas, and play a significant role in extending reading boundaries. People are willing to experiment and to tolerate books they either would not start or not stay with, as their comments reveal:

> An incentive to try books we wouldn't otherwise try.
>
> The opening sentence of *The Ice People* would have put off 100% of our group had it not been selected.
>
> Most of us have been pleasantly surprised by an unexpected choice.

Fiction tends to dominate reading group choice, but this does not mean that groups hug the Captain Corelli circuit. Three quarters of the titles listed by groups as read recently were one-offs, i.e. they had been read by only one of the 350 groups in the survey. This is symptomatic of the independence which characterizes reading groups. While they scan shortlists and reviews, they usually refuse to have their books chosen for them; and choosing can often be very time-consuming.

About three quarters of the groups we heard from meet in people's houses, but bookshops are also a venue, and libraries are getting into their stride, though provision still tends to be patchy. The library's role is one of facilitator (providing premises, sets of books to borrow, perhaps a co-ordinator), not dictator; groups usually choose from the sets available, make suggestions and determine how the discussion will run.

Perhaps one of the defining features of the reading group is its commitment to neighbourhood. In *Bowling Alone: The Collapse and Revival of American Community* (2000), the American sociologist Robert Putnam amasses exhaustive evidence to argue that people do not do things in groups any more, and that society is the poorer for it. For me, reading groups offer a heartening counter-example. They demonstrate commitment to localized networks, to the small group of known faces, a belief and pleasure in face-to-face commitment as opposed to electronic communication. Hence the power of word-of-mouth as the engine of the reading group movement. It is a determining factor in how groups start, how they choose, and why they are so keen to maintain their independence. In part they are redressing the loss of neighbourhood sociality which the church or other institutions may have supplied in the past. They can also supply a network for the uprooted, such as the expatriate community, who have long hosted flourishing groups, and for the cut-off or housebound. They currently run in day centres for the blind, in residential homes for the elderly, in therapy-oriented contexts, and in prisons (some of these prison groups are funded by the Reading Families Millennium Award Scheme).

While some correspondents emphasized the light-hearted, 'girls' night out' side of the group, I would want to see the book not just as a prop but also as a fulcrum. It affects how people talk and read:

> An understanding and knowledge of the wider issues will be developed often after reading and discussing the book.
> Hearing different people talk about the book brings it alive.
> I enjoy hearing the book's story from another angle.
> The evening enlarges the book.
> I am more sensitive to the opinions of others.

At the heart of reading group values is a belief in the importance of empathy, which influences the kinds of books that are chosen, and the way in which groups conduct their discussion. Reader–character empathy drives choice towards fiction with strong, sympathetic characterization:

> We like to discuss characters – motivations, are they likeable, what could they have done differently?

Reading groups seem to be here to stay, and they are undoubtedly having an effect on reading patterns. Many correspondents in our survey claimed that their reading habits have been significantly altered, and their words have a positive ring:

> I enjoy buying books; I now spend £100 a year on books whereas previously I spent almost zero.
> I am more patient; I give a book a chance that I might have stopped after about fifty pages.
> You read in a different way with half an eye on the meeting ahead, makes you more thoughtful.

> I have become a Reader. In earlier years I read only what I needed to for my work, and vaguely thought of novels as a frivolous indulgence. (Hartley, 2002)

Hartley gives a powerful explanation of why reading groups work. It is about choice and sharing which are fundamental to the concept of reader development.

Support for reading

National Literacy Trust

One of the most significant government initiatives in support of reading in recent years has been the National Year of Reading which ran from September 1998 to August 1999. This was delivered by the National Literacy Trust, an independent charity founded in 1993, which now runs the National Reading Campaign, the successor to the Year, in addition to other practical initiatives such as Reading is Fundamental, UK, Reading The Game and Reading Connects.

The work of the Trust is rooted in improving literacy within the education system but it also recognizes that 'everyone concerned needs to consider the broad picture and see how the home and social circumstances help lay the foundations for successful learning'. In order to achieve these aims the Trust provides:

- a web-based literacy support network which includes a range of resources, statistics and case studies
- a number of practical reading and literacy initiatives
- a systems approach: an 'analytical approach to help maximise the effectiveness of interventions to raise literacy standards while minimising unforeseen counterproductive effects'. (National Literacy Trust, 2002)

The systems approach is one which examines issues from a holistic perspective, so rather than merely looking at statistical data it ensures that causal effects are considered as well.

The National Year of Reading

The concept for the National Year of Reading (NYR) came from the then Secretary of State for Education and Employment, David Blunkett, who had the idea while in opposition. Within two months of getting into government, Blunkett had set up an advisory committee which put his plan into action. The advisory committee included representatives from the book trade, library sector, business community, media, education and voluntary organizations. The main aim was to try to create a nation of readers and to help support the raising of reading standards in schools:

> The National Year of Reading began with a vision – a vision of a society where everyone is literate and where there is a culture that opens up new, diverse and innovative opportunities for reading and writing. A crucial first step towards that vision is improving children's literacy. By learning to read and write, children acquire the foundation for their future learning and increase their chances of succeeding not just at school but when they leave school. In today's world they cannot manage without being able to read the written word. (Attenborough, 2000)

Genevieve Clarke, Manager of the National Reading Campaign, the initiative which followed on from the successful National Year of Reading, talks about the impact of the Year:

> Reader development is the proactive way in which libraries work to create the best possible reading experience for readers. The term was used before the National Year of Reading (NYR) but the year gave the concept a boost. The year gave legitimacy to the work libraries were undertaking in reader development, it reiterated the idea that it is alright for libraries to work in this area. The two-year funding from the Department for Culture, Media and Sport (DCMS)/Wolfson fund for reader development projects stemmed from the NYR. The year also promoted partnership working and the recognition that libraries had to work with other agencies in order to reach non-readers. (Clarke, 2002)

National Reading Campaign

The National Year of Reading was allocated considerable government funding of £4 million over three financial years, which allowed the project co-ordinators to allocate £800,000 to 86 projects during 1998–9. Its successor, the National Reading Campaign, also supported by the Department for Education and Skills, currently has funding until the end of March 2004. One of its key aims is to ensure that reading for pleasure and purpose maintains a high profile and is kept on the agenda in schools, libraries and within the wider community. The promotional initiatives run under the National Reading Campaign banner tend to target 'those people who stand to gain most through reading and literacy development' (National Literacy Trust, n.d.). Campaign Manager Genevieve Clarke explains how its priorities were identified:

> A consultation exercise was undertaken at national and regional level to determine the main focus of the Campaign. With more limited funding, it was decided that it was important for us to concentrate our energy on supporting those working with people who did not necessarily consider themselves as readers. Three roles were identified, with networking and information provision for practitioners seen as the most important. This is largely achieved through the website (www.readon.org.uk) and via a newsletter now published three times a year, though the success of this process depends on a two-way flow of information.

> In addition, we run promotions that focus on different parts of the audience such as Reading Champions for reluctant male readers and Swap a Book for adults in the workplace. And our third area of work is around encouraging partnership working. This often involves libraries, as in our work with the prison sector where we have tried to promote links between education departments and prison libraries. We've also encouraged more innovative partnerships such as that between public libraries and the nationwide Games Workshop chain in order to attract teenagers. (Clarke, 2002).

Promoting literacy

The National Year of Reading funded a considerable number of projects involved with promoting books and reading to children and young people. Funding was also open to projects for adult readers and this was the point at which a growing interest in reader development for adults was discernible, with the launch of initiatives such as Branching Out co-ordinated by Opening the Book.

At the same time as this focus has increased in libraries, the Campaign has made a link with the Government's more recent priority to improve the literacy skills of adults. As Clarke says:

> Just as the NYR supported the National Literacy Strategy when it was introduced in 1998, we feel that the Campaign also has a role in supporting the Government's Skills for Life strategy for improving the literacy skills of adults which was launched in 2001. In the best cases, an introduction to an enjoyment of reading can be a huge motivator and inspiration. However, there is a dearth of interesting mainstream material, fiction and non-fiction, for adults who need basic skills support. It is important to acknowledge the efforts of two publishers to rectify this situation, Barrington Stoke and New Island, who have developed an interesting model. The latter has published three series of Open Door books written specially for less confident adult readers by best-selling authors such as Maeve Binchy and Roddy Doyle. There are now plans to commission some top British writers for further series. (Clarke, 2002)

DCMS/Wolfson funding enabled the National Reading Campaign and the National Literacy Trust to work with The Reading Agency on the Vital Link initiative during 2001–2. This explored how reader development work in libraries could benefit those adults wanting to improve their skills. Nine library authorities in four different regions linked with their local basic skills providers to work with existing basic skills students and to reach out to new learners who might have been put off by the formal education system. Together they selected titles from mainstream library stock that could provide a way into an enjoyment of reading for those adults who had not previously felt confident enough to choose books for their own enjoyment. The initiative has produced a practical toolkit for libraries and basic skills providers wanting to take this work forward, a training programme and a reading promotion called First Choice (National Literacy Trust, n.d.).

Long-term strategy

Clarke focuses on the energy that can be brought to bear on the education agenda through reader development initiatives within and beyond library walls. However, there is a need for this work to be embedded:

> The focus now with the National Reading Campaign is much more strategic, particularly in light of the need to move towards sustainability. There is a huge amount still to do, but reading is holding up well against other distractions and competitors. It is vital that the way into an enjoyment of reading is made relevant to people's lives. This work to identify and engage with new audiences is time consuming and projects tend to involve small numbers, but it provides some valuable models. The sheer enjoyment of books is seen as vitally important in supporting literacy. (Clarke, 2002)

This belief also lies behind the other reading and literacy initiatives run by the National Literacy Trust, as explained below.

Reading is Fundamental

Reading is Fundamental, UK (RIF), provides opportunities for children to choose and own new books. Through schools, community groups, sports centres and businesses RIF sets up literacy projects that promote the fun of reading and emphasize the importance of reading beyond the educational imperative of developing literacy skills. The projects target areas where there is little book ownership or book reading culture so that children from these homes can know the joy of book ownership. The diversity of projects and the range of books mean that children of all ages benefit from this initiative. RIF's statistics are impressive; since its launch it 'has already set up more than 500 projects distributing 450,000 books to over 150,000 children and young people' (National Literacy Trust, n.d.).

Reading The Game

This motivational work lies at the heart of another promotional scheme run by the Trust, Reading The Game. Working with professional football clubs, this innovative initiative is piloting ways in which football clubs can support the drive to raise literacy standards and find ways to promote players as positive role models for reading (National Literacy Trust, n.d.).

Reading Connects

The promotion of a reading culture is crucial to raising literacy standards. A more recent initiative of the National Literacy Trust is the establishment of a support network for secondary schools that will help develop reading-rich environments for the whole school community including parents and support staff. Called Reading Connects, this is working with key agencies, including libraries, to promote and share good practice and develop long-term strategies for enhancing achievement through reading (National Literacy Trust, n.d.).

Booktrust

Complementing the work of the National Literacy Trust is the educational charity Booktrust, which was founded in 1926. Chris Meade, Director of Booktrust, is convinced that the strength of Booktrust lies in its independence, the impartial advice offered by the charity and the fact that it has nothing to sell, 'no axe to grind'.

Bookstart

The Bookstart project (Bookstart, n.d.) was initiated by Booktrust in 1992. Referred to by Gary McKeone (2002) as 'the most inspired and inspiring initiative in the arts', it was the first national books for babies programme in the world. It is one of the most high-profile initiatives linking libraries with health visitors, who deliver the book packs to parents at their baby's eight-month check. It relies on the support of publishers who provide books at reduced rates and, in some cases, free of charge. The project would not have achieved its high national profile, however, without the input of Sainsbury's who designated it as their major charity for the millennium. This allowed the project to roll out from a number of localized initiatives to be delivered all over the country, to all children, over a two-year period.

Breathtaker

Booktrust have taken this idea a stage further and introduced a similar scheme, Breathtaker, for adults. Recent projects have involved working:

> with isolated mothers in East Anglia, victims of crime in Birmingham and . . . young offenders . . . offering them the services of a reader in residence to recommend three breathtaking books to give them a boost and some breathing space to take a fresh view of their lives.
>
> (Booktrust, n.d.)

Arts Council of England

The Arts Council of England (ACE) in April 2002 amalgamated with the ten Regional Arts Boards for England 'to form a single development organisation for the arts' (Arts Council, n.d.). Although part-funded by central government, The Arts Council maintains its independence. The funds they distribute come from central government and from the National Lottery, the former providing £295 million and lottery funding providing in the region of £200 million. The Arts Council is concerned with all areas of the Arts and its Literature Department is relatively small when compared to other departments. The Director of Literature, Gary McKeone, talks about the work of the Arts Council in relation to reader development:

> Arts Council of England's support for reader development is based on the simple premise that reading is a creative act. The reader completes the creative circle begun by the writer and the relationship between reader and writer is essentially symbiotic. Reader development acknowledges that the role of the reader is active and participatory, not passive.
>
> Most of the work we support focuses mainly although not exclusively on the public library network. This is because libraries, democratically accessible, usually built at the heart of communities, are a natural and national network of literature centres. They are literature's equivalent of the theatre, the concert hall or the gallery with the essential difference that they are, almost by definition, socially inclusive.
>
> We are keenly aware that if libraries are to fulfil their potential, then librarians have a pivotal role to play. In essence they need to become literature promoters, confident in selecting and recommending books, imaginative in their presentation of those books, creative in programming events and ambitious to make libraries nerve centres of literature activity.
>
> The Branching Out project, run by Opening the Book, was funded precisely to tackle this agenda. This ongoing initiative aims to increase the audience for contemporary literature through public libraries. It does this by providing training and support to library staff to increase their skills in promoting contemporary literature. It uses new technology, online training and actual training days to achieve its purpose. At the time of writing, some thirty-three library authorities have benefited. We have invested over £300,000 in this project and are now looking at ways of rolling the work out nationally.
>
> One other crucial intervention in the area of reader development is our support for The Reading Agency. This new organisation unites under one banner the Reading Partnership, Well Worth Reading and LaunchPad to create a single, national reader development agency whose primary focus will be the public library network. This new agency, jointly funded by the Arts Council of England and the Chartered Institute of Library and Information Professionals (CILIP), will combine the expertise of the three separate agencies, covering all age ranges and offering a consistently imaginative approach to reader development nationally.

> Of course, reader development is not the sole preserve of libraries. It can and does happen in an eclectic range of places and through a variety of organisations. Booktrust is perhaps foremost among these. Booktrust's Bookstart scheme is the most inspired and inspiring initiative I have yet to come across in the arts. For the past three years, almost every baby in the country has received a Booktrust Bookstart bag at the eight-month health check. The bag contains two baby books, a library card and a guide to babies' books for parents. The beauty of Bookstart is that books, reading, libraries, literature are seen as an intrinsic part of a child's development. Reading is not just about pleasure; it's about progress. It's an activity, a skill that can help children improve their grasp on the world they are starting to map their way through. Reading, reader development, whatever we want to call it, can accompany us all on that journey. (McKeone, 2002)

DCMS/Wolfson

The previous chapter looked in some detail at the DCMS/Wolfson Public Libraries Challenge Fund which for two years focused largely on reader development projects operated by library services. In a speech at the launch of the Fund, Alan Howarth (then a Junior Minister at the Department for Culture, Media and Sport) acknowledged the vital role the National Year of Reading had played leading to the large sums of money being granted for the two years of the DCMS/Wolfson programme. As Clarke says:

> The DCMS/Wolfson funding was significant in attracting funding for the reader development agenda. A key outcome of this funding was the recognition of how important reader development work is. Libraries have been encouraged to develop reader development strategies. They have often started with one-off initiatives that have broadened to have a regional or national focus and eventually the move has been away from short-term project funding to a focus on library strategy; a movement from a scattergun approach to the embedding of reader development work in library service objectives and the development of reader development and reading strategies. This shift needs to continue and is fundamental if reader development is to be sustained. This move also tracks the data around performance indicators. These services are not an add on but mainstream and core. There is a need for the strategic placing of reader development in long term library service planning. (Clarke, 2002)

As Margaret Wallis, Principal Lecturer, one of the team of evaluators from the Social Informatics Unit at the University of Brighton writes:

> Since its creation in 1997 the DCMS/Wolfson Public Libraries Challenge Fund has become one of the key catalysts for change in the public library sector. The projects it has funded have introduced many library innovations throughout England, initially in the area of

> ICT's. In 2000 the focus of the Programme shifted to reader development and reading promotion work and the DCMS decided for the first time they needed to evaluate the impact of the new Programme. Margaret Wallis and Nick Moore from the Social Informatics Research Unit at the University of Brighton were invited to develop a methodology to measure the extent to which the aims and objectives of the Programme were achieved and the value and impact of the investment on reader development work.
>
> The aim of the Programme was to enhance public libraries' traditional strength in promoting reading as a skill and pleasure. Applicants for support under the Programme were encouraged to develop services that would introduce new audiences to reading-related activities. The target audiences identified by individual projects varied from the very general to the highly specific. (Wallis, 2002)

This is discussed in more detail in Chapter 8.

Paul Hamlyn Foundation

The Paul Hamlyn Foundation have recently established a new £2.6-million fund for book, reading and library projects for young people and others with limited access to books and reading, The Reading and Libraries Challenge Fund. Funding will be available from April 2003 to April 2006, under three streams:

- Right to Read – for collaborative projects that are intended to improve long-term access to books and reading for children and young people in public care
- Free with Words – to help prisons and young offender institutions provide easy access to books and reading material for inmates of all nationalities and reading levels and encourage reading for pleasure.
- Libraries Connect – for initiatives that are intended to effect lasting change in the way libraries work with communities that are not well served, such as refugees and asylum seekers.

Libraries and reader development

Chapters 1 and 2 explored the role of libraries with respect to reader development in some depth. They identified librarians as champions of reading and looked at the culture change needed for libraries to begin to take reader development work seriously. A number of the agencies and individuals mentioned above have also highlighted the pivotal role of public libraries in reader development. It is worth reiterating here in terms of the work currently being undertaken in developing both child and adult readers. Miranda McKearney, Director of The Reading Agency, argues that:

> A reader focused vision should help get libraries much higher up the national and local agenda . . . this work is a phenomenal cultural and learning force through which we can achieve a whole range of national ambitions. A force that many other government departments and initiatives could be harnessing to achieve their objectives in the way that SureStart is. [SureStart is 'the government's programme to support children, parents and communities through the integration of early education, childcare and health and family support services' (Sure Start, n.d.).]
>
> The nation needs what we do with readers, and needs to fund it seriously. What libraries do with readers is unique – it's the missing ingredient for many other policy and partnership agendas because it injects the access and motivation necessary for the delivery of key government strategies including the National Literacy Strategy. . . . Libraries have a new vocabulary to describe their work with readers, new ways of planning and executing it. There's a sounder and more innovative body of practice to draw on and new structures to work through to create regional and national reading offers – the summer reading challenge is a powerful example of this. There's new research on the value of reading and its individual and community benefits and libraries are bringing together reading and learning strategies – recognizing that the informal, self-motivated learning they promote should be central to creation of a deeper learning culture. And there's also been a re-embracing of reading's creative, imaginative role in people's lives. . . . The big challenge for the future is how to move beyond project work to embedding the work across the service and attracting mainstream, not project, funding. (McKearney, 2002)

Clarke talks about how the NYR and The Reading Campaign have boosted the central role of libraries in delivering books to readers:

> The campaigns have provided a spur to support the work already undertaken and have provided impetus for the reader development movement. This has been liberating for library staff because it has allowed them to continue to do what they feel works. Another benefit has been the growing debate about how much libraries should get involved in education but there is a growing recognition that the "reading voice" enabled by the library is a strong one, the sheer enjoyment of books is seen as vitally important in supporting literacy. (Clarke, 2002)

John Readman, Head of Libraries, Archives and Arts for the London Borough of Lambeth, considers how libraries themselves have benefited from the increased interest in reader development work:

> One of the key impacts has been the raised awareness of librarians and what they do in terms of reader development and increased awareness of the book trade, including a greater awareness of bookshops and publishers and their role in promoting reading. There

> is considerable value in the two-way relationship between librarians and the book trade. There has been a recognition that librarians are more proactive in promoting stock and know more about why people read and why they don't and they encourage other professionals to think more creatively about wider reading.
>
> There are some functional impacts in relation to the profession and libraries nationally. The process of producing library plans for DCMS has been key in raising the profile of reader development. Reader development as a result has become more embedded in the guidelines and the resulting plans. There have long been advocates for reader development work amongst the rank and file of library staff but now chief librarians are becoming involved, the process is pulling them along. So there are two key facets, the creative professional and the process, that are now converging.
>
> (Readman, 2002)

Partnerships and libraries

Some of the most innovative projects of recent years have been those which have linked together a number of key agencies. A major focus of reader development work has been increased emphasis on partnerships. Although libraries are generally socially inclusive it is not always easy for them to undertake initiatives in isolation, they need the support of other agencies. Branching Out was explored in the previous chapter as an excellent example of partnership working and many of the initiatives mentioned above have relied on working with a variety of groups to maximize opportunities and ensure sustained involvement.

Readman reiterates the unique position of libraries and the advantages they have in the book world:

> Publishers have a surprising lack of understanding of their reading market, and, have had their eyes opened to the possibilities that libraries provide in terms of information about who reads what and why. The current discussions between The Reading Agency, regional library and arts agencies with publishers have some real potential to achieve lasting outcomes for the library world.
>
> The Reading Agency has helped to make links, they have been advocates for libraries to the book world letting them know what libraries are doing and what their potential is. The Reading Agency's work with Orange has resulted in a real change. These agencies have the power to advocate on behalf of libraries to change the minds of those in the business and forefront the power of the library market. The work with Orange demonstrates the power of what can be done. There is significant money put into the event and enormous energy goes into talking about libraries. This model has the potential to be rolled out to other initiatives. The model is triangular:

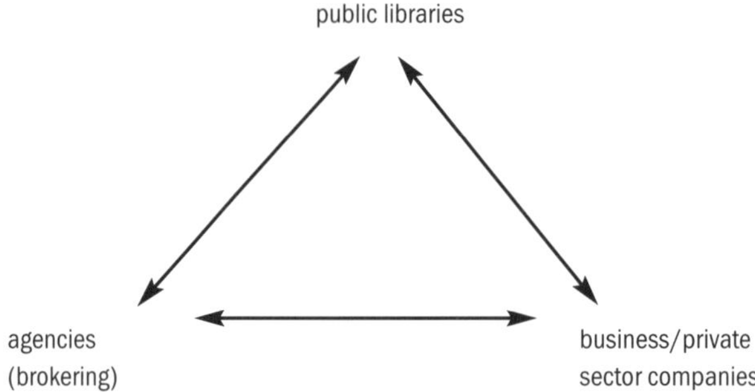

I am passionate about the agencies such as The Reading Agency and Opening the Book who act on behalf of public libraries in the wider world to enhance the role of libraries and raise awareness of them. The partnership with agencies who act on our behalf is crucial; without their support public libraries and reader development would not be where they are today, they would just be concentrating on small scale projects, although it is important to acknowledge that all the individual, small-scale initiatives have contributed to the overall strategic framework.

There has been a subtle shift in the last three to four years. A word of caution however: it is important for libraries not to become complacent. We need to raise the game further if we are serious about working with large organisations such as Orange. There is still vast disparity between authorities, with some key authorities leading the way. We need to bring the trailing authorities up to a basic level.

Libraries, agencies and partnership organisations all have a contribution to make. The agencies in particular have a national role working with regional arts boards and literature officers. This is more difficult in London although even in the regions opportunities for literature officers to network are limited.

Through the work of the London Library Development Agency the libraries in the London area are working more effectively together. This is backed up by the need for libraries to develop performance indicators and basic standards to attempt to measure, both qualitatively and quantitatively, the impact of reader development work.

Reader development work is more embedded locally in training particularly in stock knowledge and awareness. Library authorities have to fill the gap in what is not being done in professional training in library schools. Libraries need to ensure that staff know about stock. We have come a long way but there is still a lot further to go. Reader development is embedded in library strategic thinking both locally and nationally. The libraries are the natural place for reader development work but they need to raise their ability to find creative ways of using other spaces outside of library buildings for this work. Libraries also need to be clear about what the 'payback' is for them. (Readman, 2002)

The Reading Agency

As suggested above, The Reading Agency, jointly funded by the Arts Council of

England, Southern and Southeast Arts and CILIP, has been a major success story:

> Well Worth Reading, LaunchPad and the Reading Partnership, three vibrantly effective reader development organisations with national and regional remits decided to pool resources and form a single agency dedicated to reader development and literature promotion. The new agency will focus its work primarily on the public library network.
>
> (McKeone, 2002)

McKearney emphasizes the unique elements of The Reading Agency: 'no other agency works with readers with the same mixture of access, inspiration, or the same ethos of support for individual growth combined with community trust and respect and, perhaps most powerfully, no other agency is as well placed to get the benefits of reading to the disenfranchised.' She discusses the key ways in which The Reading Agency works with libraries, by refocusing on:

> libraries' USP [unique selling point] – the thing they do that no other agency does, the thing that makes them worth funding and that makes them unmissable, powerful players and partners at national and local level – their special relationship with readers. But both libraries and government seem hesitant to embrace a reader centred vision . . . focusing on the reader makes sense of libraries' function; it's a focus based on the needs of users, and it creates a strategic blueprint for a new age of library development. Reading should be at the heart of the library offer to the nation, its core work, not just an add on.
>
> We're not arguing that libraries should stop doing non-reader related activities (although on closer examination many of the services that might initially seem non-reader related – like local history, access to ICT and local information – actually turn out to be closely reader related) but we're arguing that libraries should recognise their core function is to support the reader. With this core aim quite clear all sorts of things will flow, from sound service development to better staff morale and recruitment, from far stronger marketing and advocacy to more strategic partnership building.
>
> (McKearney, 2002)

The Reading Agency's vision statement (Reading Agency, n.d.) is 'to inspire a reading nation', working with libraries to 'challenge, inspire and support them'. The key objectives and strategies for achieving this are:

> *Advocacy*
> to change the way influencers see and fund libraries' work with readers . . . gathering evidence and arguments and presenting it powerfully . . . supporting libraries, through training and the provision of materials on our web site, in developing regional advocacy strategies and materials.

Research
Research is an important area of work, because it produces the evidence base for advocacy as well as developing good practice. A good example is the research for the LLDA [London Libraries Development Agency] into reading groups which shows how belonging to a library based group gives people who might otherwise feel on the margins a real sense of belonging to a diverse community.

Innovation
To create vibrant readers' services and reach new people, libraries need to be thinking outside the box, working with new partners and exploring new approaches, so one of the key objectives is to open up new ways of working with readers and new routes to finding them. A new and important partnership is with the People's Network, exploring how to weave a powerful and really motivating new Internet element into libraries' national summer reading challenge to children.

Raising standards for the long term
To equalize access to reading and raise standards, working to support and empower librarians . . . running an extensive training programme covering everything from reader strategies to youth work partnerships, children's reading groups to marketing.

Their Reading Futures
The Their Reading Futures (TRF) initiative is ambitious, but also a very practical, long-term programme to deliver higher quality reading services for children. TRF is a way of changing how libraries work with young readers and their families, trying to take the lessons and skills learnt in some brilliant, but patchy project work and using them to transform main stream services, targeting all staff, not just children's specialists. One of the librarians trained, Peter Burns from Durham, says, 'TRF is the most important thing in children's librarianship for years. Because in the end the reading experience for most children is brokered and delivered by general library staff, at whatever level. Training, awareness and knowledge of customer care for children and young people is as crucial for the Saturday assistant, as it is for the professional in charge of the service. TRF gives a vocabulary to our staff to say: What exactly is it that we do? How can we convince other agencies in our communities that it's important? And how can our services survive and grow?' TRF has:

- agreed a nationally accepted definition of reader development to create clarity with staff or partners about exactly what the work consists of and why it matters
- created an outcomes based audit framework for library authorities to use in auditing and changing their services for young readers, drawing heavily on the work Resource is doing on the Inspiring Learning Framework
- trained 330 children's librarians in England, from library leaders at national level

to staff at local level by bringing together a Youth Libraries Group and Association of Schools, Children's and Education Librarians 'champion' in most authorities; training covered strategic outcomes based on planning, core skills and advocacy, preparing people for the extensive on-line training about to be available on the website

- developed an outline of the core skills staff need to deliver a really effective service to young readers and their families
- developed arguments, evidence and powerful national advocacy materials under six main policy headings. These will be made available on the TRF website with a framework to support library services in adapting national techniques, evidence and arguments for regional use. (McKearney, 2002)

The London Libraries Development Agency

The London Libraries Development Agency (LLDA) was created to 'develop a co-ordinated strategic vision for library and information services across London, aiming to forge partnerships and build links, to be a first point of contact for those who seek to work with libraries and making the case for libraries, using advocacy materials to stimulate debate and discussion about the role libraries can play' (London Libraries Development Agency, n.d.).

One of the current projects is Books & Business, a partnership between LLDA, Arts & Business London and The Reading Partnership. This is a year-long programme of activity designed to build stronger relationships between libraries and business in support of reader development. Longer term, it aims to transform the way public libraries work with the business community in London, on both a local and city-wide basis (Books & Business, n.d.). Two other key reader development projects, both with funding from DCMS/Wolfson and jointly managed by London Arts, are Young Cultural Creators, which also involves the Tate Gallery, and Read Routes, which operates across all of London's public library services. Their next big joint project is London's Libraries Recommend, which hopes to bring together public librarians, publishers, booksellers, authors, reading group participants and others to select their Book of the Month. This title will then be heavily publicized via all 400 of London's public libraries. Keeping London reading is one of the key aims of both LLDA and London Arts (London Libraries Development Agency, n.d.).

Reading in schools

There is an interesting, and apparently increasing, dichotomy between the teaching of reading in school and reading for pleasure. The teaching of reading is often perceived by the press, parents and the outside world to be the remit of the teacher, whose role is to present children with foolproof techniques that will ensure children will become fluent readers during their first two or three years at school. This is of course not the full picture: the importance of introducing books to children at as young an age as possible has been reinforced through projects such as Bookstart (Booktrust, n.d.) and in the work of authors such as Dorothy Butler (1998) and Margaret Meek (1982, 1991). It is vital that the concept of reading for pleasure is encouraged in school. There has been concern, recently, that government initiatives such as the National Literacy Strategy are squeezing out the fun aspects of reading and that there is little room to promote the concept of reading for pleasure, reading for its own sake. Initiatives such as USSR (Uninterrupted, Sustained, Silent Reading) and ERIC (Everyone Reading in Class), which aim to promote and encourage reading by providing the opportunity to undertake reading during the school day, have often been casualties of the time-consuming effects of the National Literacy Strategy.

How children should be taught to read, the best way to learn to read and the foolproof techniques that can be applied to all children have long been a focus of educational debate. The pedagogic view of the best way to accomplish this task has changed over the years. As Robinson notes, it was not until the 19th century in the UK that formal systems were implemented to teach the skills of reading. Early pedagogic arguments centred on the memorizing of 'certain physical features of language and using these features to decode text' (Robinson, 1997, 14), although whether 'look and say' or 'phonics' were the ideal approach was fiercely debated. More recent theorists, e.g. Goodman, have suggested that miscues and mistakes have a large part to play in the process of learning to decode text. This introduced the idea of the reading environment and the need to expose children to a range of texts and narratives so they could begin to make guesses about the texts and individual words within them. The debate polarized in the late 1980s, between the 'reading for real approach' and a 'phonics' based approach which relied heavily on graded reading schemes to allow children to progress. The former advocated that children should be exposed to a range of texts and narratives and would learn by engaging with texts in a supportive environment, bringing to bear a range of skills including phonic, look and say and their own experiences. However children learn to read it is increasingly accepted that:

> [w]here the learners have a rich experience of texts, they successfully acquire phonological awareness, contextual, grammatical and graphic knowledge; they orchestrate these textual features with their understanding of language and life. All these aspects of early reading challenge the notion that, in children's growth as literates, there is a predictable, uniform, sequential programme of lessons which ensures success. (Meek, 1998, 116)

The National Literacy Strategy and Key Stage Three Framework

Secondary teacher and researcher Glen Mynott provides an overview of the National Literacy Strategy for Key Stages One and Two and discusses the implementation of the Literacy Framework for Key Stage Three. He provides evidence to support the notion that these initiatives may not be in the best interests of children:

> The National Literacy Strategy was introduced into primary schools in 1998 with the intention of improving the teaching of literacy through regular and sustained focus on reading, writing and speaking, and listening. In September 2000 a framework for extending the strategy into secondary education at Key Stage Three was piloted in selected schools throughout the country. As a result of the pilot the Key Stage Three framework with some amendments was fully introduced into state maintained secondary schools in September 2001.
>
> The objective of the Strategy was to ensure that the teaching and learning of writing and reading skills took place in all schools beyond Key Stage One. According to Geoff Dean, prior to 1998, 'a few teachers planned challenging, progressive, programmes of language and literacy development, but in insufficient numbers' (Dean, 2002, 23). The National Literacy Strategy sets out the literacy skills that pupils should be taught in each year of primary school. These are divided into 'Word Level Work' which comprises phonics, spelling and vocabulary; 'Sentence Level Work' which incorporates grammar and punctuation; and 'Text Level Work' which involves comprehension and composition. The strategy also sets out the means for teaching these skills through the rigidly structured daily Literacy Hour. The Literacy Hour is divided into four sections: a fifteen minute introductory session involving shared text work, fifteen minutes of focused word or sentence work, twenty minutes of group or independent work, and a ten minute plenary or consolidation session (DfEE, 1998).
>
> The Key Stage Three Framework continues the objectives of the Literacy Strategy through Years 7, 8 and 9 in secondary school. The skills that pupils should be taught in these years are divided into: 'Word Level' (spelling and vocabulary); 'Sentence Level' (sentence construction, punctuation, paragraphing and cohesion, stylistic conventions of non-fiction, and standard English and language variation); 'Text Level – Reading' (research and study skills, reading for meaning, understanding the author's craft, and study of literary texts); 'Text Level – Writing' (plan, draft and present, write to imagine, explore, entertain, write to inform, explain and describe, write to persuade, argue, advise, and write to analyse, review and comment); 'Speaking and Listening' (speaking, listening, group discussion and interaction, and drama) (DfEE, 2001).
>
> The National Literacy Strategy and the Key Stage Three Framework have come in for a lot of criticism from writers, teachers and teacher trainers because of its rigidity and its suppression of creativity. The author David Almond used his acceptance speech on winning the Carnegie medal for *Skellig* in 1999 to criticise the government's obsession with testing and prescription. He argued that the National Literacy Strategy, the National

Curriculum and national tests at ages 11 and 14 were 'stifling teachers' ability to teach and pupils' ability to learn' (Ward, 2002, 2). In a recent article, Philip Pullman suggested that 'the problem with literacy strategies is that they are created by people with no sense of the joy of the written word'. Pullman lists the 72 verbs 'that feature in the sections on reading for Key Stages 1–3 of the National Literacy Strategy document' (words all associated with the technical aspects of reading) and asks, 'where's the word enjoy, I wonder? Where does that come? Nowhere, absolutely nowhere' (Pullman, 2002).

Feelings among many teachers against The National Literacy Strategy run high. Richard Marshall in an editorial for *English in Education* complains that the fact that the initiative 'is merely a half-baked set of reactionary prejudices overcooked by expensive PR should have been enough for it to have been thrown in the slop bin by now'. However, as Marshall points out, 'it's still considered staple fare' and:

> What is most surprising is the number of English teachers who have been ready to help serve up this dish, usually with a rather cynically knowing nod and wink that suggests that, yes, they know it's rotten but there's money in it and anyway – rather arrogant this – they're good enough to add enough spice and flavour to make it palatable, even nourishing. But palatable, nourishing, it isn't' (Marshall, 2002, 1).

Marshall's views are endorsed by Ted Wragg who argues that 'having a literacy hour is fine, as is offering advice, but governments telling teachers what to do minute-by minute is simply a crude means of control, the ultimate conservatism, an attempt to persuade the public that 'traditional methods' are being enforced because 'research' supports them' (Wragg, 2002, 7). He quotes the example of an inspector who 'vetoed taking children to see lambs being born, prior to writing about it, because the literacy hour required the lesson to begin with 15 minutes of 'shared text'. What a monumental idiot. Writing is the weakest part of the literacy strategy, so how about 15 minutes of shared birth as a stimulus?'

Other concerns are that the literacy hour could be damaging pupils' speaking and reasoning skills. Researchers at Durham, Cambridge and Leicester universities have shown that only 10 per cent of children's oral contributions to the literacy hour are longer than three words and only 5 per cent are longer than five words. They also expressed fears that teachers are posing fewer challenging questions – which might develop higher-order thinking – and limiting the length and breadth of class discussion because they are anxious to 'cover the ground' (English, Hargreaves and Hislam, 2002). Furthermore, it has been argued by Dominic Wyse (2002), of Liverpool John Moores University that many of the tactics used in the literacy strategy, such as beginning each daily session by stating its objective, are not supported by research. He claims that research suggests phonics is most effective at ages five and six, yet the literacy strategy imposes it until age nine. He also says that the number of grammar objectives fly in the face of research showing grammar teaching is an ineffective way to improve writing at primary level. (Mynott, 2002)

Conclusion

The concept of creative reading was introduced by Rachel Van Riel (Van Riel and Fowler, 1996) and has been useful in demonstrating the importance of the reading process and the value of the reader in the book production supply chain. The author is often perceived as the creator of a work of fiction but the importance of the role of the reader as the consumer of this product has not always been recognized.

It is evident that numerous agencies are working to promote reading and the concepts of reader development. There is increased media interest in books and reading and evidence of a reading renaissance, a renaissance that has resulted in an increased emphasis on the promotion of reading in general rather than specific titles, authors or genre. The growth of reading groups has been phenomenal. But there are still vast areas of society where this does not resonate at all and effective means need to be found to reach these groups. Evidence that proves the value of reading is still needed, as are more links with the Regional Arts Boards and other players in the reader development arena.

Many of the projects and initiatives discussed in this chapter are a direct result of partnership working. This is obviously a major way forward for reader development work: the more agencies involved in reading and the promotion of books, the less likely it is that individuals will fall down the spaces in between. A quote from Chris Meade, Director of Booktrust, provides a fitting end to this chapter:

> Creative reading is still the term I prefer. It cuts across the division of books into educational and for pleasure. It's about the individual's journey through reading and how we locate those books which speak particularly to us, and lead us somewhere special. It invites readers to talk about what their books mean to them, how they enrich their lives in that way that only books can. (Booktrust, n.d.)

References and further reading

Appleyard, J. A. (1994) *Becoming a Reader*, Cambridge, Cambridge University Press.

Arts Council of England. Available at www.artscouncil.org.uk. [Accessed 16.01.03]

Attenborough, L. (2000) The National Year of Reading, *The New Review of Children's Literature and Librarianship*, vol. **6**, 103–13.

Books & Business. Available at www.llda.org.uk/partners/index.html. [Accessed 27.01.03]

Bookstart. Available at www.booktrust.org.uk. [Accessed 16.01.03]

Booktrust. Available at www.booktrust.org.uk [Accessed 16.01.03]

Butler, D. (1998) *Babies Need Books: sharing the joy of books with children from birth to six*, rev. edn, London, The Bodley Head.

Clarke, G. (2002) Personal communication with the author.

Dean, G. (2002) Not Such a Joyless Exercise, *Times Educational Supplement*, (22 February), 23.

English, E., Hargreaves, L. and Hislam, J. (2002) Pedagogical Dilemmas in the National Literacy Strategy: primary teachers' perception, reflections and classroom behaviour, *Cambridge Journal of Education*, **32** (1), 9–26.

Fish, S. (1980) *Is There a Text in this Class?: the authority of interpretive communities*, Cambridge, MA, Harvard University Press.

Goodall, D (1991) Marketing Fiction Service. In Kinnell, M. (ed.) *Managing Fiction in Libraries*, London, Library Association Publishing, 138–57.

Great Britain. Department for Culture, Media and Sport. Available at www.dcms.gov.uk [Accessed 31.01.03]

Great Britain. Department for Education and Employment (DfEE) (1998) *The National Literacy Strategy: framework for teaching*, London, DfEE publications.

Great Britain. Department for Education and Employment (DfEE) (2001) *Key Stage 3 National Strategy: framework for teaching English: Years 7, 8 and 9*, London, DfEE publications.

Great Britain. Department for Education and Skills. Available at www.dfes.gov.uk/findoutmore/index.shtml [Accessed 31.01.03]

Hartley, J. (2002) Personal communication with the author.

Iser, W. (1978) *The Act of Reading*, Baltimore, Johns Hopkins University.

The London Libraries Development Agency. Available at www.llda.org.uk/ [Accessed 27.01.03]

McKearney, M. (2002) Personal communication with the author.

McKearney, M., Wilson-Fletcher, H. and Readman, J. (2001) Revolution by the Book, *Public Library Journal*, **16** (4), 116–19.

McKeone, G. (2002) Personal communication with the author

McKeone, G. and McKearney, M. (2002) Hard to Ignore: the Reading Agency, *Public Library Journal*, **17** (4), 105–7.

Marshall, R. (2002) Editorial: Revolting Literacy, *English in Education*, **36** (2), 1–6.

Meek, M. (1982) *Learning to Read*, London, The Bodley Head.

Meek, M. (1991) *On Being Literate*, London, The Bodley Head.

Meek, M. (1998) Important Reading. In Cox, Brian (ed.), *Literacy is Not Enough: essays in the importance of reading*, Manchester, Manchester University Press & Book Trust.

Mynott, G. (2002) Personal communication with the author.

National Literacy Trust. Available at www.literacytrust.org.uk/ [Accessed 16.01.03]

National Poetry Day (2002). Available at www.poetrysociety.org.uk [Accessed 16.01.03]

The Poetry Society. Available at www.poetrysociety.org.uk [Accessed 16.01.03]

Pullman, P. (2002) Give Them a Taste of Honey, *Times Educational Supplement*, (8 February), 23.

Putnam, R. (2000) *Bowling Alone: the collapse and revival of American community*, New York, Simon and Schuster.

Reading Agency vision statement. Available at www.readingagency.org.uk/html/about.cfm. [Accessed 17.03.03]

Readman, J. (2002) Personal communication with the author.

Robinson, M. (1997) *Children Reading Print and Television*, London, Routledge.

Rosenblatt, L. M. (1978) *The Reader, the Text, the Poem: the transactional theory of the literary work*, Carbondale, IL, Southern Illinois University Press.

SureStart. Available at www.surestart.gov.uk/new/default.htm. [Accessed 23.01.03]

Van Riel, R. and Fowler, O. (1996) *Opening the Book: finding a good read*, Yorkshire, Opening the Book, first published by Bradford Libraries.

Wallis, M. (2002) Personal communication with the author.

Walsh, S. (1993) The Multi-Layered Picture Book. In Pinsent, P. (ed.) *The Power of the Page: children's books and their readers*, London: David Fulton Publishers, 15–22.

Ward, D. (2002) Burning Bright, *Guardian Education*, (17 December 2002), 1.

World Book Day (2002). Available at www.worldbookday.com. [Accessed 23.01.03]

World Book Day Festival (2003). Available at www.worldbookdayfestival.com. [Accessed 16.01.03]

Wragg, T. (2002) Wise Words, *Guardian Education*, (16 April), 7.

Wyse, D. (2002) *The National Literacy Strategy: a critical review of empirical evidence*, unpublished. An article about the report can be accessed in the Times Educational Supplement at www.tes.co.uk. [Accessed 17.03.03]

4

Reading: an international focus

The IFLA Reading Survey

Briony Train

Introduction

This chapter considers the role and promotion of reading for pleasure at an international level. Following a brief overview of international reading research it presents the findings of reader-centred service provision in public libraries. Library staff from 18 countries give their views of the impact of reader-centred work on their library service. Additional experiential accounts are included from international experts in reading promotion for both young people and adults.

I'm a reader

Uno Nilsson (2002), from the County Library of Halland, Halmstad, Sweden offers the following tribute:

> *For teachers and children in Zimbabwe – and elsewhere*
>
> Oh yes I'm a reader
>
> Imagine what the world could be
> Imagine people who are free
> Imagine future, imagine dreams
> Look into yourself – what do you see?
> The pictures you get, the words that you use
> Are tools of your own to change or amuse
> The words that you read will improve the speed
> Of your acting and thinking to get what you need
>
> Oh yes I'm a reader
>
> Imagine a child who cannot express
> Himself, who doesn't know where to put the stress

Whose thoughts and ideas are not of his own
Somebody else will direct his bones
So give him the tools, give him the words
Make him a reader to create his own world
Read him a book to encourage your child
With thoughts and ideas bright and wild

Oh yes

The issues raised so far in this book have focused heavily on the UK, where the status of reading for pleasure and reader-centred activity has significantly increased in recent years. This increased activity is sufficiently widespread that all public library services are expected not only to promote reading as a leisure activity to current readers, but also to encourage the non-users and non-readers to enjoy books. Library staff perceptions of the impact of reader-centred work on their service are now well documented in the professional press and in internal and external audits and evaluations of, for example, the DCMS/Wolfson Public Libraries Challenge Fund for reader development.

Yet how is reading for pleasure perceived internationally? Do public libraries in other countries offer a reader-centred service? What is the nature of promotional activities taking place in libraries, and what is their perceived impact on library users? To what extent is reading for pleasure a local – or national – priority?

International reading research

An international overview of reading research reveals that reading is a key area of research in the field of education and the social sciences, including librarianship. The US National Reading Panel (1999) estimated that 100,000 research studies on reading had been published in the English language between 1996 and 1999.

The focus of a large proportion of this reading research is on the acquisition of reading skills and the cognitive processes underlying the act of reading, rather than on reading as a leisure activity. In recent years, however, a certain amount of reading research has been conducted that moves outwards from literacy learning in a formal, educational context to broader, society-based settings. Such research investigates people's reading habits, and their preferences and attitudes towards reading.

The 2002 Eurobarometer survey of European cultural activities, conducted at the request of the European Commission, Eurostat, revealed that 44.8% of Europeans read books for reasons other than work or study (European Commission, 2002).

The Australian National Reading Survey of reading, buying and borrowing books for pleasure (Nielsen, 2001) was an extensive survey of reading for all ages, and investigated reading behaviour, attitudes to reading, trends in book buying and borrowing, library usage and influences on book selection. The survey found that 78% of the Australian population read for pleasure, and also that the greatest influence on children's reading enjoyment is the attitude of their parents towards reading.

Research in this area is also conducted in developing countries, for example the UNESCO research into improving reading skills in Uganda examined how the home environment affects the reading capabilities of children in primary schools. The findings revealed that attitudes of parents affected children's reading, and that children from homes where parents were literate were more likely to enjoy reading and to be encouraged to read than those from homes where parents were illiterate. In addition, the language used as a medium of instruction and the availability of reading materials in the local language were identified as factors influencing students' future interest in reading (Obua-otua, 1997).

On the whole, international research in reading for pleasure tends to focus on children and young people, for example in the Netherlands investigations have been conducted into children's motivation and attention as primary aspects of their reading behaviour, and processes of emotion or imagination as secondary aspects (Tellegen and Frankhuisen, 1999; Tellegen, 2001).

> Because reading is a value in itself and also brings so many positive qualities and happiness to human beings, every child, every human being must have access to reading and books as a basic right. This idea has found recall in the international formulations of human rights, in article 19 of the 'Universal declaration' (United Nations, 1948) and especially in article 17 in the 'Convention on the rights of the child' (UNICEF, 1989).
>
> (Koren, 2002)

To summarize, international reading research, with the few exceptions noted, has tended to focus on the acquisition of reading skills rather than on reading as a leisure activity, and on children and young people rather than adults. Where a more sociological approach is taken, research frequently consists of surveys of reading habits or of reading as one of many cultural activities. It was precisely because of these perceived gaps in current reading research – and to attempt to find preliminary answers to the questions listed at the end of the introduction – that the IFLA International Reading Survey was conducted.

The IFLA International Reading Survey

This research was conducted in 2002 for the Reading Section standing committee of the International Federation of Library Associations (IFLA). The aim was to undertake an international scoping survey of reader-centred service provision in public libraries. This was felt to be a timely project that complemented two of the priority areas of the work of the Reading Section, namely research about reading and the development of literacy guidelines for library staff. The research findings were reported to the 68th IFLA conference in Glasgow in August 2002 (Train, 2002). It was hoped that the research would inform future discussion at IFLA and in the individual countries represented at the conference.

Aim and objectives of the research

The survey was never intended as a wide-scale attempt to map provision in all countries, but instead as a short-term piece of research, the aim of which was 'to provide a representative international overview of the extent to which public libraries provide a reader-centred service, in order to inform future service provision' (Train, 2002).

Within this aim, there were three objectives:

- to conduct an initial scoping survey of current reader-centred activity in public library authorities in a wide range of countries
- to use the data collected in order to illustrate staff perceptions of the impact of reader-centred work on their service, and to share examples of good practice
- to disseminate the information to all countries via the internet.

Research method

In order to achieve these objectives, three phases were devised using the research methodology:

- *Phase 1*: To devise a questionnaire survey that members of the Reading Section Committee could send to colleagues in a wide range of library authorities (or the national equivalent) in their own countries. Nine countries are represented on the Committee, so it was hoped that an equally wide response would be obtained.
- *Phase 2*: To select from the questionnaire data, as case studies, a sample of public libraries to be contacted and questioned further regarding their original responses.
- *Phase 3*: To analyse the data and produce a paper reporting the findings that would be available on the internet and, where necessary, in printed format.

Phase 1: The questionnaire survey

The focus of the reading survey was not on the educational development of literacy skills, but on reading for pleasure. It investigated those promotional activities organized in libraries (and elsewhere, as appropriate) in order to promote reading and to enhance the reading experience of both adults and young people. Information was requested concerning the promotional activities taking place in respondents' regions, and what they felt to be their value and impact on their organization, and on their readers. It was hoped that examples of good practice would be provided and could then be shared internationally.

The working group devised four key areas for the survey:

1. Reading policy
2. Partnerships to promote reading
3. Your reading activities
4. Staff skills and training needs.

Within each of these areas there were between two and eight questions, some closed, others requiring more information (see Figure 4.1). The survey was available online, either for online completion or to download, in a choice of English, French or Spanish.

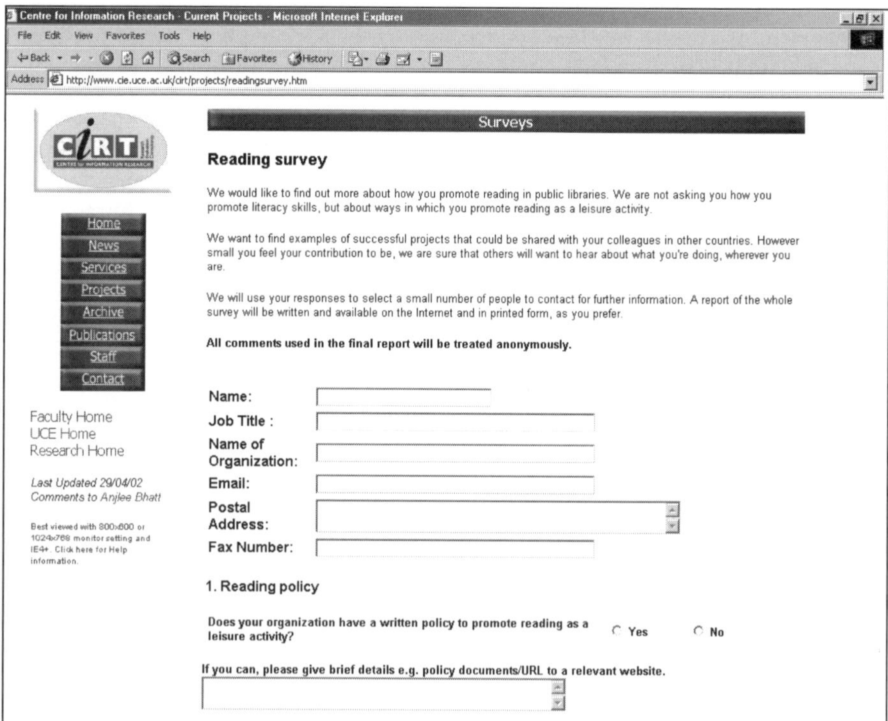

Centre for Information Research - Current Projects - Microsoft Internet Explorer

File Edit View Favorites Tools Help

Back Search Favorites History

Address http://www.cie.uce.ac.uk/cirt/projects/readingsurvey.htm

CIRT Centre for Information Research

Home
News
Services
Projects
Archive
Publications
Staff
Contact

Faculty Home
UCE Home
Research Home

Last Updated 29/04/02
Comments to Anjlee Bhatt

Best viewed with 800x600 or 1024x768 monitor setting and IE4+. Click here for Help information.

Surveys

Reading survey

We would like to find out more about how you promote reading in public libraries. We are not asking you how you promote literacy skills, but about ways in which you promote reading as a leisure activity.

We want to find examples of successful projects that could be shared with your colleagues in other countries. However small you feel your contribution to be, we are sure that others will want to hear about what you're doing, wherever you are.

We will use your responses to select a small number of people to contact for further information. A report of the whole survey will be written and available on the Internet and in printed form, as you prefer.

All comments used in the final report will be treated anonymously.

Name:
Job Title :
Name of Organization:
Email:
Postal Address:
Fax Number:

1. Reading policy

Does your organization have a written policy to promote reading as a leisure activity? Yes No

If you can, please give brief details e.g. policy documents/URL to a relevant website.

Fig. 4.1 *The International Reading Survey*

2. Partnerships to promote reading
Who do you work with to promote reading?
Please select all the relevant choices:

- ☐ Other libraries?
- ☐ Other regions?
- ☐ Publishers?
- ☐ Booksellers?
- ☐ Promotional Agencies?
- ☐ Other?

If other, please give details.

Do you think that these partnerships are beneficial to your library service?	○ Yes	○ No

3. Your reading activities

Do you promote reading in your library?	○ Yes	○ No
Do you organize special projects / activities / programs?	○ Yes	○ No

Please provide details.

Do you think that these activities have been valuable to your readers?	○ Yes	○ No
Do you have any evidence of this that might be useful to others?	○ Yes	○ No

Please explain.

4. Staff skills and training needs

Do you have members of staff with specific responsibilities to promote reading as part of their job description?	○ Yes	○ No
Is reading promotion part of the work of all staff?	○ Yes	○ No

What skills do you think are needed to promote reading to current readers?

And what skills would help to encourage non-readers to enjoy books and reading?

Do you think that you and your colleagues have these skills?	○ Yes	○ No
Do you think that training would be helpful?	○ Yes	○ No
Have you participated in any training programs to develop these skills?	○ Yes	○ No

If you answered yes, who provided the training?

- ○ Library staff?
- ○ Professional trainer?
- ○ Other?

5. Final question

Can we contact you again for more (brief) information? We would not use your names in our report.	○ Yes	○ No

Please select one of these options: Submit or Clear

Fig. 4.1 *continued*

hase 2: The case studies

For the second phase of the project, ten respondents were selected to answer a number of further questions on their individual responses and a series of more general questions on the original four subject areas:

1 Reading policy:
- How the policy has worked in practice
- How effective it has been
- To what extent it has facilitated the development of partnerships with other agencies/organizations.

2 Partnerships to promote reading:
- Reasons for the development of partnerships
- Details of financial commitment
- Benefits of the partnerships.

3 Your reading activities:
- Details of reading activities organized for adult readers or non-readers
- How evidence of the value and impact of reading activities has been – or could be – used.

4 Staff skills and training needs:
- Reasons for suggesting that certain skills were necessary to promote reading to readers or non-readers
- Details of training courses or programmes.

Phase 1: Profile of respondents

Fifty questionnaires were returned, which was an excellent response to a survey that had been distributed in this way. It was also encouraging that information was obtained from a wide range of posts, in 18 different countries:

Belarus	Finland	Namibia
Botswana	France	Norway
Bulgaria	Germany	Portugal
Canada	India	Spain
Croatia	Italy	United Kingdom
Czech Republic	Micronesia	United States.

N.B. Additional experiential accounts from international colleagues were submitted to the author for use in this chapter, and extracts from these are included, as appropriate, within the overall presentation of findings of the International Reading Survey.

Findings: Reading policy

The first section of the reading survey investigated the reading policies of respondents' public libraries. When asked 'Does your organization have a written policy to promote reading as a leisure activity?', 29 replied that they had.

Policy and strategy documents

Two respondents referred to policy documents created by their national professional organizations, either more generally 'the act of librarianship', a 'library statute' (Belarus) or a specific policy: 'We promote the Intellectual Freedom Policy of the Canadian Library Association' (Canada).

For some, the promotion of reading for pleasure is one element of the overall service strategy. This may be part of the Collection Development Policy (Canada), or the family reading strategy: 'Leisure reading falls into the [remit] of the family member portion of our policy' (USA).

In other cases, respondents referred to their service mission statement. An excerpt from that of a British Columbian public library reads as follows: 'We enrich the life of every person in our [community] by providing equal access to the world's ideas and information through books, programs and resources. . . . We welcome and support all people in their love of reading. . . . We celebrate the freedom to read, to learn and to discover.' A statement from the USA similarly promotes an equity of access: 'The Kalamazoo Public Library is committed to providing open access to opportunities which anticipate, support and respond to the international, cultural and leisure needs of people within the library district.'

Reading policies in focus: the Czech Republic

In the Czech Republic, each library has its own policy to promote reading, although the length and format of this policy varies from library to library.

Each individual policy is adapted according to local conditions and lifestyle: although the Czech Republic is a small county, there are significant local differences in the field of reading promotion. For example, in Moravia, 'people live more for their community and many community events take place there'. In Prague or the Karlovy Vary region the community focus is less strong: 'there are many visitors, tourists and foreigners in these areas'.

In the Czech Republic, non-profit organizations such as public libraries contribute a great deal to society. However, largely because of the constant pressure of budgetary restrictions, they sometimes fail to recognize the importance of promoting and marketing their reading services to the general public. Yet in the eyes of one Czech librarian, a written policy is an effective tool with which to support library staff in their promotion of reading, for the following reasons:

1 A reading policy that is based on information concerning local users' needs promotes the individual profile of the region.
2 A reading policy 'can be directly used like public information and can help to promote library services in any way'.
3 A reading policy can be used in order to demonstrate the effectiveness of the reading services of the local public library to local government organizations and other potential funding bodies.

Adapted from information supplied by Jitka Banzetova, Regional Library Karlovy Vary, Czech Republic.

Reading policy: summary

Although not all respondents' organizations had devised a specific reading policy, many included the promotion of reading within the overall service strategy or library plans. These were felt both to provide a timescale for future developments and to increase the status of reading within and beyond the organization. 'We utilize the "Equipped for the future" model of instruction which encourages adult learners to use reading to improve skills as family members, community members, and workers. Leisure reading falls into the family member portion of our policy' (USA). 'Written strategy together with some statistical data could be [a] good demonstration of the utility and usefulness of the library activities. This is very hard to show . . . because such public services have no direct – and from the view of contemporary society [this is] the most important – financial effect' (Czech Republic).

A respondent from the UK explained that such a strategy could also support the overall promotion of the reading activities of the library service: 'Our strategy has enabled us to prove that we can now make events work and we have a core audience from readers' groups which gives the staff confidence to promote elsewhere'.

Findings: Partnerships to promote reading

The International Reading Survey revealed that the 37 people who responded to this question provided information concerning a wide range of partnerships they had used or had specifically developed in order to promote reading, within and beyond their local community.

Perhaps unsurprisingly, more than three-quarters of respondents worked with other libraries: 'The District library is [the] centre of a public library cooperative system. . . . Some of [the authorities] are provided in cooperation with public libraries' (Czech Republic).

Approximately half of respondents had worked with publishers and/or booksellers (24 and 26 respectively), and approximately one-third with other regions and/or promotional agencies (18, 16).

Around three-quarters of respondents (the 37 mentioned above) gave 'other' examples of partnerships they had developed. These were extremely wide-ranging, but for ease of reference they can be divided into regional and national groups.

Regional level

Youth

Educational:

- Kindergartens, schools: 'The district library is in close contact with basic and secondary schools' (Czech Republic).
- Parents' Associations (UK).
- 'We have always encouraged teachers to book visits for classes of all ages. If necessary, we go to the schools, too. In this way we reach many children whose parents don't bring them to the library' (Canada).
- 'We have always cooperated with the schools (6–16 year old pupils). . . . We have a person who works both in the library and in a . . . team for the school . . . [she] is paid by the public library . . . the organisation working with the public library for the students has made an agreement that nobody in the region has to pay to obtain resources from each other' (Norway).

Recreational:

- 'Summer reading club' (Canada).
- '[The library] provides excursions, workshops and other meetings with the children and young adults in every age category' (Czech Republic).
- Youth clubs (Norway, UK).

Adults

Educational:

- Adult education (Botswana, Canada, UK).
- Universities: 'We have meetings at least [twice] each year discussing how we shall cooperate' (Norway).

- 'We cooperate with [the] department of non-formal education, and vocational centres' (Botswana).
- 'Literacy outreach groups', 'community literacy groups' (Canada).

Recreational/cultural:

- Arts museums (Norway).
- Authors, celebrities (Canada, Croatia, USA).
- Literacy Council (Canada, USA).
- Friends of the library (USA).
- Non-library-based reading groups (UK).
- Local government cultural departments: 'the cooperation with the 'Kulturamt', the local authority for cultural affairs: there are two or three meetings per year in order to organize the reading events over the whole year' (Germany).

Professional:

- Palau Library Association (Micronesia).
- Foreign embassies in the Republic of Belarus.
- National reader development project (Branching Out, UK).
- CLAC: Les Centres de Lecture et d'Animation Culturelle [Centres for Reading and Cultural Activities] (France).

Partnerships in focus: France and French-speaking countries

The CLAC programme is a programme to encourage reading for all in rural areas. It uses as its resource the networks of reading-related and cultural activities whose management and funding is shared between the Agency for French-Speaking Communities and the host nations.

A CLAC is a resources centre aiming to increase knowledge, access to information, leisure activities and personal development, through which a geographically restricted community can have access to the benefits of cultural and socio-cultural activities.

By the end of 2001, the Agency for French-Speaking Communities had installed a network of 213 centres in rural areas in 17 countries, largely in Africa and the Indian Ocean. Situated in areas with between 5000 and 25,000 inhabitants, they provide a rural community with access to books, to audiovisual materials and to a wide range of cultural activities.

What have these CLAC achieved since 1986? The only place for public entertainment in their area, the centres are visited by thousands of people who choose to read, to play educational or board games, to join in competitions, to watch documentary or fiction-based films, or to join in a wide range of other cultural activities.

Over 80% of readers are young people aged less than 18 years who each borrow on average 1.4 books per month. In 1999, for example, more than 1 million books were circulated throughout the various CLAC networks.

Partnership benefits

Respondents to the second phase of the IFLA research were asked to state if, and to what extent, the partnerships to promote reading had been beneficial to their organizations.

For most respondents, a primary benefit was the exchange of information, and sharing ideas with new colleagues: 'We learn things from each other – and we find [a] solution that everybody can be satisfied with' (Norway).

For others, a major benefit was that additional funds helped them to provide a better quality, and higher-profile service: 'The library is able to offer services or collections to the community that it would otherwise find a challenge to offer or not have at all. The participation in a partnership raises the profile of the library and of reading in general which is a definite benefit to us' (Canada). 'There is a benefit in public relations; in having a funding body; in interesting other authorities in reading as a leisure activity' (Germany).

One respondent felt that the benefits were felt by all despite the lack of additional funding offered by partner organizations: 'The cooperation [has] been running for more than ten years – this is a fact that can show the cooperation to have been beneficial. It is hard to explain if we have no "money" in our hands, but everybody feels that these activities are useful' (Czech Republic).

Partnerships to promote reading: summary

Respondents participated in a wide range of partnerships that had either been developed specifically in order to promote reading or that had previously existed. Most communicated regularly with other libraries, but many examples were given to describe ways in which other agencies had become involved in the work of the local library service, both for young people and adults and for educational and recreational purposes.

It was felt that in many cases partnerships led to more effective service delivery and higher quality promotional activities: 'The library is able to offer services or collections to the community that it would otherwise find a challenge to offer or not have at all' (Canada).

Findings: Reading activities

Forty-six respondents stated that they promoted reading in their libraries, and 45 said that they organized special projects, activities or programmes via which to do so.

An initiative targeting young people in particular is the Norwegian 'Troll I Ord' (Words Come True) project (Haga Indegaard, 2002). The project (1998–2001) was developed as a result of growing governmental and public concern that Norwegians were spending less time reading for pleasure than ever before. The aim of the initiative was therefore to reverse this trend.

The project was based in Stavanger Library, in the Cultural Centre, as 'the city has an active environment for authors, and one of the country's most active and best visited libraries'. A full-time project leader was employed, who worked in close co-operation with the library. The name of the project, Troll I Ord, was chosen because it 'plays on magic, mystique and fairy tales . . . refers to oral stories and reading . . . and it does not contain the command "Read!"' (Haga Indegaard, 2002).

Although Troll I Ord was largely directed towards children and young people, it also targeted parents and other adults: 'we are trying to influence the adults directly' (Haga Indegaard, 2002).

It consisted of several different sub-projects, for example:

- Storyteller workshop – for kindergarten staff
- Literary fashion show – presented at the opening of a photo exhibition called 'Young in Norway'
- Open Library on Sundays – a popular family day.

Although the first phase of the International Reading Survey did not differentiate between promotion to adults and young people, the second included the question 'Do you organize reading activities for adults as well as children? Please give examples.'

One respondent explained that the focus of reading promotion within their organization was on the young reader: 'We are especially promoting activities for children: creating a very special . . . environment at the Young People's Library, where children and teenagers enjoy the freedom to make . . . choices' (Bulgaria).

A second felt that there was no local demand for adult-centred activity: 'Activities for adults are not regular. . . . There is no such need [for] these types of activities . . . there are many cultural events in the city and inhabitants are [able] to choose according to their taste and mood' (Czech Republic).

However, other respondents provided a wide range of information concerning ways in which the promotion of reading for pleasure included an adult audience: 'In my role as the Readers' Advisory Librarian I am a frequent speaker to community groups and as such am constantly promoting great reading to adults' (Canada). 'We organize lectures and book presentations for adults' (Germany).

A particularly detailed response was provided by a Finnish librarian, who described three separate events to target an adult audience:

> For adults we have literary conversations about books and author visits. The Adult Education Centre takes care of most . . . of them; we provide the place, service and advertising. We organize literary evenings perhaps once or [twice] a year . . . and then we have . . . every November a Scandinavian literary event (now, I think, in seven or eight countries), which is called *Candle Night*. In libraries of all partaking countries we read the same text at the same time (in our own languages) and then discuss it, tell stories, sing or listen to music. The themes are different each year.

Reading activities in focus: the USA

Public librarians in the USA have renewed their commitment to celebrating and supporting the general reader over the last two decades. One of the main ways in which this commitment has been evident is via their establishment of partnerships and programmes that support the general reader.

The Center for the Book in the US Library of Congress was established in 1977 to promote books, reading, literacy and libraries. It has acted as a catalyst to establish state book centres in 47 states, reading promotion programmes and partnerships. Each state centre develops activities that promote its own book and print culture. The Washington Center for the Book launched a highly successful community programme in 1998, 'If All Seattle Read the Same Book . . .', which has caught the nation's attention and is being replicated in communities across the USA. Examples include Los Angeles, California reading *Fahrenheit 451* by Ray Bradbury; St. Paul, Minnesota reading *Profiles in Courage* by John. F. Kennedy; and all of the state of Virginia reading *Sophie's Choice* by William Styron (McCook, 2002).

Support for reading, both basic literacy and recreational reading for experienced readers, is a significant aspect of the librarian's role and of the public's perception of the library's role. Therefore, the act of reading and the role of reading in people's lives are topics that warrant study and reflection (McCook and Jasper, 2001). During the last two decades a growing number of US public librarians and scholars have reflected on the complex act of reading, sought to develop sources that assist them in guiding readers, and have participated in partnerships that have ensured a growing audience for these services (McCook, 2002).

The perceived value of the activities to the readers

Forty-seven of the 50 respondents thought that their reading activities were of value to participants, and 40 felt that they could provide evidence of this value.

The discussion of the International Reading Survey at the IFLA conference in Glasgow 2002 reflected that this was one of the more difficult areas of the Survey. It was felt that it is easy to have a 'feeling' for success, to feel that something we have organized has effectively reached the target audience. Yet how can this feeling be quantified? How can the evidence be found to convince senior managers and funding bodies that an initiative is worth continuing for a further period?

Despite the difficulty of doing so, 40 of the 45 respondents were able to supply evidence of the impact on participants of their reading activities. A large proportion of the evidence that respondents felt able to provide was quantitative, for example in terms of stock circulation, membership and event attendance figures.

Stock circulation

Comments from respondents included:

- 'Statistics of issues generated by some book promotions' (UK).
- 'Increase in circulation of young adult materials' (US).

Three Canadian respondents noted that circulation figures altered according to the number of promotions on display at a given time:

- 'We find that circulation dramatically increases during the Reading Challenge and the Summer Reading Club' (Canada).
- 'Circulation decreases when we don't offer programmes and don't have displays set up' (Canada).
- 'There is a direct relation between successful promotion and use of collection and services' (Canada).

A respondent from Bulgaria agreed: 'I [display] books which were at the library collection for two years, they were not read at all. When young people saw them together with pictures they are interested in reading them' (Bulgaria).

Membership

Three respondents reported increased membership of the library service in general or of reading groups as evidence of the value of the reading activities they had organized. One referred to the 'increased use of the library' (Canada), a second to 'new family members' (UK), and a third observed: 'When new people come to hear authors, if they are not library members, they take out membership' (Canada). A fourth commented that promotional events organized in her library had resulted in a 'take-up of reading group membership' (UK).

Attendance

Two US respondents referred to 'attendance' figures and 'participation numbers' they had collected, whereas two from the UK used less specific terms: 'Large numbers of Dads involved, . . .[a] steady build-up of audiences for events and [an] increase in [the] number of reader groups' (UK).

Evaluation as further evidence of impact

In addition to considering circulation, membership and attendance as indicators of the impact of reader-centred activities, many respondents referred to 'evaluation' or listed specific evaluative activities that they had conducted in order to formally monitor the impact of promotional events on the audiences. Some collected formal data using 'event monitoring forms' (UK). 'Our early childhood literacy program . . . last year gathered baseline information on incoming kindergarteners' reading readiness levels, and will now continue to assess those levels. We have also engaged an outside evaluator for that program' (USA).

Others felt that collecting anecdotal data was also a useful way to obtain evidence:

- 'Positive feedback from parents' (Canada).
- 'Increased . . . interest in reading groups' (UK).
- 'Teens enjoying the library and saying so' (USA).
- 'Students ask for titles, or recommendations for books' (Micronesia).
- 'Every year teenagers tell us they have read books they would not have read' (UK).
- '[The reading activity] gets customers speaking about reading and its importance in our lives' (USA).

Dissemination

The second questionnaire asked the ten respondents to describe ways in which the previously listed evidence:

- had been used, e.g. to inform senior managers
- could potentially affect funding for future activities
- had been disseminated to the readers themselves – library users, events audiences?

Six respondents stated that they informed senior managers of the value and impact of their reading activities, although the extent to which this occurred varied considerably, as the following examples illustrate:

- 'I regularly inform senior managers' (Bulgaria).
- 'Response to these programmes from the public is passed on to the Management Group. Hopefully it is then used in their decision-making processes' (Canada).
- 'We report about all events . . . to communal senior managers' (Finland).
- 'Senior managers and board members know about all our programmes. The Head of Children's Services is a member of the Management Team and also sits on the Coordination Team advising the Board's Strategic Planning Committee. I have used such evidence to sustain book and programme budgets in tight times and increase them in good times, get funding for special initiatives such as the

children's millennium project, and gain approval to open our own children's bookstore' (Canada).

The potential impact on funding allocation was less frequently acknowledged, and it seemed that responses to the question 'Could the evidence affect funding for future activities?' were cautiously made: 'Yes maybe, but this is a slow process' (Bulgaria), 'As far as we know, no' (Germany), 'I hope so, but I have no good examples' (Norway).

A more positive response came from the UK: 'Yes, now we have more confidence that events will work and [will] be worthwhile. [We are] getting more ambitious'.

Dissemination to the reading audiences

The subsequent dissemination of evidence concerning the impact of reading activities on the readers themselves was similarly tentative, with one exception:

- 'Only through readers' groups' (UK).
- 'No, not yet' (Germany).
- 'Not specifically' (Canada).
- '. . . No, we have not contacted readers' (USA).
- 'Yes, all the time, we discuss very often' (Bulgaria).

Reading activities: summary

Almost all respondents organized specific activities via which to promote reading for pleasure, both for adults and young people, and almost all thought that these activities were of value to their recipients. Considerable evidence of this value was provided, both quantitative (stock circulation, membership and attendance figures) and qualitative (readers' feedback, anecdotal evidence, qualitative questionnaires).

Internal evaluation of reading activities was also being conducted in many cases, and findings were being disseminated to colleagues, senior managers and the general public, although the latter process was tentative.

It is clear that reading activities and their promotion are felt to be very closely connected to all library activity. As one librarian commented: 'Even [though] the library services have been enlarged so much recently, the main object of library activities – reading – is kept, and my opinion is it will be kept, side-by-side with modern technologies' (Czech Republic).

Findings: Staff skills and training needs

Almost three-quarters of respondents (34) had members of staff within their organization with specific responsibilities to promote reading as part of their job description, and a slightly higher number of respondents (37) stated that reading promotion was an aspect of the work of all staff.

Skills required to promote reading

Respondents were asked to list firstly those skills they felt were required to promote reading to current readers, and secondly those skills they felt would help to encourage non-readers to enjoy books and reading.

Before presenting the data, it would be useful to ask 'Who is the non-reader?'

- A person with low literacy skills?
- A non-library user, someone who possesses the skills to read but chooses not to?

Both kinds of people could legitimately be described as 'non-readers', yet both evidently have very different needs, and face very different potential problems when considering the public library service.

It is interesting that some respondents approached the issue from the point of view of encouraging children to develop the reading habit from an early age, whereas others directly addressed the reading or non-reading adult, having adopted strategies to introduce the target groups to the pleasures of reading. Examples of such strategies and the skills to support them are listed below.

The reading child

- 'Knowledge of the contents of books and of children today: grandmother's favourites are very seldom suitable for our kids who live in such a different world' (Finland).
- 'I think [that] the most important thing is the librarian's personality, especially when working with young people in a fast-changing world . . . because of this I think the librarian should possess very special skill' (Bulgaria).
- 'If training can be provided on children's library services this can help because if children learn how to be habitual readers at an early age, this problem of reading will be solved' (Botswana).

The non-reading child

- 'A wide knowledge of and appreciation for children's literature. An understanding of cognitive development, an understanding of the community, children's needs and interests' (Canada).
- 'Storytelling, story hours, knowledge of books and picture book slides, very good sense for children's needs, patience . . .' (Germany).

The reading adult

- 'The members of departments for adult readers [to] have reading promotion as a part of [their] work' (Czech Republic).
- 'You need to be able to discuss books both formally (booktalks and discussions) and informally in the stacks' (USA).
- 'Knowledge of stock and new titles, confidence to promote material to members of the public' (UK).

The non-reading adult

- 'Some understanding of why not everyone wants to use the library, being able to work with those that are socially excluded' (UK).
- 'You need to go out into the community to promote reading to those who do not have a reading habit' (USA).

Participants' responses to both questions can be divided into the following themes:

- Personal skills
- Professional skills.

Personal skills

For many respondents, the skills required to encourage both the reader and the non-reader to read would not be found in a job description, but could instead be described as 'personal skills', personality traits that, if possessed by a librarian, would perhaps be more likely to provide such encouragement:

- 'showmanship' (Canada)
- 'enthusiastic and creative staff' (UK)
- 'enjoyment of people and empathy for them' (Canada)
- 'being able to talk to all types of people' (UK)
- 'good powers of persuasion!' (Canada)
- 'a positive kind personality' (Bulgaria)
- 'sens de l'écoute et de l'accueil' ('good listening skills and a welcoming approach') (France).

One librarian gave the following full response to the question, a response that illustrates her strong belief that empathy and respect are two vital skills required in order to effectively reach the non-readers:

> You have to respect them, and find out [what] kind of subject or themes they are interested in. Maybe a movie built on a book can help them to get through a book? People who have [a] problem learning to read are not stupid, it is important that people working in the libraries know that. If you have this kind of problem it is important that people encourage you and show that you are great when you have managed to read something, even if for most of us this is no problem. (Norway)

Professional skills

Respondents to both questions clearly felt that marketing and promotion were critical ways of developing and encouraging the reading habit: 'promotion' (USA), 'advertising' (Croatia), 'media presentation' (Italy), 'advertising techniques' (Micronesia).

Outreach work

Respondents recognized the importance of outreach work, particularly when promoting the library service to non-readers, many of whom would not be regular users:

- 'Frequent *outdoor* presence of the library' (Italy).
- 'Knowing who your readers or potential readers are or the different groups in your community that need attention' (Namibia).

Communication skills

A further skill that is useful when conducting outreach work or any work to encourage non-library users is the ability to communicate effectively. For some respondents, this was described as 'communication skills', for others the definition was more complex:

- 'librarians with knowledge about how children think and feel' (Norway).
- 'reading aloud to children of all ages' (USA).
- 'enthusiasm and excellent communication skills, enjoyment of people and empathy for them' (Canada).
- 'some level of psychological knowledge' (Bulgaria).

However, it was also felt that these skills were equally important when promoting reading to current readers: 'being able to talk to all types of people' (UK); 'public relation skills' (Italy); 'highly developed interpersonal skills' (UK).

Book knowledge

For some respondents, a skill that is frequently overlooked is book knowledge, having an awareness of all resources that are available to encourage the current reader and the non-reader. From the responses they gave, however, it would seem that almost all librarians felt that to have knowledge of the materials was insufficient to encourage the non-reader to read. Although the word 'knowledge' was used several times, equally frequently cited were terms such as 'interest', 'love', 'enthusiasm', 'passion', 'appreciation'.

Readers

- 'Good knowledge of the library collection' (Canada).
- 'Knowledge of stock and new titles' (UK).
- 'You have to read the books that you are going to sell' (Norway).

Non-readers

- 'Staff members themselves should have a love for books and reading; a sound knowledge of a large number of authors and the type of books they write is a must' (Namibia).
- 'Knowledge of [the] range of books that they [non-readers] would enjoy/are relevant to them' (UK).
- 'Read, read, read and read more books!' (Micronesia).

Once the knowledge of available reading materials has been acquired, respondents felt that equally valuable was the ability and confidence with which to encourage and recommend books to others:

Readers

- 'Confidence and interest in books' (UK)
- 'A willingness and a high level of enthusiasm about books and reading is critical' (Canada).

The non-reader

- 'Awareness of varied interests to "hook" non-readers '(UK)
- 'The ability to determine their interests and recommend related books, [and] follow-up so that these people know someone is interested in their reading' (Canada).
- 'To be able to help them find something to support their interests and show them

the library collections as full of useful, interesting and needed information and knowledge' (Czech Republic).

- 'The modern library is directed towards the model where users are the main characters. We must proceed from their information requirements' (Belarus).

Staff skills in focus: Finland

Irja Rinne, Chief Librarian from Posio Communal Library, Finland, states that in her library service, reading promotion and readers' advisory work is for all staff 'an important part of their job'. It is her view that the older members of library staff – 'the middle-aged personnel' – promote fiction reading for pleasure as a matter of course, that they 'base their skills on personal interest': 'We often have a habit of "dropping hints" of books we have read'. She feels that younger members of staff are perhaps less confident promoting reading in this way.

Training courses have therefore been devised for all members of staff, 'to promote reading for pleasure', and are held every year. Irja summarizes her work as follows: 'I feel that the task of leading a small public library in Northern Finland is demanding and often hard. But meeting . . . a young person who shares my pleasure to read and to enjoy reading – could there be a higher reward?' (Rinne, 2002)

Training

Interestingly, although 40 respondents suggested that they and their colleagues possessed the necessary skills to promote reading for pleasure, 45 felt that training would nonetheless be helpful to them. Approximately two-thirds of the group (33) had previously participated in training programmes to develop these skills, training having been provided by the following agencies: library staff (7), a professional trainer (10), both (8), other (workshops; conferences; literature development workers; booksellers; adult and continuing education colleges) (7).

The sample group is too small from which to draw any significant conclusions, although it is interesting that the largest group had hired a professional training provider, which at least suggests that training in reading promotion is a sufficient priority to merit expenditure.

To further investigate the issue of training and professional development in this area, three additional questions were asked in the second survey:

- If you said that you had staff training for reading promotion, was this one course for a specific purpose, or do you have an ongoing training programme?
- How effective do you think that the training has been? Please explain your answer.
- How, and to what extent, is the training information passed to other staff?

The sustainability of training programmes

Sadly, only two of the ten respondents reported that they had an ongoing staff training programme in reading promotion. A Canadian librarian gave the following detailed response:

> All staff joining the children's library team have to complete a project involving reading and critiquing picture books. All staff members have a range of age levels they must be able to make reading recommendations for and therefore read from the collection as part of the job. New books are made available to staff before going to the shelves. We send staff out to relevant workshops whenever they are offered. We talk about books and how to promote them and use them in programmes all the time as part of our daily business in a children's library. (Canada)

A librarian from the Czech Republic said that previous training in reading promotion had been available, but that due to recent budgetary cuts, 'now we have training programs only for IT and computer skills'.

The effectiveness of staff training programmes

The response to this question was similarly mixed. One librarian clearly stated: 'The effect is not really measurable' (Germany), although a second respondent was more positive: '[We're] getting there, I feel as if we have to keep plugging away at it all' (UK).

The most positive response again came from one of the Canadian librarians, who described the actual outcomes of training sessions provided within her organization: 'All of my staff can and do make sound reading recommendations to our patrons. We get lots of requests for recommendations and lots of positive feedback from patrons who enjoyed our choices. We also spend time showing parents how to choose books their children will like, so we have a higher satisfaction rate and more repeat business'.

Dissemination of training information to other staff

Within the organizations participating in training programmes, the main method of cascading training information to colleagues was via staff meetings, usually weekly. Alternative dissemination methods included the following:

- one-to-one training with the Head of Service
- workshops with private training providers
- 'assigned readings' (Canada).

It was acknowledged that dissemination is not a straightforward task, and that it can be difficult to measure the extent to which all staff are aware of training issues. Speaking of the dissemination of such information to colleagues within her local authority, one librarian stated: 'Often, I suspect that it's not [being disseminated], but we can only keep going!' (UK)

Staff skills and training needs: summary

There was a considerable depth of response to the questions concerning the staff skills required to promote reading for pleasure to readers and non-readers. Librarians who focused their responses on children and young people were concerned that promotional skills were crucial, and those who considered both children and adults often described a different approach for each age group. As a Bulgarian respondent suggested:

> I think we have to search for a new meaning of 'reading', maybe trying to discover what 'reading' means for children and young people. . . . I am convinced that young people discover the pleasure of reading by the intermediary of the computers and adults discover computers by the intermediary of reading . . . we have to think about differences between habits of reading for different ages.

A particularly thorough response was provided by a respondent from Belarus, who listed many skills that she felt were required of all library staff in order to effectively promote reading to both the current reader and the non-reader:

- 'general knowledge of science and its applications
- information culture and communication culture skills
- professional ethics
- being good at service promotion and search of documents using modern technologies
- taking into consideration information needs of users and their social and psychological distinctions
- constant self-education and acquiring new knowledge and skills
- possessing personal characteristics needed for social and library work
- possessing special professional skills (functional)
- direct contact with users through communication
- involvement of users in library events and displays'.

The International Reading Survey: in summary

The Survey revealed a considerable amount of interesting data from 18 different countries, pertaining to reading policies, partnerships, promotional activities and staff skills and training. Activity to promote reading for pleasure is wide ranging and far reaching.

It is suggestive that a significant number of respondents to both phases of the International Reading Survey (between one-quarter and one-third, depending on the question) had clearly considered the questions only in terms of services to children and young people. The questionnaire contained no explicit instruction to focus only on this age group: 'We would like to find out more about how you promote reading in public libraries. We are not asking how you promote literacy skills, but about ways in which you promote reading as a leisure activity' (Train, 2002, 6).

The growth of reader development activities has enhanced public library service provision to all age groups in the UK (see Chapter 2), and reading as a cultural activity is regarded by many as a potential means of achieving social change. Socially inclusive projects have been initiated and sustained, and in a number of cases such work has become part of core service provision.

However, even in countries where literacy rates have always been high, there has been a gradual decline in reading and library use in favour of other cultural activities. For example, a Eurobarometer survey of Europeans' participation in cultural activities (European Commission, 2002) noted that fewer than half of respondents (44.8%) had read any book for pleasure in the past 12 months.

In order to combat this decline and to ensure that the public library service retains its relevance within society, it is vital that reading resources are equally allocated and promoted to people of all ages.

The International Reading Survey was small in scale and only ever intended as a scoping survey, an indicator of international reader-centred activity. It would be inappropriate to make generalizations concerning the nature and impact of such activity, based only on 50 examples from a total of 18 different countries.

For example, although comparisons across European countries are quite feasible, how can we compare the reading culture in Africa with that in the UK, when the annual output of new titles from each varies so greatly? How can examples of good practice be shared, be at all relevant, when the working environments of librarians in each country differ so greatly? Today's sociologists draw our attention to the ever-increasing division between the 'haves' and the 'have-nots', between the 'information rich' and the 'information poor'.

Yet as the findings of this survey have illustrated, it should not be assumed that library staff in financially poorer nations are less able to promote reading for pleasure, or that such activity is automatically straightforward for the wealthier library services. Irrespective of their nationality, many of the 50 respondents regularly face the same issues of staff training, of developing partnerships with non-library organizations and of embedding short-term projects in the organizational infrastructure. They share the same objectives: to make the public library service available to all members of their local community and in so doing to encourage reading for pleasure.

The theme chosen by Barbara Ford for her 1997–8 American Library Association presidency was 'Global Reach, Local Touch'. She emphasized the importance of international co-operation and communication, suggesting that librarians across the world should share their experiences and expertise with one another, using the digital age as a means of freeing them from 'geographic limitation' (McCook, Ford and Lippincott, 1998, 3). Similarly, Wedgeworth encouraged all library staff to be aware of the work of international colleagues, to have 'a global perspective' (McCook, Ford and Lippincott, 1998, 6).

In fostering this wider perspective and appreciation of the local relevance of the work of our international colleagues, we become aware that 'libraries function not in isolation, but as part of complex cultural systems that have a global reach' (McCook, Ford and Lippincott, 1998, 231). Such an awareness could play a vital role in breaking down barriers caused by misunderstanding and misinformation.

> Increasingly, many issues, such as those involving the environment, health, the economy, population growth, and poverty, are global in scope. By acting locally, however, each proactive step that individuals and groups take in their own communities helps to address the challenges that cross national boundaries. Individually, we might be able to influence only a small area, but collectively these individual actions have a much wider ripple. (McCook, Ford and Lippincott, 1998, 5).

Reading for Pleasure: Four countries

Let us conclude with experiential accounts from librarians in four different countries – Australia, Canada, the Netherlands and Norway – all of whom give examples of ways in which reading for pleasure is promoted by their public library services. Although the four countries inevitably have different priorities for their library services, each account reflects the national recognition of the status of reading, and the efforts being made to promote reading as a cultural activity, to 'market reading as a source of lifelong pleasure'.

Australia

Academic Gayner Eyre, from Charles Sturt University, Australia writes:

> Reading promotion in Australia has, until recently, been the province of individual libraries and schools. To completely understand the role of libraries in the promotion of reading in Australia, it is necessary to understand something of the structure of the library system. The National Library of Australia is situated in Canberra. Each of the states has a state

library, which offers training and support to libraries in local authorities within that state.

In Australia, many secondary schools have teacher-librarians, dually qualified in education and librarianship. There is a strong emphasis on reading promotion, often co-ordinated through school libraries. Schools play a very important role because of the vastness of Australia and the remote nature of some communities.

One of the developments in promoting literature and reading within schools has been the use of 'literature circles'. This term describes a method of social reading, the aim of which is to promote critical reading skills. More recently there have been developments concerning the incorporation of ICT into the literature circle experience. Trinity Grammar School in Sydney, one of the pioneers of literature circles in Australia, experimented with shareware software and developed a website which led to 'Book Raps' – inter-school discussions via electronic media.

Publishers and booksellers also contribute to the promotion of reading through activities such as author tours, book festivals and also through individual initiatives. For example, a cyber book launch was held in May 2000 by the University of Queensland Press, one of the leading publishers of fiction for young adults in Australia. James Moloney's novel *Touch Me* was 'launched live on the Internet by students at a high school in Brisbane, using electronic streaming technology' (ACCU/UNESCO, 2002). This was followed by a live chat session between the author and 200 students.

The largest and most significant reading promotion is the recent 'Books Alive' initiative, which was ongoing at the time of writing. The campaign is part of a $240 million package, the Book Industry Assistance Plan (BIAP), funded and co-ordinated by the Australia Council, the arts funding and advisory body of the Federal Government. Although part of the total initiative is to support the book industry in Australia by offering textbook subsidies to primary schools and grants to primary school libraries, the four-year 'Books Alive' segment concentrates on reading for pleasure. Its aim is to 'promote the intrinsic value of books, reading and literacy (particularly for children) and the books of Australian writer' (OZCO, 2002). Objectives of the campaign include:

- Encouraging participation in, appreciation of and enjoyment of reading
- Developing readers amongst non-traditional readers
- Promoting the value of literacy, particularly to children and young people
- Promoting Australian writers and writing.

No discussion of Australian reading would be complete without mentioning reading within the context of indigenous peoples of Australia. The Government has recently expressed concern over the acquisition of reading skills by aboriginal children in remote areas, and there is a move within educational and publishing circles to redress this.

(Eyre, 2002)

Canada

Dinah E. W. Gough, Head of Children's Services, Oshawa Public Library. Canada, writes:

> The section of the Oshawa Public Library's collection development policy concerning children's collections begins: 'Children's materials collections are designed to encourage reading, celebrate the literature of childhood, stimulate imagination . . . to empower, entertain and delight.'
>
> We energetically advocate reading for pleasure. Half of the main children's department's $70,000 materials budget is spent on new picture books and novels. We regularly display selections of recommended titles for children at different age levels, and a big bin of family read-alouds is always front and centre. We produce theme and by-age booklists so that staff can locate and introduce one title for a reader the first time and then send the reader away with a list of twenty more titles he is likely to enjoy borrowing on subsequent visits.
>
> Every month we feature two additional displays. Some recent themes: survival stories; more books for fans of Harry Potter; and 'Being Boys: humorous stories about growing up male.' We try to include both fiction and non-fiction in displays, having found that many readers, especially boys, prefer the latter category as a source of recreational reading.
>
> Every summer we register children for a summer reading club (sponsored across Canada by TD Bank), and emphasize the fun of reading over the quantity read, offering weekly club meetings where the members can enjoy book-related crafts and activities. During the school year we schedule orientation visits for classes from city schools. Part of the purpose is to do some skill building so that children become comfortable using the library, but the main reason is so that we can read stories to the younger children and book talk to the older ones.
>
> A patron entering the children's area can expect any staff member to be able to make good reading recommendations. This standard is achieved through a combination of selecting staff for knowledge of children's literature and on-the-job training. Staff also carry books out into the community, to schools and parent groups, talking about reading to children and showcasing books children will love. We schedule author visits as often as we can afford to, and combine the talks with autograph sessions to bring book-makers and book-lovers together. Our millennium project was a two-month celebration of Canadian children's literature, with many author visits and related events. Our main branch runs a small on-site children's book store which stocks high quality titles at the lowest possible prices and encourages patrons to buy books for home libraries and give as presents.
>
> Our children's collections are broad-based and heavily used by students, but direct curriculum support is not an objective. Our primary function is to nurture readers. We do all the usual imparting of facts to parents – and anyone else who will listen – about the need to read to children so that they will have the skills to achieve a bright future. But our favoured and most successful method of getting this message across is to market reading as a source of lifelong pleasure. (Gough, 2002)

The Netherlands

Marian Koren, Head of Research, NBLC (Netherlands Public Library Association), writes:

In general, reading in the Netherlands seems to be on the decline. Many media reports refer to the nightmare of 'de-reading' (ontlezing). Its alarming message has had some effect: a national reading policy was created, and a budget set aside for a number of reading promotion programmes.

The library service and the school

There is a clear division of tasks when it comes to the various aspects of reading. Learning to read takes place in schools; libraries support reading for pleasure. In spite of many efforts by librarians, schools seem reluctant to accept and include the library as a fully-fledged partner.

A number of libraries now follow the same longitudinal method as is applied in schools: the library-based programmes follow the young pupils throughout their school career with an attractive programme of activities.

New services

Dutch libraries have been creative in finding new ways to encourage children and young people to read, even when there is little reading tradition or encouragement at home. One of the approaches is to have children suggest books to their peers, especially appealing when this can be done digitally.

Great attention is being paid to very young children. Peutermaand, a month-long initiative from Groningen, now takes place in eight provinces and may become a national promotion, convincing parents and adults that a child is never too young for the library or books.

New users: from babies to seniors

The Netherlands Public Library Association (NBLC) has initiated programmes for babies and toddlers in order to encourage the enjoyment of language, rhyme, songs, pictures, storytelling and reading aloud.

Reading to or with seniors is a recent phenomenon, especially welcomed by homes for the elderly. Library services include new book programmes with the focus on local history or life biographies. Libraries facilitate the choice of books, train volunteers, and cooperate with institutions for the elderly. Some projects on reminiscence training have also started. Those seniors who can no longer read for themselves, or have little reading tradition, enjoy being read to by volunteers, librarians etc.

Export of Dutch reading promotion

Some concepts and programmes of reading promotion have been developed successfully in the Netherlands and have been imported by other countries. One example is the concept of a separate Foundation for Reading Promotion.

Recently, a new impetus has been given to book and reading promotion in Flanders, Belgium. Several organisations including libraries have joined their forces in the new Stichting Lezen Vlaanderen, with government subsidies of 397,000 euro. The Flemish government also supports projects for reading culture with 249,000 euro.

Another Dutch export-article has been the Children's Book Jury, a reading promotion campaign, in which children themselves vote for their favourite book. Authors are very pleased to receive this 'alternative' award. Sweden has adopted the formula and implemented it successfully five years ago. (Koren, 2002)

Norway

Astrid Todnem, Literature Advisor, Stavanger Public Library, Norway, writes:

Stavanger is a small city of about 120,000 people. The Stavanger public library is part of the Sølvberget cultural centre, situated in the city centre. Stavanger City Council states that "Stavanger should be the foremost city of literature in the country.' Sølvberget aims to 'encourage local, national and international art, culture and literature; to be an arena for the new and experimental.'

I work as a Literature Advisor at the Stavanger public library, where I have shifts at the issuing counter as well as being the library's representative in the coordination and planning of three different literature festivals.

Chapter 02 is an international festival for literature and freedom of speech. It has a high international profile, and offered two literature seminars last year. One put the situation of the Balkans in the limelight, the other dealt with Iranian literature, looking at the overlap between the traditional and modern ways of life.

Stavanger public library also joins forces with a local restaurant to host 'The Literature Week at Cafe Sting', now in its seventeenth year. This festival consists of live readings by Norwegian authors presenting newly published work, thereby creating a venue where the author and reader can meet.

The library is also in cooperation with the Stavanger cinema, *Kino Z*. The cinema helps by making film posters and other promotional materials available for the library displays. When *Bridget Jones's Diary* was released on film in summer 2001, for example, not only was Helen Fielding's work on display, but also a range of other authors whose theme is 'the quest for love'. This year plans are being made to stage a role-play on library premises based on parts one and two of the *Lord of the Rings*.

We also host activity days around a specific theme. Last year there was a separate 'men day', to inspire and motivate the male audience through consciously using traditional male clichés in the making and marketing of the day. This included a large display including crime fiction, male cooking, sports and hobbies, with the slogan 'You're not a real man until you've at least thought about crossing Greenland'.

I run three different reading groups. Two consist of retired people who meet every fortnight, while the third one has younger members and usually meets once a month. The first two groups mainly read new and current literature. I provide tips and background material so that the members can choose different books to read. The members of the younger group often want to read the same book.

I very much believe in taking the book from the shelves in order to display the cover. Even more so I believe in personal contact with the reader, to show my own preferences in recommending books. I call it 'to push books', that is to take the necessary step away from the counter to the customers, and together start browsing the shelves.

(Todnem, 2002)

Acknowledgements

The author would like to thank all those who took the time to complete the IFLA reading survey, and to Anjlee Bhatt, University of Central England in Birmingham, for creating the online version of the survey.

References and further reading

ACCU/UNESCO (2002) www.accu.or.jp/index.shtml. [Accessed 13.03.03]

European Commission (2002) Europeans' Participation in Cultural Activities: a Eurobarometer survey carried out at the bequest of the European Commission, Eurostat. Available at http://europa.eu.int/comm/public_opinion/archives/eb/ebs_158_en.pdf. [Accessed 13.03.03]

Eyre, G. (2002) Personal communication with the author.

Gough, D. E. (2002) Personal communication with the author.

Haga Indegaard, L. (2002) Personal communication with the author.

Koren, M. (1996) *Tell Me! The rights of the child to information*, The Hague, NBLC.

Koren, M. (2002) Personal communication with the author.

McCook, K. de la Peña (2002) *Librarians and Reading for Pleasure in the United States*, text written for the author, August.

McCook, K. de la Peña, Ford, B. J. and Lippincott, K. (eds) (1998) *Libraries – Global Reach, Local Touch*, Chicago, American Library Association.

McCook, K. de la Peña and Jasper, C. (2001) The Meaning of Fiction in Public Libraries, *Acquisitions Librarian*, **25**, 51–60.

Nielsen, A. C. (2001) *A National Survey of Reading, Buying and Borrowing Books for Pleasure.* Available at www.ozco.gov.au/issues/booksalive/ac_nielsen.html. [Accessed 13.03.03]

Nilsson, U. (2002) Poem read at IFLA (International Federation of Library Associations) 68th conference Glasgow, Section for Children and Young Adults Open Section, August 2002.

Obua-otua, Y. (1997) *Improving Reading Skills in Primary Schools in Uganda*, Kampala, UNESCO.

OZCO (2002) A Biannual Snapshot of Arts Policy Research: arts research in progress or planned across Australia, May 2002. Available at www.uzca.gov.au/resources/publications/research/rippa/pdfs/rippa%20example.pdf. [Accessed 13.03.03]

Rinne, I. (2002) *Reading: an international focus*, text written for the author, July.

Tellegen, S. (2001) Why Do Children Enjoy Reading?, *School Libraries in View*, **15** (3), 14–18.

Tellegen, S. and Frankhuisen, J. (1999) *Lost in a Book or Absorbed by Computer Games: some results from an empirical exploration, conference on children's literature and the fin de siecle, University of Calgary, Canada*, Amsterdam, University of Amsterdam, Department of Communication Science.

Todnem, A. (2002) Personal communication with the author.

Train, B. (2002) *International Reading Survey: presentation of findings*, Birmingham, University of Central England. Available at www.cie.uce.ac.uk/cirt/projects/past/IFLAreport.pdf. [Accessed 13.03.03]

UNICEF (1989) *Convention on the Rights of the Child*. Available at www.unicef.org/crc/crc.htm. [Accessed 13.03.03]

United Nations (1948) *Universal Declaration of Human Rights*. Available at www.un.org/Overview/rights.htm. [Accessed 13.03.03]

US National Reading Panel (1999) *Teaching Children to Read*, US Department of Education.

5

Cultural and multicultural perspectives on reading

Judith Elkin

Introduction

The UK has been a richly diverse multicultural, multi-ethnic, multilingual, multi-faith country for decades. The belief that people in the UK should be educated to be aware of the positive values of this rich mix in society has been expressed by many individuals over the years. By 2003, one might expect that such ideas would be well embedded in education and society at large. Some of the passionate words and ideas being expressed by writers, educationalists and librarians in the late 1960s and early 1970s are still timely and worth revisiting today. Many of the contributors to this chapter reflect on the need for ongoing debate.

This chapter highlights the value of reading within a multicultural society and explores issues concerning multiculturalism, racism and language from the perspectives of writers, librarians and a range of individuals concerned with celebrating diversity in society through reading. The chapter concentrates on the situation in the UK but its messages are applicable to all societies.

Rosemary Stones' (1999b, 3) use of the word multicultural is largely followed here: 'the association of "culture" with a lifestyle, a language, a religion – expressed in music, art, custom and ritual, literature, cooking, philosophy etc – make it the most appropriate way of describing our society and preferable to the narrower if more accurate "multi-ethnic" or the vaguer and perhaps more questionable "multi-racial"'.

Racism today

The Inquiry into the Stephen Lawrence murder highlights the insidious and ongoing existence of racism in society. It defines institutional racism as:

> The collective failure of an organization to provide an appropriate and professional service to people because of their colour, culture or ethnic origin. It can be seen or detected in processes, attitudes and behaviour which amount to discrimination through unwitting prejudice, ignorance, thoughtlessness and racist stereotyping which disadvantage minority ethnic people. (28)

And emphasizes the need for:

> every institution to examine their policies and the outcome of their policies and practices to guard against disadvantaging any section of our communities. . . . Racism . . . conduct . . . words or practices which advantage or disadvantage people because of their colour, culture or ethnic origin. Its more subtle form is as damaging as its overt form.
>
> (Home Department, 1999, 321)

The Working Group Against Racism in Children's Resources (WGARCR, 1999) reflects on the principles that brought the group together 15 years previously:

> The messages are as true now as then . . . There has been a tendency over recent years for policies to overlook why our children have to struggle so hard for a place in the sun . . . All children should be seen: much of a child's early development is through play; all children need to see themselves represented positively in play materials; racism is discriminatory and damaging to all children and therefore must be combated; it appreciates that all children are different, and that this uniqueness must be valued; it fosters every child's self esteem, recognizing that skin colour, language, religion and culture are part of a child's identity; it empowers every child by nurturing positive self image.

WGARCR campaigns strongly for the rights of young people:

> We know that some young children upon arrival at the nursery are already saturated with the exclusionary ideological underpinnings and value judgments found within the popular culture. Within popular TV programmes, videos and Disney films, black children, disabled children and non-stereotypical girl role models are almost non-existent. Young children are aware of their gendered, racial and physical identities at an early age. What young children need is an affirmation of their identities not just from a loving and supportive family but also from the powerful public popular culture outside their home. Positive images of diversity within the powerful and public arena of popular culture [are] critically important since this will help all children to normalize diversity. Through engaging with popular culture children soon learn who is valued and included by society and who does not count and who is excluded from society. . . . The lack of black characters as well as disabled and non-stereotypical female characters found in many popular TV programmes tells young children that white, male and able bodied is powerful, normal and desirable. (WGARCR, 2002)

A recent article in *The Guardian* on race sees Britain as a country in transition – a new country in the making. It reflects on the opportunities and disadvantages experienced daily by 4 million non-white Britons, noting 'a country where mixed-race relationships are on the rise, where obstacles to public success are being quietly pushed back'. It quotes American Henry Louis Gates Jr, Chair of Afro-American Studies at Harvard and a lifelong advocate of affirmative action:

> It's a class escalator; if you cut the electricity, no one moves. . . . There are black CEOs [in the U.S.A], yet 35–40% black children live at or below the poverty line; roughly the same as when Martin Luther King was killed. . . . I don't think it's for us to tell black people how they should live their lives. But it's important that some members of the middle class feel responsibility towards the larger black community. Many of us do in my 'crossover' generation – those who entered historically white institutions after the civil rights era.

He also highlights how the politics of race can never be separated from the language used to describe it: 'My grandfather was coloured, my father was a Negro and I am black' (The Guardian, 2002).

Language

Language and use of language thus continue to be an issue:

> In Britain there have been some clear shifts in 'acceptable' language – 'coloured' is now a 1950s period piece, while discussion of 'immigrants' was eventually, if slowly, superseded as increasingly high proportions of ethnic Britons were born here. More recently, the unifying 'black' umbrella identity has been increasingly challenged not only by Asian, Afro-Caribbean and black Africans but increasingly by Pakistani, Bangladeshi, Gujerati, Sikh, Nigerians and other groups seeking to stake claims to a distinctive place in the British race debate. (The Observer, 2001, 2)

Writer Beverley Naidoo (1994, 10) believes that:

> discrimination on the basis of 'race' is still deeply prevalent throughout Britain. But unlike during my own childhood, there are more possibilities today of young people hearing other voices which challenge racism and which value diversity and equality. Language is a powerful tool in shaping our ways of seeing.

Multiculturalism

Where do the boundaries between racism and multiculturalism lie? Farrukh Dhondy is eloquent and thought provoking on the subject:

> Culture is not easy to define. . . . And yet there are few people today who would not agree that the word is a spectrum of differentiated cultures and has been since records began.

. . . As a reality, multiculturalism is as old as our various written histories. As an idea (or a cluster of diffuse ideas), 'multiculturalism' is new. It is essentially an act of recognition of diversity and, immediately beyond that, of committed judgment, one frame of reference looking at another and having to come to terms with it.

The confounding of multiculturalism with anti-racism is understandable, but it's the merest of contemporary coincidences and a mistake. . . . Anti-racism is a simple and self-evident creed, however many skirmishes remain to be fought on its terrain. As an idea, multiculturalism is transnational and it has nothing to do with race. Its first law is that cultures clash. Its second law is that cultures may clash in one and the same person and can do so with spectacular literary results. (English fiction in the post-sixties period was saved from a premature death by the emergence of writers who brought together, as part of their sensibilities, the culture of other societies and the traditions of English writing.) The second law of cultural absorption and hybridization means that some of us are the beneficiaries (the self-pitying have even called themselves the 'victims') of the last great geographical formation of multiculturalism that is the colonial adventure of the modern era. The frustrations of the first generation [of immigrants to Britain from the old colonies] produced the early 'multicultural' publications. There were stories and poems, some nostalgic for the countries left behind, as in the novels of Sam Selvon or the poems of James Berry. Then came the protest in subtle and unsubtle forms – the poems of Linton Kwesi Johnson, various novels written in anger. With very few exceptions the protestors debased the idea of multiculturalism for a while. They indulged the notion that their 'artistic' expression was a branch of anti-racism, another battle won in a war of racial gesture.

Beneath this, another lava was bubbling which broke to the surface in the Rushdie affair. A clearly identifiable upper middle class émigré Indian/Pakistani wrote a novel in the wonderfully inventive western genre he had espoused. The novel is quick with literary device and wit. It has several stories, some of them British and anti-racist, some of them autobiographical, in which we empathise with the young immigrant boy puzzled by the brute culture of public school, and one of them about the conundrum of power and prophecy faced by the prophet Muhammad. Everyone knows what hell broke loose. Muslims in Britain burnt the book, people rioted in India and Pakistan and were shot, the Ayatollah issued his order of death and multiculturalism announced its first murder bounty. It was the first major skirmish of international multiculturalism . . . To the protestors and burners, here was a novel written across the class and colonial divide, across cultural assumptions that came naturally to different sets of people concerned with the book. For all its humorous anti-racism and 'commitment' it came from a tradition which made literature out of heresy and ironies out of sacrilege. It seemed to mock their only source of pride in their crushed existence in Britain. Liberal Muslims protested in their turn.

This is the third law of multiculturalism, that of action and reaction in a war of judgment. . . . Multiculturalism forces us to see that the co-existence of cultures can be

> difficult, even impossible. Some religions cannot co-exist in the same mind or in the same framework of ethical reference. . . . Multiculturalism is about a realization that humans are one race and despite the fact that we have drunk at many fountains we have common thirsts. (Dhondy, 1999)

Reading within a multicultural society

This was echoed recently by Naidoo (1999, 10–11):

> A rich diversity of books is essential if we wish to provide young readers with a broad 'intertext' through which to make connections, to compare, contrast and hopefully to question the 'maps of life' and the worlds being presented to them through literature. . . . In our fragile global environment, we need young people who can cope with ambiguity, understand alternatives, recognize different perspectives at the same time as feeling committed to the idea of a common humanity. . . . Fiction can be a starting point for exploring questions about one's own identity as well as that of others, for exploring commonalities as well as conflict and clashing perspectives. The great strength of fiction is that it offers a realm removed from immediate reality and yet it can provide a prism through which we can see ourselves and others. . . . Questions of gender, race and class – pushed aside in the early nineties by functionally minded managers – are still rearing their heads, demanding that we engage with them.

One can argue that the effect of books and reading on children, as they develop and grow rapidly, is particularly critical, but the positive benefits of reading in a multicultural context are equally relevant to adults. For children, books can demonstrate the value of different cultures and show the similarities between children playing, learning and growing up anywhere. Curiosity in children about their country of origin and the language and culture of their parents and grandparents can be encouraged. Readers can explore their history and feel pride in belonging to two cultures; in books they can find confirmation that they are valued. Books have the power to involve people in previously alien backgrounds, cultures and religions and give a sense of pride in their own cultural and religious heritage. Books can foster racial and cultural understanding and offer positive role models. Whatever the reader's race, sex and circumstances, stories are the medium through which the individual can come to terms with their existence and become that supreme being, their own person.

The author's personal concern with this complex and ever-changing area began very practically in 1969, when working for Birmingham Public Libraries. The local Language Centre was exploring the idea of an exhibition of craft books, which could be used to demonstrate teaching of language through practical work: woodwork, paper modeling, puppet making. This led to a realization of how few attractive, exciting books there were for 'immigrant children' (sic) in schools. The only books the children were offered in schools were Ladybird books: simple, unimaginative and pedestrian. A working party of librarians and peripatetic teachers working with non-English-speaking children was set up to find books suitable for early second-language learners of any age; books that were simple in construction and language without being condescending or babyish and that would encourage and stimulate reading. The group was conscious that children, when originally learning to speak and read, have plenty of time to learn through play, listening, repetition and experience; there is very little time with a second language, even just to acquire basic language. Simple stories provided an ideal vehicle for this. After experimenting and observing children using the books, a selective bibliography was produced, to accompany an exhibition aimed at teachers:

> For children growing up in a multi-racial community, books can play a vital part in the development of awareness and understanding. . . . We live today in a multi-racial society, and the provision of books and other materials must be an integral part of any educational system. (Birmingham Public Libraries, 1969, 3)

This was the beginning of a mission to ensure that libraries, schools, publishers and writers were made aware of the need for multicultural children's and adult books. This built on the concept of books as bridges to international understanding, a concept which underpinned Jella Lepman's work, founding the International Youth Library in Munich in the immediate post-World War 2 period. She believed that: 'the earlier in life we lay the foundation for international understanding and tolerance, the sounder will be the bridges built later and the more ready for peaceful traffic and exchange back and forth' (Lepman, 1964).

Professor of Psychology David Milner in his influential *Children and Race* (1975) and *Children and Race Ten Years On* (1983) highlights the special role of books:

> It is the active quality of reading which marks it off from other forms of entertainment or instruction. Reading requires constant action and creativity from the reader in order to turn words into mental images. These images are powerful creations, idiosyncratic, particular to us, and in which we have some investment. . . . The content of children's books is therefore uniquely important. This is one of their first glimpses of a new reality. One that is very vivid, personal and private. How this world is peopled affects their ways of seeing the real world. . . . It is possible to demonstrate that positive images of black people in children's books positively affect the racial attitudes of black and white children alike. (Milner, 1994, 9)

Attitudes in books – looking back

In the late 1960s and early 1970s, there was a recognition, particularly in the USA and UK, that readers had the right to a body of literature which reflected naturally the varied experiences and rich cultural diversity of society. There was deep concern about racism, covert and overt, particularly as it was being presented to children through books:

> Racial prejudice is being fostered among children by the books they read at school, particularly in text books by implying the superiority of all that is white.
>
> (The Teacher, 1971)

> It is very difficult to find positive or leading figures who are black . . . in children's books . . . black people invariably play secondary, negative, exotic, comic or brute roles . . . these attitudes expressed over and over again, gradually distort our children's perceptions until the stereotypes as well as the myths become accepted as a reality, even by the subjects themselves. (Kuya, 1975)

> Most children's books present a world in which all characters, at least the significant ones, are white . . . the message that such books carry for black children is that they do not matter or count. . . . The reader must assume that blacks do not experience whatever storybooks deal with. They don't go shopping with their mothers or take a trip to the zoo; they don't have dreams about monsters; they don't have birthdays; they don't exist in the role of fairies, clowns, astronauts or the baby Jesus . . . traditionally the black person is portrayed as a servant, a maid, a janitor or villain.
>
> (Community Relations Commission, 1976)

Two books, *Black Skin, White Masks* (Fanon, 1968) and *The Forsaken Lover* (Searle, 1972), highlighted the problems children were facing through prejudice and misunderstanding:

> a culture must provide an early basis for the identity of a child. He needs to feel as he grows towards adolescence, that there is a structure of meaningful wider belongingness behind his relationship with himself and his family, some supporting social strength which he can trust. (Erikson, 1972)

Bernard Coard (1971) demonstrated how the British middle-class culture pressurized black children to:

> hate his colour, his race, his culture, and to wish he were white (32). . . . The black child's true identity is denied daily in the classroom. In so far as he is given an identity, it is a false one (28). . . . Pride and self-confidence are the best armour against the prejudice

> and humiliating experience which they will certainly face in school and in the society (39).

Milner was also concerned about children's racial identity:

> Children's racial identity is complex. Basic recognition and awareness of racial differences begins around three years of age. This recognition and awareness is soon supplemented by a growing evaluative orientation: the appearance of positive feelings for the child's own racial group, and somewhat negative feelings towards other groups. Race, even more than age or gender, illustrates the relationship between attitudes towards the self and towards others . . . children absorb, through the socialization process, both a view of the world and view of their place within it, that is both social attitudes and social identity.
>
> (Milner, 1994, 9)

Guides to the literature

Although there was awareness of the danger of the dominance of negative images in books for children and the need to find more positive, sensitive images, there were no bibliographies or literature guides available during this period and little apparent interest in multicultural materials among publishers and booksellers (apart from specialist and community booksellers). Early work was being done in Lambeth, where children's librarian Janet Hill was attempting to demonstrate the role and value of librarians in a multicultural society and encourage them 'to be aware of the problem of identity which faces the black child growing up in our society; of the deep roots of prejudice, and our slow awareness of this – too slow to save that child from hurt, rejection and bitterness' (Hill, 1973, 135).

Her bibliography, *Books for Children: the homelands of immigrants,* (Hill, 1971*)*, was annotated and highly critical, demonstrating frighteningly clearly the dominance of negative images in children's books.

In parallel, the author was researching the, albeit limited, range of children's books with positive images. This led to a range of articles and bibliographies (Elkin, 1971, 1976b, 1980, 1985a, 1985b, 1986; Stones, 1994; 1999a) over the ensuing years. These, alongside Hill's work, proved influential in terms of national awareness-raising, development of multicultural and anti-racist policies in schools and libraries and encouragement of publishers to begin to fill gaps in the literature, in the belief that:

> We should no longer be tolerating books which offer a racist perspective and which prolong and promote prejudice amongst children. If books reflect society, they are also one of the forces which shape it, a vehicle for combating racism, providing positive challenges to damaging stereotypes and prejudiced attitudes, for encouraging understanding and offering new and optimistic possibilities. . . . Racial bias in books is dangerous in two

> ways: it offends, humiliates, threatens and insults minority groups; it serves to inhibit their learning and therefore damage their life chances and it affects the perceptions of the white majority by offering less than half the truth about other members of society and encourages and confirms feelings of superiority. (Elkin, 1976a)

The National Union of Teachers (1979) was active in developing guidelines:

> education has a vitally important role to play in creating for our future citizens a society where cultural diversity is welcomed and racial harmony will flourish. . . . The most valuable resource of all is the teacher's attitude of mind; it is hoped that these guidelines will stimulate critical appraisal of learning materials and textbooks and help foster a positive attitude amongst the teaching profession towards education for a multi-ethnic, multiracial society.

Rosemary Stones (1999b, 4), reflecting on progress over the previous 15 years, suggests an ongoing need for such guides:

> *A Multicultural guide to children's books* was first published in 1985. The second edition followed nearly ten years later and sold out almost at once. It has continued to be much requested and this, together with the heated discussions on continuing racism in our society that followed the tragic murder of Stephen Lawrence, prompted us to undertake once again the task of updating and republishing the Guide.

Attitudes in books – now

If the guides to the literature are still needed, does multicultural literature still need champions to promote it? Naidoo believes so:

> When talking about literature for adults, there is no separate category of multicultural literature and literature generally has been enormously enriched by writers from a wide variety of backgrounds, e.g. Ishiguro – they are part of the domain of literature. The fact that multicultural literature is still required as a category in the children's book world is an indictment. Why? Discrimination and racism are still there even if shifting. The body of literature is much broader now than 20 years ago; it has enriched us all. There is a richer discourse now, we hear more voices but many of the issues are still profoundly there . . . [racism] is here and affects everyone. September 11th – a terrifying wake-up call to the West – showed that everyone is affected, disaffection affects everyone.
>
> (Naidoo, 2002a)

Critic and author of more than 80 books for children, Mary Hoffman worked in the field of multicultural and anti-racist books in the early 1970s. Has Mary seen any changes in the area of multicultural children's books over the last 20 years?:

> it is easier to see developments in picture books in terms of the numbers of children of colour or non white children now appearing. Thirty years on and 11 years after *Amazing Grace*, it gets easier to do all the time, maybe because publishers are more responsive. . . . But there is still a dearth of illustrators able to depict children of colour. This is frustrating for writers. Similarly there are very few writers or illustrators of colour working in the field. More illustrators need to be able to depict children of colour. (Hoffman, 2002).

She still believes we need a much wider range of different types of family in stories and picture books:

> When I go into inner city classrooms, I meet children of all sorts of combinations of mixed-race partnerships. Books in the UK are only just catching up and we still have very few books depicting children of mixed race, despite a very rich mixture in the population. It is not just about colour, it is even more about what constitutes the family, particularly within extended families and different family constitutions, for example single families and children brought up by grandparents. We're missing out on that richness and diversity. Books need to catch up with the world and reflect the reality within which children and their families live and the experiences of readers. Thus, multicultural fiction is as important as ever; we are still a xenophobic nation. Look at the recent race riots in Oldham; this is not about people coming in to the country, but rather people who have been here for generations. (Hoffman, 2002)

Publisher Verna Wilkins reinforces these sentiments. She believes that:

> the situation for black children and books has moved on, although not a great deal. . . . Traditionally, black children [in books] have been omitted or stereotyped in equal measure. Black children today have no history of being equally represented. . . . Children learn, at a very young age, that colour, language, gender and physical ability differences are connected with privilege and power. . . . Racism, sexism and handicapism have a profound influence on their developing sense of self and others. . . . I want to share ideas with children and make teachers think about what they are doing in the classroom.

She believes this is as important now as it was 30 years ago:

> We are preparing children who will be adults in the new millennium – we are preparing them for a world that we are unsure of because we cannot foretell what it will bring. We know that it will be a world in which technology has moved to change lives and lifestyles irrevocably – a shrinking, interdependent, multicultural world. We must pave the

> foundations for children to live and learn in a world where equal opportunity does not have to be argued about because it is the status quo.

She cites one recent INSET (In Service Training for Teachers) with teachers, where there was no suggestion in the publicity that this was a 'multicultural' inset but teachers questioned why the exhibition of books showed mainly black children. She challenged the teachers: 'If you take white books and white illustrations into the classroom, do you say these are white books? No! – but that is still the norm in many classrooms, regardless of the make-up of the children in that class. Teachers must be encouraged to take stock and reconsider what they are doing on a daily basis. . . . But perceptions need changing now. It is heartbreaking that so little has changed' (Wilkins, 2002).

The recently published, *Learning for All: standards for racial equality in schools*, draws attention to finding ways to 'ensure that non-inclusive teaching materials are used in an inclusive way (for example materials which assume an "all white" audience might be used to explore issues of stereotyping, ignorance and prejudice)' as part of the section on Resources: 'The school takes active steps to ensure that resources in all areas of the curriculum are inclusive' (Commission for Racial Equality, 2000, 29).

Multicultural literature

Multicultural literature is still a fairly young force in children's literature: 'Most of the people who work with young readers would acknowledge that over the last generation it has enriched the resources of many schools and libraries in the UK, giving children access to images and narratives from a wide range of cultures, and familiarizing them with the existence of different languages and traditions' (Hunt, 1994).

One of the pleasures of reading over the past decade has been the emergence of a new generation of British-born black poets and writers (Jacqueline Roy, Malorie Blackman, Benjamin Zephaniah, Jackie Kay, etc.). Their work speaks authoritatively to a young audience for whom multicultural realities are, by and large, taken for granted. These writers give insights and opportunities to readers of all ages:

> While young children will love the variety of rhythms and pluralism of ideas bounced about by John Agard, Grace Nichols and James Berry, as teenagers and adults they will be seriously challenged by these same poets questioning how our humanity is diminished by cultural bigotry. Traditional African folktales that delight young children can begin to lay a basis for older readers engaging with a writer like Chinua Achebe and his depiction of a traditional world being torn apart under colonialism. Mildred D. Taylor's short stories for young readers not only provide a pathway to her own writing for teenagers but to Maya Angelou, Alice Walker, Toni Morrison and other black American writers. Anita Desai

> and Jamila Gavin encountered in the middle years will begin to open windows into subtleties and complexities within India and beyond, to be more fully explored in adult-oriented fiction. (Naidoo, 1999)

The 30 years of the Booker Prize has coincided with the extraordinary development of Commonwealth literature, although the winner of the Booker of Bookers, Salman Rushdie, has asserted that Commonwealth literature does not exist. The term, he argues, yokes together a heterogeneous collection of authors who ultimately have little in common except their tenuous link with Britain. Even so, there has not been a year when at least one book on the shortlist could not be described under that heading:

> There may be no such things as Commonwealth literature, but there are certainly individual writers from post-colonial environments whose work has manifestly changed attitudes to fiction and our knowledge of the world. . . . In Britain we have come to understand better the multi-cultural nature of our society. The Booker Prize has played a significant part in this process, for what are writers but the articulate voice of nations. (Niven, 1998, 41)

Booker Prize winners have included V. S. Naipaul (Trinidad and Britain), Nadine Gordimer (South Africa), Salman Rushdie (India and Britain), Thomas Keneally (Australia), J. M. Coetzee (South Africa), Keri Hulme (New Zealand), Peter Carey (Australia), Ben Okri (Nigeria and Britain), Michael Ondaatje (Canada and Sri Lanka) and Arundhati Roy (India). Shortlisted writers have included Chinua Achebe (Nigeria), Anita Desai (India), Romesh Gunesekara (Sri Lanka and Britain), Abdulrazak Gurnaah (Tanzania and Britain) Timothy Mo (Hong Kong and Britain) and Rohinton Mistry (India and Canada).

Multicultural writers talking

Let us listen to the voices of writers, inevitably contributing a hugely diverse range of perspectives as they talk about their views on writing and reading; but also reflecting an energy and a passion for writing within this broadly defined multicultural literature field.

Jackie Kay

Scottish writer Jackie Kay born to a white birth mother and black Nigerian father, was adopted and brought up in Glasgow:

> Everybody there was white and I was black so I didn't really fit in. . . . I'm really interested in . . . the borders between England and Scotland. Black and white, gay and

> straight. It seems to me that everything interesting and exciting exists on the margins of these borders. If you look at all the trouble in the world, it's concentrated in the margins between things. . . . I like the in-between land and what I'm really interested in writing about is how that affects people, when they feel they belong and they don't belong, when they fit in and when they don't fit in. A lot of us have that experience, being slightly outside of things. Reading and writing are like two sides of the same coin, you toss one up in the air, you get heads or tails and one's reading and one's writing. For me, they can't be separated . . . the point of living is to read. I think that reading is as important, if not more important, than writing. Reading is a mirror, books reflect yourself, you can find yourself in a book and you can also just get so much escape and so much pleasure. . . . Sometimes you feel exposed when you're reading, you feel the writer actually knows you. That's such a wonderful intimate feeling. (Sunday Herald, 2000)

John Agard

Author and poet John Agard speaks about talking to children in school:

> These moments linger in children's minds. They forget the information, but the human contact lingers. . . . You're there to bring a flavour of your culture in the human sense. For teachers who want to explain to children abstract concepts like 'imagery' and 'metaphor' Creole is a marvellously rich source. Imagine a 'duck-belly' bike, imagine playing 'fling-to-fling' (throwing a ball to each other), imagine a 'hard-ears' child (stubborn), Caribbean children should be made to feel proud of that heritage. (Agard, 1985)

Grace Hallworth

Grace Hallworth, author and travelling storyteller, talks about sharing stories with handicapped adults and elderly persons, and with audiences at social gatherings, such as weddings and funerals, as well as day-to-day story-sharing sessions for children in schools and libraries:

> Whether I am invited to participate in multi-cultural programmes or to encourage an appreciation of stories, my concern is with *all* children. For all today's children should have their horizons given psychological and physical breadth if they are to be equipped to perform effectively in a world where the target for the future is the exploration, and probably habitation, of worlds in space. An important beginning to acquiring this kind of dimension is the exploration of human diversity and its many aspects.
>
> (Hallworth, 1985)

Mary Hoffman

Mary Hoffman believes that a writer can depict different ethnic groups honestly, whatever their own background, writing from a personal point of view. Mary's first picture book, *Nancy No-Size* was the first children's book to feature a child of colour, from a mixed-race family. Issues of skin colour are shown in the context of Nancy being 'not too big and not too small'. Mary herself is not black or mixed race, although she is aware of issues through her own family and through her work in schools. The story grew out of Mary's own family context; her husband is half Indian and skin colour was a real interest for their children, comparing skin colours with cousins and friends. The mother in the story is black and the father white, but the illustrator, Jennifer Northway, based the pictures of the father on her own white but dark-skinned husband. The book was banned in some libraries and Mary got letters from angry parents, many of whom had assumed that both parents in the story were supposed to be black. This was not helped by the publisher's refusal to use the term 'mixed-race family' in the blurb.

Amazing Grace, the first of a series of books about the eponymous heroine, was published in 1991 and sold reputedly one and half million copies worldwide. When visiting the USA in the mid-1990s, Hoffman was told that it was the first children's book with a black child on the cover that had walked out of the shop with people of many different colours. Caroline Binch, the illustrator, is not black but has a wonderful skill in her depiction of the strength of black characters, particularly when working with live models. Hoffman found that *Amazing Grace* was on a 'Books to avoid' list in the USA because she was white and therefore her book was deemed to be inevitably dishonest. Happily, checking *Amazing Grace* on the web, she was astonished by hundreds of postings from all over the world, all positive. She believes 'it does not matter what colour the writer or illustrator is; what matters is the story and its impact and meaning for the reader.' She has had numerous letters from black mothers to say how important her books have been to, particularly, their daughters in making them feel good about themselves: 'If the books are authentic to the reader, that is the test' (Hoffman, 2002).

Mary pays tribute to Frances Lincoln, 'a commendable and very proactive publisher'. Frances Lincoln asked her to consider writing a book about refugees, realizing that this was a much under-represented group in books. This coincided with Mary's growing interest in asylum seekers. As part of her research, she spent a year working part-time with asylum seekers in a homelessness centre in Barnet. The book, *The Colour of Home* (2002), is particularly poignant because Frances Lincoln died suddenly and very young the year before the book was published. Mary hopes that Frances would have approved of the book and pays tribute to the publishing house which remains true to Frances's memory. Mary cites Malorie Blackman's *Noughts and Crosses* as an important exploration of prejudice: 'It forced me to face my own prejudices, as I had to constantly remind myself which way round the characters were. This is a real eye opener for many readers' (Hoffman, 2002).

Malorie Blackman

> A number of things made me want to write books for children . . . the dearth of books featuring black children as the main protagonists was a spur to becoming a writer. I grew up reading books that ignored black children. Apart from anything else, it was very lonely. . . . I enjoy reading children's books – the imagination and diversity of them is constantly astounding. My aim is to write for ALL children. Some adults have trouble believing that, but it's true. Children approach each new book, idea, thought, action, with an open mind – until they are sadly taught otherwise. But the letters I get from children who have enjoyed my books make it all worthwhile. (Blackman, 1994)

Anita Desai

Indian writer Anita Desai muses on her writing:

> I was really writing these books for myself as much as for the children who would read them, but it occurred to me that a writer can help his readers to make choices, to think before they choose, and to choose what is beautiful and kind and valuable out of all the chaotic confusion that the world presents. . . . I have more readers in England than I do in India – if my books have any 'message', I felt these messages were for Indian children (in *The Peacock Garden*, that Hindu and Muslim children should be able to live in harmony; in *The Village By The Sea* that the environment is of great value to us and should be protected and appreciated, not destroyed) and I am astonished that children in a foreign country have responded to these ideas so much more warmly. . . . It has shown me that children all over the world have much more in common than what keeps them apart; they are more willing to share than I knew. (Desai, 1985)

Benjamin Zephaniah

Black poet Benjamin Zephaniah writes:

> I wasn't like normal children; normal children played doctors and nurses, they built things with lego bricks or they dressed dolls. I had an obsession with words and rhyme. I wanted to enter other people's minds and spread ideas all over people. There was nowhere to go, no-one to talk to, until I discovered a friend who had the same feeling as myself. We would go to secret places and perform poems to each other only stopping to debate the issues of the day and consider issues crucial to the poet and poetry . . . like, what rhymes with orange. The poetry we loved had to be performed, we had to get out and meet our

> audience face to face, we wanted them to understand us. We were extremist, we wrote when we were extremely happy or extremely angry. (Zephaniah, 1994)

Beverley Naidoo

Beverley Naidoo grew up in South Africa. In her early books for children, she claims that she was crossing borders, going back to childhood, a highly racialized childhood, where everyone was caught in the boundaries:

> I wanted to challenge the racism of society. For a long time South Africa was a very sick society. No justice, no equality, no democracy. Only white people had power and they made everything depend on skin colour. My South African fiction is an attempt to explore perspectives and voices which my apartheid childhood prevented me from seeing and hearing. I was a white child looked after by the mothers of black children who were forced to live without their mothers: my own experience was of being brought up by a white mother, my biological mother, and a black mother. My second mother was a black cook-nanny who saw that I was washed and fed and was always around to talk with me when my own mother was busy. Yet I was brought up to see her as a servant and to call her 'Mary'. While all white adults had to be addressed as either 'Mr' or 'Mrs' or 'Aunty' or 'Uncle', I was brought up calling all black adults by their first names, which was extremely rude. . . . As a child I also accepted that the person who looked after me ate her food off a tin plate and that her own three children lived far away. I never really thought what it must be like for them to be without their mother. One day she got a telegram and collapsed in front of me. Two of her small daughters had got diphtheria and died. I remember being sad and shocked – but I still didn't ask *why*? I could not have caught diphtheria because as a white child I had been inoculated. *Journey to Jo'burg* is dedicated to the memory of those two young children and their mother. My books are located at a particular point in time, reflecting the themes of that time. That is what I want readers to engage with. (Naidoo, 2002a)

Journey to Jo'burg was an exploration: 'through memory of my own childhood under apartheid. *Chain of Fire*, (1987), was a state of emergency novel, carefully researched using material smuggled out of South Africa for me.' *Journey to Jo'burg* was banned in South Africa and only unbanned in 1991, after Nelson Mandela was released from jail. It is still not well known in South Africa:

> On my first journey back to South Africa in 1991, I had a tremendous experience. I was with a teacher working with children who had dropped out of school. She used *Journey to Jo'burg* as a 'workshop book' but without telling any of the children that I was the writer. There was still a curfew and there were still tanks on the streets. I was able to witness the power of the book, as the teacher introduced themes and the children acted out their feelings

> and reactions. . . . I talked to as many young people as possible about what it meant for them at that point in time, what were their hopes and fears. (Naidoo, 2002a)

In 1991, she was immersing herself in the early post-Apartheid era, hearing the voices and connecting emotionally with the subjects. During this time, she recognized what Nadine Gordimer called 'witness literature' – exploring issues of the day, critical issues for human beings of the day, of that particular point in time and in that location:

> That is my underlying aim – and maybe the ultimate aim of literature - to explore common humanity; to speak to us across time and space, to explore.
>
> I wrote *No Turning Back* to reflect on the hinterland, to explore ways in which the wider political world impacts on society. [*No Turning Back* was written in 1995, on the eve of the first democratic elections in South Africa: There was an assumption that everything was going to be fine. Yet it takes generations to recover.] *No Turning Back* took a child living on the streets, suffering from one of the most heinous crimes of Apartheid, the break up of the family/breaking the bond of the family/ breaking up the deep ways that families come together. . . . I felt it was time to move on, to move to a novel exploring the themes of change and the histories we carry with us. How do we turn conflict into friendship? (Naidoo, 2002a)

Naidoo has since moved to look at other worlds, recognizing that away from South Africa there are deeply serious issues in other areas. She began to explore her concern about refugee children, with *The Other Side of Truth.* She expresses considerable pleasure at a letter from a teacher:

> At present, 72 children in Year 6 are doing an Author Study. We have become totally absorbed in your books *Journey to Jo'burg*, *No Turning Back* and *The Other Side of Truth* to the point where we are celebrating with a 'writer's workshop' in the school hall for a full day in July. . . . Your story *The Other Side of Truth* has been voted as the 'book that changed my life' by all the children in my class. We have read it (obsessively) for the last month, unable to do anything else but read and discuss it, plus its underlying theme. The characters Sade and Femi have opened up a new world for the children and myself as we are now aware of the harrowing plight of refugees . . . our efforts have resulted in my class joining an active campaign to secure asylum for a family from Eritrea. . . . Our souls have been enlightened as a result of reading your books.

Naidoo was enormously pleased to win the Carnegie Medal for *The Other Side of Truth:*

> a recognition that a novel coming out of the African tradition was worthy of this prestigious award – here was a chance to give voice to what had led me into writing *The Other Side of Truth* and to the recent disturbing growth in hostility towards refugees.

> . . . I am encouraged too that there are still committed young people's librarians who believe that high quality fiction is a powerful force for the next generation to make leaps of imagination, with heart and mind, into exploring our common humanity.
>
> (Naidoo, 2002a, 2002b)

Publishers talking

Let us turn to the voices of two publishers, for their views on publishing in a multicultural society.

Tamarind

The author Verna Wilkins set up her own publishing house, Tamarind, in 1988. She was then the only black publisher in the UK. In 2002 she remains the UK's only black publisher of children's books. Verna was born in Grenada, where her headteacher father was instrumental in introducing Caribbean history to a curriculum dominated by England's past. Her motives in creating Tamarind reflect this antecedence. Her observations of her children's early schooling in England confirmed her conviction that society's low expectations of black learners and their exclusion from classroom literature were linked factors which had to be confronted simultaneously:

> Just as my students didn't expect their lecturer to be black or female, my kids were not expected to be high achievers at school. They both learned to read early, but all the signs of their excellence, such as their impatience with the stuff they were given to read, were interpreted as signs of disruptiveness. Nothing at all in their early reading reflected their existence. Writers, of course, write about what they value, not what they are ordered to write about, and it gradually dawned on me that the only person I could trust to write authentically about the lives of my own kids and others like them was me. I can't say I started off as a good writer; writing was made necessary by the need to publish what I knew had to be published. (Hunt, 1994)

Verna claims to be a reluctant publisher, but one unfettered 'by the filtering that takes place in publishing – they can't see beyond what they view as mainstream'. She has proved that you can sell black books: 'provided you get it right . . . but black people have had to suffer for generations, why should they suffer in children's stories?' This was what was happening in most children's books and, she suggests, is still happening now: 'black children have to be exceptional in some way, never ordinary.'

She recognizes the importance of black writers, writing from within and having credibility for black children. She does not condemn white writers but thinks:

> books must have credibility for the child reader – even *Amazing Grace* which has sold in huge numbers has a character who has to overcome racism to succeed – how sad for black children. There is a chasm here: 'Just let me be OK – let me be ordinary.' Do black children who have to struggle in real life, really need to struggle in books, too? (Wilkins, 2002)

She spends a lot of time in schools, talking to teachers and pupils. This includes collecting images of black children to share with illustrators, and encouraging children to see themselves as future illustrators as well as writers. These practical steps to resist the visual caricaturing of black children and to make a difference are paralleled by a policy of rejecting problematic depictions of black culture in Britain. All of Tamarind's resources represent black people as self-confident and unselfconscious achievers. Against the suggestion that this evades issues of racism, Verna asserts that her work empowers black children more subtly than books which display a piety and earnestness that children are not receptive to. Her objective is a seamless celebration of human potential:

> I don't see myself as a victim nor do I want black kids to be stereotyped as such. If you present young children with a book full of racism it's like dumping them in a thicket of thorns without a machete. For heaven's sake give them the weapons to deal with it first. Give them confidence, give them delight in reading, give them images of themselves as powerful people.
>
> We produce picture books that enhance black children's sense of self and personal value. Books which show children of colour confidently and unselfconsciously getting on with their lives. Books in which success is normal. Books that are fun. . . . We choose our illustrators with care. We are acutely aware of the characteristic signs of 'shorthand' used by illustrators to depict children of various ethnic groups, and the stereotypical situations set up for families of colour. We do not produce 'black books' or books for black children – we aim to provide a seamless celebration of human potential. All our books are for all children. (Wilkins, 2002)

She talks about a recent visit to a poor Irish/Caribbean Catholic school in London, a school with low expectations of children. She talked to Dove class about her method of working: she gets up and writes until she has to stop to empty the fridge into her stomach, when she needs a break. Then she is ready to return to working again. She talked to them about writing the story of Stephen Lawrence, how she cried as she wrote the story. How did these children respond? They were inspired to write a book, 'a wonderful mixture of fact and fantasy' about Verna emptying the fridge into her stomach. In the fridge were some eggs and these hatched in Verna's stomach into dodos. Verna had four wishes, which she mainly used to empty the fridge out of her stomach but the last wish was that the people who killed Stephen Lawrence were brought to justice. 'When children are handed the power, they identify with the written word, they can use their imaginations, they can mix fantasy and fact, they can understand what stories mean to them and they become authors in their own right.'

She thinks that 'it is frightening that we are not getting children to read'. Her book *Dave and the Tooth Fairy* has sold a quarter of a million copies around the world: 'It challenges perceptions – the tooth fairy is black. Children accept this and black children are uncontrollably elated, even speechless!' She recounts, with pleasure, the book being the focus of one school's book week: 'a black book unconsciously as the focus of book week – exactly what should be happening but very rare.' The Headteacher and eight pupils dressed up as the interview panel to fill the vacancy for the Tooth Fairy. The teachers, dressed as tooth fairies, were closely questioned about their credentials: 'It was a wonderful stimulus for the children's imagination, taken way beyond the original book itself – this surely is what good books should be about – stimulating the children to think differently' (Wilkins, 2002).

Mantra

Mantra was set up in 1984, by a triumvirate of Indian professionals, combining the skills of a barrister, a management consultant, a social worker and a classical Indian dancer. They were motivated by anxieties similar to those that originated Tamarind:

> As parents of young children we were concerned that there was nothing available that reflected either the cultural heritage of our children or their experience of growing up in Britain. Mantra's commitment to raising the self-esteem of Asian children, challenging stereotypes (particularly of Asian girls) and promoting bilingualism has been applied to a broadening range of genres as its original audience has matured, and a wider readership developed. The way racism is dealt with depends so much on the author's intentions, and what we're trying to do is to tap into the enormously varied perspectives and the immense talent of the Asian population, to get new young authors writing confidently about their own experiences. (Chatterji, 1994)

Mantra's mission is

> to provide a global perspective to all children and we leverage the power of language to achieve this. As language is central to the lives and culture of children, we specialise in a unique form of publishing – dual language books. This was conceived as a resource primarily for schools and libraries, catering for the minority communities settled in Britain, and as a valuable tool for language awareness, injected a multicultural dimension to the classroom. We have responded to the changing demographics in Britain with a growth in titles published in as many as 25 dual language editions, including Albanian, Arabic, Bengali, Farsi, French, German, Russian, Somali, Urdu and Yoruba. The genres too have

grown. We continue to publish dual language editions of popular classics, as it is important that these titles too are available in different languages, but we are now originating more of our own titles. In recognition of the fact that bilingual children in Britain often have better oral than written skills in their home language, we have also published audio CDs to enable all bilingual children to enjoy stories in their home language. We continue to consolidate the primary range but recognise that many dual language books are young in content. In order to engage children's interest as they grow older, we are now publishing a new bilingual series of adventure books accompanied by audio CDs for children aged 9–12 years. The range of languages and the resources Mantra offers is unique and reflects the way that dual language concepts cut across all barriers and cultures. (Chatterji, 2002)

Contribution of libraries

It is clear that there is an underlying theme running throughout this chapter which is the belief that libraries, in particular children's libraries, have a role to play in ensuring cultural diversity in reading:

> It is essential that libraries reflect the needs of the communities which they serve. Libraries have a role to play in society; libraries should reflect the information, reading and research needs of their whole community, regardless of gender, ability, class, race and be aware of the great richness of cultures in society. . . . Libraries in the past, by totally ignoring the communities they ought to be striving to serve, by ignoring the specific needs of minority groups, by offering support purely to a mainstream culture and almost inevitably inferring the inferiority of any other culture, have been accused, quite rightly, of being racist. (Elkin, 1976a)

This was certainly applicable in 1976, but is it still true today? Two experienced colleagues, Geoff Mills, Head of Community Libraries for Birmingham Library Services, and Grace Kempster, Director of Information services for the British Council, were asked to comment on how the role of libraries has changed within a multicultural society. Their personal perspectives are quite different but complementary and provide the concluding sentiments for this chapter.

Geoff Mills

> Libraries have never been more important to a changing society than now. More people are expecting libraries to provide access to materials that develop their feelings of self-esteem and belonging in a society where the traditional intolerance of differences remains strong. People are reading to learn, seeking role models, positive images and information on the cultural heritage of themselves and their communities. A new

generation of library users expects something much different – access to relevant, diverse and hidden literatures previously unavailable or unpromoted in libraries. Libraries remain the best place for informal access to reading and learning, with the priority given to pre-school children undisputed, and the opportunity to offer resources with positive images of a multicultural society.

Libraries need to be pushing at people's awareness and perceptions of society, promoting thinking on diversity and cultural awareness, and ensuring that everyone has the opportunity to read broadly. It's about reminding people that they live in a multicultural society, or even not letting them forget. Libraries have a role in demonstrating that public money is being spent on strengthening a healthy and inclusive society – that intolerance and prejudice is no longer acceptable or relevant. Sadly the library profession as a whole is not engaging in this role, reflecting the national lack of interest in promoting the strengths of a multicultural society.

There is, however, a new emphasis on the reader, and the availability of external funding for libraries has enabled a range of innovative developments. The work in Birmingham Libraries through the Black Family Reading Project and the development of services to the Bangladeshi community is demonstrating that if a service is prepared to spend time listening, building up trust and adapting the design of services, it can make an impact on people seeking to develop their feelings of self, their aspirations towards learning for themselves and their families, and access to their cultural heritage.

This is most starkly illustrated in the potential for libraries to open up access to resources for people of dual heritage. The complexity of people's needs for reading and information in order to understand their circumstances and potential is striking. Libraries can help people discover their identity in relation to cultural or social norms. Where else can a 'white' mother, wanting information on African Caribbean cultures for children go? Some areas or communities have greater support structures and are able to absorb 'issues' – it's tougher in white communities or isolated estates. This all became much clearer in a recent awareness workshop for library staff on the needs of people of dual heritage. I commend this approach to anyone – it seems to encapsulate all the issues and pressures of a multicultural society within a single person. It prevents individuals and services from putting resources and services into compartments, and thus the temptation to prioritise or stereotype, and promotes the role of libraries as a place for readers to consider their unique experiences. And it challenges libraries to help people consider the impact of racism on feelings of identity and to discuss design of inclusive services.

Libraries remain the place for resources with positive images and quality writing that reflects a multicultural society. The social inclusion agenda is really challenging library authorities to take a fundamental look at the way services are presented to ensure that things are not designed in such a way as to exclude people from access – regrettably they still do on many occasions. At times libraries are the only general service in a community offering resources for minority interests, whether it be promotions of black writers in

Black History Month in a majority white area or the introduction of a collection by lesbian and gay writers. To many people today the image of libraries seems dated and short of investment but their strong and important role is recognised, when the marketing works, by all ages and groups in the community. (Mills, 2002)

Grace Kempster

The Value of reading to promote global understanding and diversity

The British Council through its 2005 Strategy is transforming itself into the world's most effective cultural relations organization by winning recognition for the UK and ensuring enduring and sustainable partnerships worldwide. The undercurrent to all our work is that the UK is not a fixed point but dynamic and that we seek to form relationships with other nations, regions and communities of the UK today in all their dynamism and diversity. Also, we focus more of our work on the next authority generations – the young people and young professionals who will be the movers and shapers of their countries.

It is clear that with global changes in our Information Age, the ways in which people can and do connect has been transformed. The Internet and its spread means that people can literally be in touch across the world, even virtually meeting using video-conferencing. They do not have to go through intermediaries like the British Council – they can connect direct. Just as these opportunities enable the world to get closer to the communities of the UK, so too does it enable people in this country to have global perspectives and multiple identities: I am a global citizen, a European and also a resident of Manchester and Surrey.

At one time, the lending libraries of the British Council were the only way in which you could learn about the UK. You read the classics and maybe some of the best current writing. Your children likewise might have been exposed to this filtered view of UK life all dependent on British Council budgets and choice. Now we have the revolution of knowing someone living here and now, no intermediary or time delay. This may seem as though the technological advance could make the use of books and reading redundant/ people can meet virtually, talk with them in a mutual exchange. However, I would suggest that it is the burgeoning of a new era of global reader to reader recommendation. There are already reading groups which have multi-country spread and membership.

Our Animating Literature plans (British Council, 2002) for Europe demonstrate the power of multi-country reading groups to spread rather than restrict reading enthusiasm. One has to consider how the child-led Harry Potter phenomenon caught on through the penfriend and e-friend networks worldwide. If reading conversations can be global, so too can the resultant reading hungers and demands for books. I think it is a question of reader development leading reading. One hopes that the world of publishing with books on demand and instant translations can keep up.

In summary there is a new paradigm for international cultural relations – exchanges which are equal, the power of conversation and talking to shape and re-shape views and perceptions. The British Council is playing its part in connecting readers with readers – but so are many others both virtually and actually. The results may be the deepening of knowledge and understanding which only the reading experience fixes. It matters enormously for our futures. (Kempster, 2002)

Conclusion

Multicultural literature is much richer now than it was 20 years ago and there is a much broader range of culturally diverse reading matter. However, its accessibility and promotion, particularly in schools and as part of the literacy agenda, is limited and racism remains rife in schools and in society. The multicultural educational agenda which one might have predicted would have made a significant impact on racism in society has largely disappeared and been subsumed by the much broader citizenship agenda, not entirely satisfactorily. Increasing evidence of racial tension and institutional racism in the UK have many underlying causes, but it is possible to suggest that the educational agenda has failed to face issues of racism at an early stage of young people's development and that this has a detrimental impact on their lives as adults. Books still have a significant part to play in creating citizens who can live in harmony in a culturally diverse society.

Children's books discussed

Blackman, M. *Noughts and Crosses*, London, Doubleday.
Desai, A. *The Peacock Garden*, London, Heinemann.
Desai, A. *The Village by the Sea*, London, Heinemann.
Hoffman, M. *Amazing Grace,* London, Frances Lincoln.
Hoffman, M. *The Colour of Home,* London, Frances Lincoln.
Hoffman, M. *Nancy No-Size*, London, Methuen.
Naidoo, B. *Chain of Fire*, London, Lions.
Naidoo, B. *Journey to Jo'Burg*, London, Harper Collins.
Naidoo, B. *No Turning Back*, London, Penguin.
Naidoo, B. T*he Other Side of Truth*, London, Penguin.
Wilkins, V. A. *Dave and the Tooth Fairy,* London, Tamarind.
Wilkins, V. A. *Giant Hiccups,* London, Tamarind.
Wilkins, V. A. *The Life of Stephen Lawrence*, London, Tamarind.

References and further reading

Agard, J. (1985) Author profile of John Agard. In Elkin, J. (comp.), Trigg, P. (ed.), *The Books for Keeps Guide to Children's Books for a Multi-Cultural Society, 8–12*, London, Books for Keeps, 31.

Beverley Naidoo: Beverley Naidoo invites you to 'read novels and stories set in South Africa, the land of her birth, and in England, the country that became her home of exile'. Available at www.beverleynaidoo.com. [Accessed 13.03.03]

Birmingham Public Libraries (1969) *Books for the Multiracial Classroom*, Birmingham, Birmingham Public Libraries.

Blackman, M. (1994) Author profile. In Stones, R. (ed.), *A Multi-Cultural Guide to Children's Books 0–12*, London, Books for Keeps, 30.

British Council (2002) Animating Literature plans. Available at www.britishcouncil.org/animatingliterature/. [Accessed 18.03.03]

Burnside, A. (2000) *Outside Edge*, Jackie Kay in *Sunday Herald*, (2 April 2000), 8–13.

Chatterji, M. (1994) Two Multicultural Publishers. In Stones, R. (ed.), *A Multi-Cultural Guide to Children's Books 0–12*, London, Books for Keeps, 12–13.

Chatterji, M. (2002) Personal communication with the author.

Coard, B. (1971) *How the West Indian Child is Made Educationally Sub-Normal in the British School System: the scandal of the black child in schools in Britain*, London, New Beacon Books.

Commission for Racial Equality (2000) *Learning for All: standards for racial equality in schools, for schools in England and Wales*, London, Commission for Racial Equality.

Community Relations Commission (1976) *Starting out Right*, London, Community Relations Commission.

Desai, A. (1985) Author profile. In Elkin, J. (comp.), Trigg, P. (ed.), *The Books for Keeps Guide to Children's Books for a Multi-Cultural Society, 8–12*, London, Books for Keeps, 31.

Dhondy, F. (1999) Many Fountains, Common Thirsts: towards multiculturalism. In Stones, R. (ed.), *A Multi-Cultural Guide to Children's Books 0–16*, London, Books for Keeps, 6–8.

Dixon, B. (1977) *Catching Them Young*, (2 vols), London, Pluto Press.

Dunant, S. (1998) Brought to Book, *The Guardian Weekend*, (23 May), 32–5.

Egoff, S., Stubbs, G. T. and Ashley, L. F. (eds) (1969) *Only Connect*, Toronto, Oxford University Press.

Elkin, J. (1971) *Books for the Multi-Racial Classroom*, London, Youth Libraries Group of The Library Association.

Elkin, J. (1976a) *Public Library Services for Ethnic Minorities*, Paper presented at one-day conference, North West Polytechnic of London, unpublished.

Elkin, J. (1976b) *Books for the Multiracial Classroom*, 2nd edn, London, Youth Libraries Group of The Library Association.

Elkin, J. (1980*) Multiracial Books for the Classroom*, 3rd edn, London, Youth Libraries Group of The Library Association.

Elkin, J. (1985a*) Multiracial Books for the Classroom*, 4th edn, London, Youth Libraries Group of The Library Association.

Elkin, J. (1985b) *The Books for Keeps Guide to Children's Books for a Multi-Cultural Society,*

8–12, London, Books for Keeps.

Note: Combined and totally revised editions were published in 1994 and 1999 (Stones, 1994; 1999a).

Elkin, J. (1986) *The Books for Keeps Guide to Children's Books for a Multi-Cultural Society, 0–7*, London, Books for Keeps.

Elkin, J. (1999) *Wide Reading and Full Literacy are Fundamental to the Child's Personal, Emotional, Social and Educational Development and Quality Literature needs to be Exploited and Promoted particularly through Libraries which Provide the only means of Universal Access, regardless of Wealth, Class, Culture, Gender or Age*, PhD thesis, University of Central England, Birmingham.

Erikson, E. (1972) In Searle, C. (ed.), *The Forsaken Lover*, London, Routledge and Penguin.

Fanon, F. (1968) *Black Skin, White Masks*, London, MacGibbon and Kee and Paladin.

The Guardian (2002) *Profile*, 6 July, 20–3.

Hallworth, G. (1985) *The Library, a centre for promoting international understanding*. Paper presented at UNESCO/IFLA conference, Salamanca, Spain, June, 1985, unpublished.

Hill, J. (1971) *Books for Children: the homelands of immigrants*, London, Institute of Race Relations.

Hill, J. (1973) *Children Are People: the librarian in the community*, London, Hamish Hamilton.

Hoffman, M. (2002) Telephone interview with the author, 14 August.

Home Department (1999) *CM4262-II (Revised): The Stephen Lawrence Inquiry*: report by Sir William Macpherson, London, Stationery Office.

Hunt, G. (1994) Two Multicultural Publishers. In Stones, R. (ed.) *A Multicultural Guide to Children's Books 0–12*, London, Books for Keeps, 12–13.

Kempster, G. (2002) Personal communication with the author.

Kuya, D. (1975) *Sew the Dragon's Teeth*, rev. edn, Liverpool, Merseyside Community Relations Committee.

Lepman, J. (1964) *A Bridge of Children's Books*, translated from the German by Edith McCormick, Leicester, Brockhampton Press.

Mills, G. (2002) Personal communication with the author.

Milner, D. (1975) *Children and Race*, London, Penguin.

Milner, D. (1983) *Children and Race Ten Years On*, London, Ward Lock.

Milner, D. (1994) Children and Race Identity. In Stones, R. (ed.), *A Multi-Cultural Guide to Children's Books 0–12*, London, Books for Keeps, 9.

Naidoo, B. (1994) Challenging Ways of Seeing? In Stones, R. (ed.), *A Multi-Cultural Guide to Children's Books 0–12*, London, Books For Keeps, 10–11.

Naidoo, B. (1999) Heritage or multiculturalism? In Stones, R. (ed.), *A Multi-Cultural Guide to Children's Books 0–16*, London, Books For Keeps, 10–11.

Naidoo, B. (2002a) Telephone interview with the author.

Naidoo, B. (2002b) Winning the Carnegie Medal 2000, *Youth Library Review*, **31**, 14–15.

National Union of Teachers (1979) *In Black and White: guidelines for teachers on racial stereotyping in textbooks and learning materials*, London, National Union of Teachers.

Note: Appended is a checklist for using books for multi-ethnic education which refers to the more detailed set of criteria and guidelines for evaluating books for use in the multiracial classroom produced by the World Council of Churches Workshop on Racism in Children's and School Textbooks and reprinted in *Children's Books Bulletin,* June 1979.

Niven, A. (1998) *A Common Wealth of Talent in Booker 30: a celebration of 30 years of the Booker prize for fiction, 1968–1998*, London, Booker plc.

The Observer (2001) Race in Britain 2001: 12-page special edition, *The Observer*, (25 November).

Philip, N. (1981) *Times Educational Supplement*, (13 February 1981).

Searle, C. (1972) *The Forsaken Lover*, London, Routledge and Penguin.

Stones, R. (ed.) (1994) *A Multi-Cultural Guide to Children's Books 0–12*, London, Books for Keeps.

Stones, R. (1999a) *A Multi-Cultural Guide to Children's Books 0–16*, London, Books for Keeps.

Stones, R. (1999b) Multicultural Publishing at the Turn of the Century. In Stones, R. (ed.), *A Multi-Cultural Guide to Children's Books 0–16*, London, Books for Keeps.

The Teacher (1971), Prejudice on the Printed Page, *The Teacher*, (19 November).

Townsend, J. R. (1969) Didacticism in Modern Dress. In Egoff, S., Stubbs, G. T. and Ashley, L. F. (eds), *Only Connect*, Toronto, Oxford University Press.

Wilkins, V. (2002) Telephone interview with the author.

Working Group Against Racism in Children's Resources (1998) *WGARCR Newsletter*, **6**.

Working Group Against Racism in Children's Resources (1999) *WGARCR Newsletter*, **8**.

Working Group Against Racism in Children's Resources (2002) *WGARCR News & Advocacy Update*, (Spring).

Zephaniah, B. (1994) Benjamin Zephaniah: poet and vegan. In Stones, R. (ed.), *A Multi-Cultural Guide to Children's Books 0–12*, London, Books for Keeps, 28.

6

Special needs/special places

Judith Elkin

Introduction

The previous chapter looked at the value of reading and reader development within a multicultural society. This chapter looks at the value of reading and reader development for people with special needs, whether they are physical, mental or associated with being excluded from society in some way, and celebrates diversity through reading. It includes a section on programmes in countries where literacy and reading are playing a role in empowering individuals, after years of poverty, neglect and the ravages of war.

What are special needs?

The term 'special needs' is generally applied to a wide variety of individuals who have special learning and reading needs as a result of a handicap of some kind, or as a result of being excluded from society or confined in some way, for example hospitalization, being in care, imprisonment or being confined to the home. This covers a very wide range of needs, which may vary for people at different points in their lives. This chapter looks at a variety of needs and how reading may contribute to an individual's personal growth and development, and even their survival.

Desmond Spiers, one-time Library and Information Officer, National Library for the Handicapped Child, summarized the question of who is a person with a disability rather neatly yet broadly, when referring to children with disabilities:

> The range of disabilities is wide and includes motor, visual, aural, intellectual and emotional impairment. Many of us probably have disabilities which are not even acknowledged as such, . . . Some children never use 'print', but they will still be valid readers by the use of sound or video cassettes. A child who understands and correctly uses a vocabulary of thirty words is as much a reader as the child with a vocabulary of 3,000 words. . . . Resources [for children with special needs] include books (in print, Braille, sign language, symbols, large print, Clear Vision, tactile, picture book, large format, pop-up, lift-the flap, cloth, rebus, board, bath, wooden, sound, dual languages), sound tapes,

> videos (with or without subtitles) and films. The use of each source is multiple: large print books, for example, for visually impaired children; reluctant readers; children with a mental handicap; large format books for children with poor motor control in fingers, hands and arms; children with a visual impairment; children with a language problem. At the same time the use of each resource is universal: all children may enjoy any of the material.
>
> (Spiers, 1992, 90–1)

Similarly, all adults may enjoy any of the materials cited by Spiers above and, just as importantly, will need support in accessing appropriate materials.

Value of reading for people with special needs

The value of reading for people with special needs has been accepted for centuries. The inscription over the library at Thebes – 'Healing Place of the Soul' – attests to the historical recognition of the soothing and healing power of literature. Spufford (2002, 31) applauds Bruno Bettelheim's interest in the ancient Indian practice of 'prescribing a story to the troubled in mind, for them to sift and contemplate: his endorsement of story as therapy made him a pioneer'. Yet, Gold (1990) questions why:

> fiction, the richest and most complex source of imagery, of models of human experience, remains largely unexplored as a healing power in affective problems and disorders, in depression, life crises, family dysfunction and so on (31). . . . The most convenient way to express catharsis is by reading fiction and poetry. To read a novel in which the reader loses the sense of separateness, lives with the characters, becomes part of their life and setting, laughs and cries with them and takes on a life in the fiction; to do this can often lead to a catharsis at the conclusion of the novel, when it is sadly, reluctantly, gratefully closed and put away (121).

Gold (1990, 279) suggests that the remarkable thing about reading in such situations is that: 'people find what they need in what they read. What strikes one reader as significant or memorable in a story may be quite different from what another reader takes from the same book'.

Gold also (1990, 290) looks at the importance of reading for people with physical disabilities, feeling that it is essential that there be an opportunity for people to explore:

> life management, achievement and usefulness, satisfaction and pleasure, in the face of significant physical impairments, restrain and discomfort. Mental power can flourish in the face of physical limitation. Spiritual and emotional and sensory satisfaction are possible . . . without understanding what the limitations of handicaps are, people with handicaps

> cannot have the possibilities of achievement opened to them. . . . Stories and descriptions can articulate the unspeakable, for them as for everyone. The reader who has a disability can control the speed and intensity of his response and match it to the emotional energy and readiness he has available . . . the experience of reader control is in this case a demonstration in practice that the reader is not helpless; the reading process itself invites mental action and activity and feeds back a positive sense of accomplishment.

Marshall (1988, 114) adds:

> Adults and children alike tend to think that no one else has this difficulty, this disability, this worry or fear and, paradoxically, it can be comforting to talk or read about others who have gone through a similar experience. . . . Trying it out, experiencing vicariously, knowing someone has been there before you, seeing how it was tackled, can be comforting, informing, reassuring, releasing by externalising the internal problem.

Beverley Mathias writes compellingly about the importance of reading for children with particular needs. Although she is concentrating on children, in her role as the Director of REACH: National Advice Centre for Children with Reading Difficulties (a UK charity which closed on 31 July 2002, after 18 years of operation, because of lack of funds), many of her comments implicitly recognize the value of reading for all ages and indicate how children who, for whatever reason, do not learn to read can be storing up problems for later life. She demonstrates the importance of early developmental work with children, to avoid the antisocial behaviour that can affect teenagers and adults later in life. She is sensitive to the need for children with handicaps of different kinds to have easy access to a wide variety of reading matter:

> Being able to read is a skill so universal that most people don't think twice about it. Not being able to read is a hidden disability that can affect all areas of living. For a child, the inability to make sense of the written word is frustrating – it lowers self-confidence, alters behaviour, and affects the child's future expectations of employment. The spiral moves down not up as the child sinks further and further into an educational desert.
>
> But what if you ask the child what reading is? The child will tell you it's 'dumb', that they don't need to read, that they can't read and don't care, and very occasionally confess that they would like to read but don't know where to start. They will say that reading is for tests; something you only do at school. So how does a child develop such a negative view of reading? When did the problem begin? It might have been with early undiagnosed difficulties. One child in every seven has undiagnosed hearing loss, many children have sight problems easily corrected. The problem might have started with a trauma such as the death of a family member, or a pet. It might have begun as anti-social behaviour in the first year of pre-school or school and allowed the child to be termed a 'trouble maker'. Then it might be that the child finds it difficult to process information, to comprehend

> spoken or written instructions, so the child is labelled again.
>
> The right approach to reading can help these children – all of them – to achieve. Reading should be the right book in the right format for the right child at the right time.
>
> Books are not just print, they are sound and vision, large print, large format, CD-ROM. Books can be read using eyes, ears, hands, and fingers. Adults caring for these children at school or at home need to change their own thinking so that what is offered to the child is something they will want to read, and can read. They need a more personal, innovative, lateral, sometimes multi-tactile approach to words and how they work. Reading pictures should never be dismissed as a precursor to reading print. An illustrator can tell a story without words just as powerfully as a written text. These books allow a child to read the story they see without struggling to master the print.
>
> Reading should be a pleasure not a punishment, and there is joy, satisfaction, and achievement in encouraging any child to read independently, but even more so when that child has special needs. (Mathias, 2002)

In the context of reading for adults with special needs, reading might be defined as being about the right book in the right format for the right adult at the right time and in the right place. Almost inevitably, libraries and librarians play a significant role in ensuring this is a reality.

Reading and people who are visually impaired

There are 1.75 million blind and partially sighted people in the UK, most of whom are affected with sight problems for the first time late in life. Ninety per cent of them are over 60 years old. Many visually impaired people enjoyed reading when they could see, and want to continue to read. To be able to participate fully in education, work and cultural life, blind and partially sighted people ought to be able to read the same material as everyone else at the same time and in whatever way best suits each individual: in large print, on a tape, by means of synthetic speech from a computer or Braille. Access to a library, locally, nationally or, indeed, both, is likely to be essential to maximize opportunities for reading in the different formats now available, although not always easily accessible.

National Library for the Blind

Helen Brazier, Chief Executive, National Library for the Blind, writes:

> A survey by RNIB revealed that two thirds of audio library users read more after their sight deteriorated. Other people discover reading as a new hobby that passes the time. In either case, it is welcomed as an activity that they can pursue independently. NLB readers, young and old, describe the importance of reading as a way of finding out about

the world or of enjoying vicarious pleasures. Visually impaired people have the same reading needs as everyone else, only they read in a different way, depending on personal preference, circumstances and ability. The most widely used alternative formats are large print and audio. About 10,000 people read Braille. Some people make print books accessible at the point of use with CCTV which magnifies print, or with reading machines and computers which can convert text into speech.

There are, however, numerous barriers to reading for visually impaired people in the UK. The principal problem is lack of choice. Less than 5% of UK published output is transcribed into an alternative format, and this process may take months if not years. Most books are transcribed by charities, and there is perceived to be only a small commercial market for large print and unabridged audio books. Hence the quantity of material is small and historically the range has been limited. Secondly, it is hard to access what little is available. There is no complete and accessible union catalogue of books in alternative formats. It takes persistence to find out about the special collections managed by numerous charities throughout the UK, and then the individual reader has to join each service separately. Thirdly, the remoteness of service providers has forced visually impaired people into a position of dependency. Catalogues (print or online) are frequently inaccessible or unusable, and the type of information provided, ostensibly to help readers choose, isn't very useful, with the result that they are less inclined to take risks. Furthermore, visually impaired readers are rarely taken into consideration when libraries plan activities such as reading groups.

NLB leads the way in developing an accessible web-based catalogue, and 2003 sees the launch of Reveal: the National Database of Accessible Resources, which will hugely improve access to information about books. Technology also enables readers to make independent choices using online tools such as the accessible version of Forager (now whichbook.net), and interaction with writers and readers via NLB's accessible website (National Library for the Blind, 2002). They can also manage their reading autonomously with the Personal Bookshelf feature of the online catalogue.

(Brazier and Corrigan, 2002)

Reader development and the visually impaired

Helen Brazier has been involved in recent years with the Branching Out project, in which the NLB works alongside 33 participating library authorities. Writing about the importance of reader development and the visually impaired, she says:

Working with partners in the voluntary sector, with public libraries, and with the reader development consultancy Opening the Book, the NLB has seen lately how reader development can transform the situation for visually impaired people. Braille readers have welcomed the greater range of books available since NLB implemented a policy of 'widening choice' in book selection to include first-time authors, gay and lesbian writers,

> writers in translation, and so on. Branching Out showed how effective promotion created a larger market for large print and audio titles. Readers who use Braille, large print and audio have welcomed the sampler books produced by the project called A Touch Of . . . , which comprise short extracts on tempting themes such as A Touch of Velvet and A Touch Ticklish. They provide an opportunity to taste something new without commitment. (Brazier and Corrigan, 2002)

The NLB has taken an active role in supporting public libraries to provide inclusive activities, such as the reading groups and events which took place as part of A Touch Of . . . creative reading festival in 2001. Thanks to the work of Branching Out and Share The Vision (2000), awareness of the needs of visually impaired people has dramatically improved. Helen provides a charming quote from one of NLB's readers: 'you are engaging us all to take more part not just be passively at the end of the delivery. That is nice.'

Reading and the elderly

Many elderly people feel disempowered, yet still have tremendous personal resources and needs. Hoy (1984) highlights the increase in the number of people over retirement age and asserts that they hold within themselves a vast wealth of resources, skills, knowledge and experience. Hoy cites the establishment of library clubs for senior citizens in Leicestershire which enabled librarians to exploit resources and alerted all staff involved to the variety of needs, interests and abilities of elderly people and to develop new techniques in serving this group.

Recall

This is echoed in Help the Aged's tape/slide programme Recall, about London over the past 80 years. It was used by the librarian at Edinburgh Royal Infirmary to provide the basis of a reminiscence therapy programme. This gave patients the chance to talk about themselves and their experiences and made them feel that they had something worthwhile to contribute, giving them a sense of respect and dignity. The Recall programme was supplemented with more locally relevant material which included a collection of pensioners' stories and reminiscences, and a large-print song book (Forrest, 1990).

Reading and people with multiple handicaps

Ring (1986) describes a state-of-the-art library at Winchester House, a skilled nursing facility for severely handicapped residents in Libertywill, Illinois. A full range of library services and materials is co-ordinated by a professional librarian and 50%

of the residents are reached through the thoughtful and creative application of special media. Opportunities for residents to realize their full potential are provided. The library is having a positive effect on the residents' health, is improving their general outlook, and is minimizing the regimentation associated with institutional life.

New Zealand writer Dorothy Butler is well known for her seminal book, *Babies Need Books* (1998). *Cushla and Her Books* (Butler, 1987) is an inspirational book about how books helped her multiply handicapped granddaughter and her parents to cope with the stressful early years of her life. Born with a chromosome deficiency, asthma and eczema, Cushla was a sickly baby, who fed and slept poorly. She had hearing, sight and mobility problems and was constantly distressed; her early development and growth and prognosis were poor.

Books began to play a part in Cushla's life from the age of four months: 'Filling in the long hours during the day and night necessitated some parental ingenuity, and desperation certainly played a part. The baby would look at a book; she constituted a totally captive audience, and reading the text gave her mother something constructive to do. Cushla's mother turned to books naturally, at this time, for help' (18). The habit of using picture books with Cushla came to occupy a considerable proportion of her waking hours from about the age of nine months. Cushla's mother came from a family in which reading was an everyday occurrence:

> It was natural, therefore, that books should be used as 'time-fillers'. . . . Moreover, Cushla was unable to occupy her time and attention in normal ways – crawling, pulling herself up, exploring objects encountered, tasting and watching everyday activities. Without one-to-one help it is likely that she would have relapsed into a state of almost total non-involvement (27).

Cushla and Her Books documents the way that picture books, stories and poetry were entrenched in Cushla's everyday life and how, as a result, her language and cognitive development rapidly reached and overtook that of the average three- to four-year-old:

> How can one assess the contribution of her books to the quality of Cushla's life? It seems clear that access to such a wealth of words and pictures, in a setting of consistent love and support, has contributed enormously to her cognitive development in general and her language development in particular. . . . But, perhaps, most of all, Cushla's books have surrounded her with friends; with people and warmth and colour during the days when her life was lived in almost constant pain and frustration. The adults who have loved her and have tried to represent the world to her when she could not do this for herself have played their parts. But perhaps it was the characters themselves who went with her into the dark and lonely places that only she knew. . . . And perhaps they will always be with her; Peter Rabbit and Grandmother Lucy, Mr Gumpy and James, James, followed

> by a procession of cats and kings, tigers and bears, with Davy and Emma and Naughty Agapanthus bringing up the rear. If so, she will be well fortified. (Butler, 1987, 102)

Butler quotes Cushla's own words, recorded when she was three years, eight months old, spoken as she settled herself on the sofa, her rag doll in her arms and the usual pile of books at her side: 'Now I can read to Looby Lou, 'cause she's tired and sad, and she needs a cuddle and a bottle and a book' (102).

Writing in a postscript to the book, with Cushla then six, Butler reflects on Cushla's reading ability (now reading fluently and silently):

> Cushla was not 'taught' to read, unless the provision of language and story, in books and out of books, can be called a method. I believe it can, and that it is the best method of all. It produces children who experience reading as a joyous process, natural to the human state; children who absorb ideas as sponges absorb water. That this ingestion helps such children to find meaning in the complex and contradictory experiences that constitute life is self-evident (105).
>
> Seven years ago, before Cushla was born, I would have laid claim to a deep faith in the power of books to enrich children's lives. By comparison with my present conviction, this faith was a shallow thing. I know now what print and picture have to offer a child who is cut off from the world, for whatever reason. But I also know that there must be another human being, prepared to intercede, before anything can happen . . . no authority prescribes reading aloud for chronically ill babies whose handicaps are thought to be mental as well as physical (107).

Aidan Chambers (1985, 12) is much moved by Cushla's story:

> Language formed her; indeed it was language that first woke her to the world against everything that the medical experts said could happen. It was language in books on which she grew to know the world she could hardly see or hear for herself. It was hearing language read aloud, and sung too, from the books held almost literally at the end of her nose that taught her how to read for herself. Literature without any doubt gave Cushla Yeoman images to think with, and now she is a lively child able to live with spirit and joy against every adversity a damaged chromosome and a distressingly disabled body could put in her way. But she has done it, and literature helped, only because there were adults around her who knew what had to be done and did it, often against the advice of expert opinion and gloomy prognosis.

Reading and looked-after children

Cushla was lucky to have caring adults around her, so that, as Chamber says, language could wake her to the world against severe odds. Having access to books and someone to share them with are recognized as two of the most important factors in the development of a child's literacy. Children without that secure, caring environment, for example looked-after children, may well be deprived of books and reading opportunities, leading to behavioural problems and further deprivation in terms of educational attainment and self-confidence.

The Who Cares? Trust

The Who Cares? Trust (n.d.) is a national charity working to improve public care for the 60,000 children who are separated from their families and living in residential or foster care. It promotes the interests of children in public care and works with all those interested in their well-being in the UK. The recognition that having books in the home, and an experience of sharing books with an adult, are two of the most important factors in the development of children's reading has underpinned much of their work, for example the following projects.

A Book of My Own project

A Book of My Own project (Who Cares? Trust, 1994) aimed to help improve the reading ability of young people looked after by local authorities. The report recommended that young people should be empowered to select and buy their own books, as well as have access to an adult to support them and listen to them read. The evidence of the report showed that literacy and access to books can act as a gateway to educational attainment and improved self-confidence.

The Right to Read project

Leading on from this, the Right to Read project recognized that many children in public care have few, if any, books of their own; they may know what they want to read but can find it hard to get hold of books. The Right to Read project was funded by the Paul Hamlyn Foundation in association with the National Literacy Association. It hoped to use the enjoyment of reading as a way to improve literacy and involved four key elements:

- Starter libraries of 50 books were placed in 40 residential homes and staff were encouraged to make a reading area that was comfortable, welcoming and accessible at all times.
- Roadshows were held to give advice to foster carers and residential workers on how to choose and use books to enable children to learn while enjoying the experience.
- Children were awarded book tokens, books and other gifts to mark a particular

effort or educational achievement of any kind.
- The Trust produces the *Who Cares? Magazine*, which reaches 30,000 children in public care. A special edition had a Right to Read insert and covered reading, creative writing, puzzles and celebrity interviews about books and reading.

The children's excitement and pleasure were noted almost immediately and carers felt the project had helped to improve their relationship with the children: 'I feel that although all children and young people are encouraged to read whilst in the care of the local authority, this project has given reading for pleasure a much higher profile in the care system. We can only build on this for the future welfare and life chances of all looked-after young people' (Jones, 2001).

The Network

The Network, a project tackling social exclusion in libraries, museums, archives and galleries, was established in 1999 with seedcorn money from the Library and Information Commission, following a research project, Public Library Policy and Social Exclusion (Resource, 2002). Originally, it included public library authorities in London and the south-east; by late 2002, it had 76 organizational members in England, Scotland and Wales. One of the spin-off projects is the following.

Access to Books and Reading Projects for Young People in Public Care

The Access to Books and Reading Projects for Young People in Public Care project began in Autumn 2002. John Vincent (2002), the Network's Networker, writes:

> More and more library authorities are beginning to work with looked-after children (along with other initiatives to tackle social exclusion) without necessarily developing the expertise in doing so, particularly in terms of creating sustainable working partnerships with other service-providers and fully understanding the specific needs of looked-after children. The aim of this project is to enable library staff to appreciate the specific needs of looked-after children and to make and sustain the necessary contacts to deliver effective services to them, in particular: to increase library staff awareness of the issues involved in working with looked-after children; to equip library staff with the skills to develop sustainable partnerships to support working with looked after children; to enable library staff to develop outreach and other ways of working outside the library buildings; to equip library staff to 'cascade' this training to their colleagues.
>
> This is done by assessing the needs of library staff in terms of, for example, information and training, to enable them to make successful links with and provide services for looked-after children and producing a training package that can be cascaded to other staff. This is followed by a series of training courses on a regional basis to create

> 'champions' who can then cascade the training themselves. This work is being carried out in conjunction with four or five 'trial' authorities (including the London Boroughs of Enfield and Merton, West Sussex County Library Service, and York City Library Service).
>
> (Vincent, 2002)

The major problems Vincent anticipates from the project are: 'the reluctance of many library staff to work outside their traditional role, especially with a client group that may be seen as "challenging" or "difficult"; the lack of time to allow staff to become really familiar with this area of work and the lack of money to pay for training'. It is hoped that these problems can be tackled head-on, by: 'making library staff more familiar with working with looked-after children, equipping them with the skills to deal with "challenging" behaviour and using the network of "champions" who can deliver localised training, to minimise the time needed for training' (Vincent, 2002).

Reading and victims of abuse

Victims of early abuse are also vulnerable in terms of later behavioural problems, educational attainment and self-confidence. Librarians are increasingly being drawn into multi-disciplinary child protection work. The Guardian (2002) reports that all staff on the issue desks of Nottingham libraries are now trained in spotting potential victims of child abuse. They have also learned how to offer a listening ear to members of the public worried that a child might be at risk.

Polese (1994) highlights the benefits and pleasures that books can bring to children who are being physically or sexually abused and believes that reading can help abuse sufferers to cope with difficult lives. He conducted a study of adults who had been abused as children and found that many saw books as a saviour during that time: 'To pick up my book was to hold onto a piece of sanity'. . . . Everyone in my family was addicted to something. My drug of choice was reading. I don't even know what I read. I just read to get away from my own desolation and pain'. Many said that books enabled them to see the possibility of a different, and more normal, way of life: 'I feel like I grew up in the Moffat and Austin households. From them I learned that family life could be warm and supportive. It gave me something to try for with my kids' (156).

Sufferers are often inspired by particular characters with the most attractive characteristics being perseverance and resourcefulness. Anne from *Anne of Green Gables* was the most frequently cited character in Polese's study, with the sufferers admiring her ability to use her inner strength to overcome neglect and emotional abuse: 'One can't help but see the goodness in Anne that she doesn't see . . . through loving and understanding Anne, I learned to do the same for myself' (157). Another reader admired Cinderella because she got a happy ending: 'I knew that was fantasy but it gives you hope, you know, and you stay open to good things happening. I figured if she could make it so could I. And I have' (157).

Some sufferers also found solace in horror books, with a Stephen King fan saying: 'What happens to the characters in his books was somehow more horrible than what was happening to me. To read about others' terror and fear lessened mine' (157). The pleasure of reading horror books is explained by King himself who suggests that reading about horrible things happening to others helps people to cope with their own everyday problems and stress.

Pamela Stephenson (2001), in her biography of husband Billy Connolly, reflects on the importance of reading in his early life:

> Billy has found various ways to heal and make adult sense of all his early abuses, but back then, when there was little safety anywhere in his life, what saved him? For one thing, he absolutely loved reading. Not his schoolbooks – he thought they were very dull, although the class would sometimes be read to on a Friday, and that was quite soothing. *White Fang* and adventure stories from Canada and the Yukon were popular (47).

She refers to the comprehensive library system in Glasgow, and Billy's local branch library:

> It was wonderfully warm inside, and full of people of all ages, especially elderly folk. Every newspaper was there, mounted on a board with a special cord for turning the pages. Billy had worked through the infants' section years ago, steamed through the boys' corner (*Just William*, Enid Blyton and all sorts of adventure stories), and when he became twelve he was finally able to swagger up the street with not one, but two books. That's when he discovered Tibet. Once he came across *Seven Years in Tibet* he was completely hooked, fascinated by its isolation from the rest of the world (48).

Community programmes

Preventative programmes may well avoid some of the situations described above. Recent paediatric literacy programmes in the USA aim to change parents' thinking about reading, with healthy babies, good parenting and family literacy as the goals. These bring together children's libraries, doctors and community volunteers to promote the importance of reading aloud to children early and often. Feldman and Needlman (1999) look at models for these programmes and how they are being implemented, focusing on a programme offered by the library at the Rainbow Babies and Children's Hospital in Cleveland, Ohio, USA, where training highlights ways to make books come alive for children and strategies to encourage children and parents to participate.

Kars and Doud (1999) describe a programme started in 1997: Kalamazoo Public Library and Bronson Methodist Hospital, along with community organizations in Michigan, collaborated to create an emergent literacy programme. It provides volunteer readers at community sites, prescribes reading aloud for healthy child development and gives books to children at well-baby visits, providing a cloth book for every child born in the county. In addition the programme offers workshops on reading and book-sharing skills for parent groups and provides book collections and volunteer readers to child care centres.

Reading in hospital

For people in hospital reading can be a tremendous solace for all kinds of reasons:

> For someone in hospital, 'shut up' inside the four walls of a room, reading can be a marvellous escape, a way of forgetting his or her illness, anxiety and pain for a while. For a moment, a book also offers a way of entering into a special relationship with a mediator, the librarian, a friend. . . . Reading or being read to . . . can contribute to the patient's well-being and even recovery. The provision of reading matter is now a recognized part of the quality of the hospital facilities for patients. (Guerin, 2000)

Reading can play an important role in helping people suffering from catastrophic illness by showing how others have coped with similar situations. Reading can give insights into the feelings and responses of others in a similar situation and help understanding that other people experience similar fears, frustrations and worries. Simon (1984), looking at library services to patients in psychiatric hospitals, viewed the library as 'a refuge from the institutional aspects of psychiatric care'.

Reader development in hospitals

Imagination Time

Imagination Time (n.d.) is an innovative children's reader development pilot project in London hospitals, organized by LaunchPad, in partnership and with funding from Walker Books and the Arts Council of England. It provides access to books and related arts to children in hospital who are missing out on this provision because they are not attending school and do not have access to their local public library. Fifteen London library authorities and 21 London hospitals were involved in the project in 2001. Activities included hospital visits by library staff for storytelling and book sessions, and author and illustrator sessions on the wards. The author and illustrator sessions created a sense of a special occasion and made the children feel important, while library staff shared their skills with nursing and hospital play workers and learnt about how to adapt their work in hospitals. The project received positive feedback from hospital staff: 'The storytelling is fascinating to listen to and really makes the parents and children escape . . . the children really benefited from the sessions, regardless of their disabilities, they really responded to the contact be it verbal or physical.' Parents, too, responded well: 'Last week my daughter was rather poorly and the library visit encouraged her to get out of bed and take part in the activities.'

Reading therapy in hospitals

Matthews and Lonsdale (1992) conducted research into the use of reading therapy with children in hospital. They identified three types of reading therapy (17):

- growth reading – to promote growth and well-being; to enable the child to come to terms with and profit from their time in hospital
- factual reading – use of factual or educational materials to deal with specific problems such as information on procedures
- imaginative reading – the use of a fictional or imaginative experience similar to that of the patient to arrive at an understanding of and possible solution to the problem.

Interviewees, including librarians and hospital staff such as play workers, thought that reading was used to replace fantasy with fact, counsel patients and children, alleviate fears and anxieties and bring the outside world into the hospital: 'reading is a way of getting to know the child – also an opportunity for a cuddle . . . a book communicates. A child communicates with a Cindy doll, but a book speaks to a child' (18). Reading was seen as an integral part of play therapy and not separate from it but it was felt that there needed to be greater awareness of reading therapy. It was also clear that short-stay patients were no less in need of reading and reading therapy than long stay.

Walker and Jones (1986) examined death in current children's literature and looked at how reading helped children deal with the possibility of death and to feel less isolated: 'children, through reading, realise that others share their plight . . . their feelings are within the range of normality. And it is a relief to know that others suffer as they do. When children feel less isolated, they lose some of their embarrassment about the situation' (16).

Reading and people in prison

Reading for people confined to a prison environment is likely to rely heavily on library provision, within the prison itself. This poses certain challenges for the librarian, not least the issue of working with, at least initially, an often uncommitted and frequently low-ability readership.

Sullivan (1998) states: 'The convict's first thought, as he sees and hears the gates close around him, is of escape. Reading is one primary strategy for escape and survival when the gates slam shut' (113). Cox (2002) adds, 'reading is a powerful key to all our imaginations . . . where better to encourage it than among those whose world is otherwise confined by a claustrophobic compound of cells and corridors, gates and grills' (49).

All prisons are required to have a library and enable prisoners to use and exchange books (HM Prison Service, 2002). The library at HMP Belmarsh has set up a reading group (Cox, 2002), aiming to improve reading and communication skills, encourage wider reading and stimulate thought. The group has helped prisoners to be more confident in leading discussions and forming and justifying their opinions and their reading tastes have also expanded. One prisoner said that they appreciated the chance to challenge the stereotype of the prisoner as a 'mindless thug'.

Sue Wilkinson, Prison Library Manager, Her Majesty's Prison, Birmingham, writes about the importance of reading in prisons:

> For many men and women in prison, reading for pleasure is a new experience. In their lives 'outside', they do not use libraries or do much reading. Things change in prison. Prisoners will come to the prison library initially simply because it is somewhere to go – a different set of walls to stare at. It is not surprising, however, that many people who were never motivated to read before discover the value of the reading experience whilst in prison. Reading becomes an important activity 'inside'. In any prison, there is a vast amount of unoccupied time, with little to fill it. There is also limited freedom of choice in prisons. The day is regimented, and there are few opportunities for the prisoner to express personal preferences. This is not so in the library. There, the reader can take control. He or she can choose whichever books they want, and, more importantly, for whatever reason they want – they may want to read the book, copy the picture on the cover, pose on the landing with War and Peace tucked under their arm, or use the book to prop up their wobbly bed. Whatever the reason for that choice, the reader is the only person who knows – an important freedom in prison.
>
> Some people find the concept of prisoners having this freedom of choice quite worrying. They think that prisoners' reading should be directed to 'improving' and educational books, and that they should not have access to certain types of fiction, quite ignoring the fact that prisoners are exposed to a wide variety of media, such as TV and newspapers. It is quite ironic that the book should be seen as such a powerful influence when reading is commonly regarded as a passive activity.
>
> Reading gives a prisoner a much-needed sense of privacy – the book provides an exclusive, private space. For a person who is physically confined, reading offers limitless opportunities to 'escape'. With a book, a reader can go anywhere, be anyone – the hero,

> the villain, the lover or just an interested bystander. Reading for pleasure is often perceived as having little value, particularly in prisons, where the emphasis is on formal learning. However, all reading is a learning experience, and all reading contributes to the mental well being of the individual. Books can pass the time when you are bored, and relax you when you are stressed. Boredom and stress are key factors in prison life.
>
> Making reading choices is not always easy for prisoners. For many, a library full of books is an unfamiliar landscape, and the way that libraries are arranged and the jargon that we use can seem exclusive and off-putting to someone who is not sure of the meaning of 'fiction' and 'non-fiction'. If there is nothing to guide them through the maze readers in prison stick to safe choices, usually true crime or horror, or look for things that they remember reading or having read to them at school, which, of course, may not be what they want to read now. Other factors also make choosing books difficult for the prisoner. In many prisons, the time that inmates can spend in the library is strictly limited, leaving them with little time for any serious browsing. Many prison libraries, particularly those in older prisons, are housed in inadequate accommodation, giving staff little space to display books attractively, and little opportunity to create a pleasant and restful environment. (Wilkinson, 2002)

Reader development in prisons

As Wilkinson says, time is an issue, with vast amounts of 'unoccupied' time but with limited time available for browsing in the library and inevitably reduced time to spend with families. This is an essential problem which reader development initiatives can readily address, as can be seen below.

Inside Books

In 2001, the Prison Libraries Group of CILIP (The Chartered Institute of Library and Information Professionals) delivered the 'Inside Books' project, the first national reader development project for prison libraries funded by the DCMS/Wolfson Reader Development programme. The project was managed on the Group's behalf by Opening the Book Ltd. The aim of Inside Books was to explore how the theory and practice of reader development could be adapted and applied to the prison environment. Three readers in residence were placed in four prisons to set up reading groups and develop models of good practice. These were then disseminated to prison librarians via a series of regional training days and a reader development manual which was produced as part of the project. As Wilkinson reports:

> The most powerful recommendation in prison is that of another prisoner. Inside Books enabled reading group members at the pilot prisons to recommend books to other prison library users via the Inside Books sampler, which contains reviews and extracts from 10

titles from HarperCollins (who produced the sampler), and a list of a further 90 titles from different publishers. The emphasis was on contemporary fiction across a range of genres. 100 copies of the sampler were distributed to each English prison.

The Inside Books project has had a profound effect on reader development in prison libraries. For the first time, prison library staff had access to top quality training from experts in the field which related specifically to their work in prisons. So often, public library training and reader development initiatives do not translate well into the prison situation. The reader development manual – the first of its kind – provides a lasting source of inspiration, containing tried and tested models which really do work in prisons. Reader development has now become an established part of prison library provision. Many prisons now run regular reading groups, and some have linked in with reading groups in the community 'outside', exchanging reviews and in some cases, inviting 'outside' group members into the prison.

Inside Books also piloted the use of reading groups with people who are normally excluded from the reading experience. Successful groups have been established with adult beginner readers, where the emphasis is on the pleasure and excitement of reading, rather than the technical skill. The reading group provides a social atmosphere which takes the pressure off the reader and gives the potential for developing not only reading skills but also communication and writing skills. One prison library has recently started an informal group with patients from the prison hospital who all have severe mental health problems. Again, the emphasis is on enjoyment of reading, and using the reading experience as a means of social contact.

It is, of course, impossible to adequately evaluate the benefit that prisoners derive from reading, and the effect that it has on their lives. It is perhaps best left to Jean, who was a member of a prison reading group, to express what reading means to her: 'Books are the only consistent thread in my life. They have been my friends, they have taken me to worlds and places I could never otherwise hope to see. They have introduced me to thousands of characters – some I loved, others I hated – people I would never have met in my real life. Books have been my teachers. Through them I have found safe havens away from pain and despair, learnt history, politics, science. Books are part of me.'

(Wilkinson, 2002)

FATHERS

As well as encouraging prisoners themselves to read, some prison libraries are helping prisoners to become more involved in their children's reading development. Gartree Prison in Market Harborough, Leicestershire, runs FATHERS – Fathers as teachers, helping, encouraging, reading and supporting (Beaumont, 2000). The scheme aims to break the cycle of low literacy and imprisonment by encouraging prisoners to be better parents and to be positive role models for their children. It also hopes to promote better social behaviour, improve self-esteem and empower children with better literacy skills. Prisoners can read stories on to tape for their children, or introduce the librarian reading the story. Children are also encouraged to bring their school reading books to read to their fathers at visiting times. One inmate believes the scheme has been a big success and says, 'when I was at home I used to read stories to my daughter every night before she went to bed . . . after two years of missing dad's bedtime stories she can now settle down to them again' (Beaumont, 2000, 45).The scheme has helped to open up new channels of communication between fathers and their children, while the reading at visiting time has given the children a sense of importance and increased self-esteem.

The Big Book Share scheme

The Big Book Share scheme at Nottingham Prison has also encouraged inmates to record stories and contribute to their children's reading development (Kings, 2001). As well as encouraging their children to read, the prisoners are also becoming more confident and aware about choosing and sharing children's books.

Reading in prisoner-of-war camps

The value of books in the extreme conditions of prisoner-of-war camps is highlighted by Shavit (1999). Close to 100,000 Americans and 135,000 British and Commonwealth servicemen were held in prisoner of war camps in Germany during World War 2 and the Red Cross tried to ease their confinement by providing them with books. While many of the prisoners simply used reading as a way to relieve the boredom or to improve their mind, others appreciated the sense of escape that books gave them.

Families were allowed to send books to the camps and one prisoner explained the excitement of waiting for the deliveries: 'the contents of the weekly food parcel and the quarterly clothing parcel did not vary much. Books, therefore became the great standby and a means of escape from the confinement of the barbed wire' (Saunders, 1949, 118).

The demand for books was high and never fully met by the camp libraries and books were borrowed at an immense rate: 'The opening of our small library was a real shot in the arm for now we could slip away from this prison. It was only a mental escape but it still allowed us to break free from our internment' (Williams, 1991, 121). 'We could not have lived without books. They were the only sure support, the one true comfort. . . . In reading one had a pleasure of which, like sleep, one could never be deprived' (Kee, 1982, 126). 'Books were the best escape. You vanished into whatever world was theirs and hours fled by. . . . I read to kill time and for entertainment' (Westheimer, 1992, 130).

> Many people do not read much, but if they were deprived of all reading material they would suffer greatly. I am sure that thousands of books in our library were responsible

> for providing constructive, mind-saving diversion from the mental fortunes of POW life.
> (Military Intelligence Service, 1945, 131)

Aida (1999) also recalls the pleasure that a particular book brought him during his time in the Japanese army in World War 2. *Songs of a Fish* was a collection of essays by Professor Kazuo Watanabe who was a quiet advocate of humanitarianism and liberalism in Japan. Having lost his copy during the battles, Aida found a copy next to the body of a dead soldier in Burma. He found the book painful to read because it reminded him of a world of ideas that he thought he would never see again: 'all these things which I was deprived of in reality would appear before me with a paradisial quality and clutch at my heart with anguish and longing. . . . I wanted to touch it everyday and would worry if I hadn't done so' (218). During his time in a PoW camp, the book was circulated and one prisoner even copied it on to toilet paper and had it bound as a second copy, with the price on the back as 'one million yen'. Aida thought that all the prisoners experienced the same kind of homesickness as him when trying to read it but also like him could not bear to be parted from it. The book was left at the camp on his release and he has only recently acquired a new copy. He now experiences a different set of feelings when reading the book and said, 'it seems to me that I was then reading a different book – or rather I was reading it under a light completely different from that of the present' (218).

Bibliotherapy

Bibliotherapy, or reading therapy, is the formal 'scientific' approach to much of what has been discussed earlier in this chapter. It has largely been recognized as a treatment in the USA but is also gaining some recognition in the UK. Bibliotherapy is defined by Clarke (1988, 1) as 'the therapeutic use of books or other materials with individuals or with groups of people' and described by Schlenther (1999) as 'identification with a character or situation and the projection of oneself into it, catharsis-experiencing of emotional release, insight and integration'.

Gold (1990) gives ten psychological consequences that he has ascertained arising from the use of story and poetry in therapy: language growth, life information, identification, modeling, cognitive shift, problem solving, immunization, feelings, normalization and sharing. He summarizes the benefits of using reading:

> to promote changes in perception that can heal and make whole, that can move people onto new and fertile ground for the growth of new life (342). . . . Fiction and poetry are the appropriate materials for therapy because they are products of, and a key to, the storymaking faculty of human cognition and they evoke feeling, and feeling must be evoked if we are to work with human emotions. Language is the human link between thought and feeling; story is the most memorable organization of language (343).

Coomaraswamy (1988) highlights the benefits of bibliotherapy, by citing a patient suffering from recurring episodes of clinical depression and serious suicidal intentions. Describing the help that she gets from Somerset Maugham's *Of Human Bondage*, the patient says it is:

> an opiate in resisting my blackest despair. I read it so compulsively that I was able to banish my suicidal thoughts. It got me through my two darkest hours and scotched my intentions to seek permanent oblivion from my inner torment. . . . Reading changes my experience and helps me to change direction. I read until my mind changes my black thoughts to more positive trends (74).

RAYS

The RAYS (Reading and You Scheme) at Calderdale and Kirklees public libraries is using bibliotherapy to help a range of groups including people with mental health problems, the elderly and refugees. People who have been suffering with anxiety, stress and depression are referred to the bibliotherapist by their GPs and are given one-to-one sessions as well as being encouraged to join group sessions. One client, who was struggling with confidence, depression and bereavement after a difficult marriage and the sudden death of her boyfriend, found solace in love poems: 'I found it very moving to have someone else express my thoughts and feelings, to know someone else has felt the same grief.'

Local writers have been contributing poems for the groups and one client said: 'These are my soothers – I get them out to read when I'm feeling stressed.' Another client who had just left hospital said: 'This is my first trip outside since coming out of hospital and I wanted it to be to the reading group.' One of the groups is for young Asian women who have been outcast from their community: 'This is the first book I have read. You got just the right one for me, I was in the story, oh, so exciting. It was real life, it shows you. That is what I want to read about' (Murphy, 2002a).

A group for carers has recently been set up, and one carer who has been working with the bibliotherapist said: 'I was in that book and I didn't want to finish it. I wanted to be that person. Reading is the best way of relaxing I know. It's very stressful looking after someone and this [reading] is time out for me' (Murphy, 2002b).

Developing literacy: informal programmes to promote reading

Many of the situations detailed above are the result of societal or family breakdown, poverty or illness. In many areas of the world, extreme breakdown of society, of governments, of families, as a result of the ravages of war, famine, disease, the devastating effects of AIDs, make life ever more hazardous. While reading cannot solve all ills, in many developing countries, literacy and reading can offer opportunities for human development and empower individuals. There is often only limited access to libraries or reading materials, particularly among the lowest socio-economic and poorer or rural communities; yet these are the people who need them the most. To counteract this, there are numerous informal programmes aimed at promoting reading to people in developing and marginalized communities throughout the world; many rely on individual local missionary zeal, passion and commitment to bring peace and harmony through books and a belief that books can bring a little light and hope into lives: 'Myriads of small fires burning throughout every part of every developing country must surely be more effective than a few scattered large fires that in the long run burn themselves out' (Elkin, 1999).

Academic Kingo Mchombu sees reading as a critical activity for the future within the developing nations:

> In the context of Maslow's hierarchy of basic human needs: physiological, safety, belonging and love, esteem and self-actualization, cognitive and aesthetic needs, a child who is always hungry, or faces life-threatening situations daily, is not likely to develop an interest in reading. However, it is possible to organise reading activities and consolidate on reading behaviour by finding materials which relate to needs such as: physiological, security, love, competence, curiosity and hunger for knowledge and beauty, using these as building blocks to sustain and expand the child's curiosity. (Mchombu from Namibia, 1999)

This section will explore some of the more successful and unusual initiatives. The quotes and information are taken from leaders of the specific projects as quoted in Elkin, 1999, unless otherwise stated.

The projects recognize a growing desire to give a personal and community dimension to reading, to give children a happier childhood and, more generally, to re-humanize communities that have in many cases been dislocated by violence and poverty, and to give or restore a voice to those who have none. Becoming a reader and learning to behave like a reader are parts of the social process. Yet, in many countries, reading has traditionally been seen as a very formal process. Reading for pleasure implies that reading for choice should take the place of the prescribed reading of school textbooks. Within this context, with literacy and education seen as a passport from poverty and marginalization, reading:

- empowers
- transforms futures
- is essential to mending lives
- is powerful and energizing
- belongs to intimacy, especially between mother and child
- needs to be linked to the child's basic needs
- should be active and personal

- provides readers with the means of controlling their lives by making them accountable and increasing their awareness
- improves the quality of life by providing information about hygiene, ecology, family life, etc.

South America

Nicaragua

Nicaragua, as most Central American countries, is poor in socio-economic terms. After decades of conflict and confrontation, Nicaragua is in a post-war period, only some ten years since the end of the civil war. There is no energy or running water in some areas. As a result, many family environments are violent. There is a circle of poverty that does not allow children 'to have dreams or see ways of living differently'. There are huge disparities between rural and urban children. Communities are in the process of losing their identity and collective memory; the oral tradition is declining. In reading promotion programmes with pre-school children, one of the basic components is the oral tradition and there is work going on with community educators to make recordings before the oral tradition is lost and communities lose their identity.

The Books for Children Foundation is a private and independent organization, which organizes simple programmes, based on the principle that everyone must be able to read and write well. The concept of reading in Nicaragua in general is still a very formal one. Words are used to discipline rather than to care, in an atmosphere of shouting and violence; neither educational nor the family environment are promoting caring; 'children are disabled little adults.' In this environment love and affection are needed as the mediator rather than discipline and there is a need to give children access to many and diverse types of books. The Foundation aims to stimulate projects around reading, including the Mobile Classroom Library project.

Since 1993, the Mobile classroom library project has provided books to 160 schools, each with about 150 books, aiming to promote reading, by finding space, providing books and furniture and including the local community, for example grandparents, in telling stories. The project provides books, pays teachers and encourages voluntary reading. The main criteria for the books selected are their cultural relevance, aiming to provide access to universal literature as a basic right for children.

Three years ago, the Menaguan Street Children Project began to provide bookbags for the street children, many of whom are regularly beaten, sniff glue and have alcoholic parents; they have probably never been to school. The project visits two to three times per week, bringing children 'a little moment of happiness' and giving them a rewarding occasion by treating them with love and care and offering them the possibility to relate: a rare occurrence.

Peru

The Rural Libraries of Cajamarca Scheme covers 15,000 square kilometres of tough highland terrain and is served by 600 voluntary farmer-librarians. They travel down to the valley town of Cajamarca, collect up to 40 books at a time and return with them to their remote rural homes, often three days' journey away:

> On their backs travel copies of the Peruvian Constitution, books on law, medicine, local agriculture, plant remedies, history, stories and customs of the region, all for people who could never in a million years afford to buy them and who would otherwise never even see them. In a subsistence economy where there is no electricity or telephones, this defiantly low-tech trade in words has, over the past 27 years, brought with it expertise on everything from health to bee-keeping, along with a remarkable sense of local identity and culture. (Dunant, 1988)

Funded by Christian Aid, the scheme was genuinely subversive when it was set up in 1970s rural Peru, where, for the native population, the book had long been synonymous with conquest and oppression:

> For centuries native Peruvians have been afraid of books, because they walked hand-in-hand with those in control. . . . To keep us illiterate was to keep us quiet. As the novelist and anthropologist Jose Maria Arguedas said, 'An Indian who can read is a dangerous Indian.' If reading and books could be seen to improve life, to make a practical difference, then one might create not only a greater appetite for literacy, but a sense of self-esteem to go with it. (Dunant, 1988)

Morocco

A project in the remote High Atlas mountains aims to bring literacy to communities. When asking the local community why they wanted to learn to read and write, project leaders were told: 'I want to become a human being'. The first project built two houses of culture and a library. The aim is to spread the project, create a network, preserve the oral tradition and promote reading of books and new types of documents. A significant issue in terms of sustainability is discovering people from the local community who can be trained as animateurs, storytellers, literacy workers.

Mali

Mali, one of the poorest countries in Africa, has managed to achieve a network of public libraries, set up 20 years ago. The emphasis has been on the oral tradition and on children, both those in school and those not. Teachers in each village choose a 'librarian'. This can be problematic when the librarians act like teachers and need convincing that reading is more than the acquisition of good grammar. A priority is young children, aged about three, but it is difficult for mothers to take an active part in the library, as often they are too busy and may be illiterate. Ideally what is needed is family reading outside school and an opportunity to relate reading to the family tradition. Therefore, the oldest child in a family is encouraged to read to the youngest, thus giving access to picture books in small, intimate groups. The library organizes weekly programmes, including storytelling, devoted to small children and mothers, or older children. The library uses places where people gather, for example in houses or health centres where women meet, to show books to the very young and demonstrate the importance of reading. Use of solar energy in libraries allows them to open after dark. This allows children who cannot study at home to use the library: 'The library gives light' in two senses!

Asia

Thailand

The *Thailand Portable Libraries project* began in 1979 to mark the International Year of the Child. The project, based initially at Srinakharinwirot University, began with the aim of providing recreational books to school libraries in remote areas:

> We were to travel in remote districts bringing necessary food for the 'book hunger'. After a short distance on the road leading towards this goal, however, we realized that there would be no end to the satisfaction provided by the books brought. There would always be a hunger for more. We go on with our journey therefore and have joy in our hearts.
> (Singkhamanan, 1999)

The project designed and developed wooden boxes, about the size of a suitcase, containing 200–250 books. When opened, the boxes functioned as a display unit complete with shelves (books facing outwards). This could be placed in any quiet corner, indoors or outdoors, but always somewhere conducive to contemplative reading activities. The first major problem was the lack of books in Thai for children, with very few writers and illustrators. This was solved through the project running workshops on writing, editing and illustrating. Students of children's literature on librarianship courses at the University began to collect traditional tales, initially from Andersen, Grimm and Beatrix Potter, and rewrote them for Thai children. From this a publishing tradition grew, with a guaranteed market, stimulating quality production. The book chain had been created and has survived to this day with the ongoing enthusiastic support of many volunteers. Another problem was that, while children may love to read, many teachers did not and therefore were not encouraging children in their love. The project introduced storytelling techniques and reading animation workshops to stimulate interest in stories, using dramatization and puppet shows. The phrase: '"Use one book one hundred ways, use each one one hundred times, each time use with one hundred children" became the motto for the project' (Elkin, 1999).

Conclusion

The needs of people who are visually or aurally impaired, physically or mentally disabled, hospitalized, institutionalized, or traumatized by accident or abuse are very different. Maybe it is here that reading comes into its own, in terms of its healing and therapeutic powers and the particular emphasis on readers finding the right book at the right time in the right place. It is here, too, that the librarian as facilitator and advisor becomes so important in ensuring access to a wide range of reading materials.

References and further reading

Aida, Y. (1999) Songs of a Fish: the book as solace in extremity, *Logos*, **10** (4), 216–19.

Ball, F. (1995) Special Needs: meeting the demands of information and imagination, *School Librarian*, **43** (2), 54–5.

Beaumont, D. (2000) Spreading the Reading Message in our Prisons, *Public Library Journal*, **15** (2), 45–6.

Brazier, H. and Corrigan, L. (2002) *Reader Development and Reading for Pleasure for People with Visual Impairment*. Personal communication with the author.

Budin, M. L. (1998) What We Know to be True, *School Library Journal*, **44** (12), 38–9.

Butler, D. (1987) *Cushla and Her Books*, London, Penguin Books.

Butler. D. (1998) *Babies Need Books*, London, Penguin Books.

Chambers, A. (1985) *Booktalk: occasional writing on literature and children*, London, The Bodley Head.

Clarke, J. M. (1988) Reading Therapy: an outline of its growth in the UK. In Clarke, J. M. and Bostle, E. (eds), *Reading Therapy*, London, Library Association Publishing, 1–15.

Coomaraswamy, S. D. (1988) Therapeutic Reading and Personal Development. In Clarke, J. M. and Bostle, E. (eds), *Reading Therapy*, London, Library Association Publishing, 68–81.

Cox, A. (2002) Getting Insiders Reading, *Library Association Record*, **104** (1), 48–9.

Dunant, S. (1998) Brought to Book, *The Guardian Weekend*, May 23, 32–5.

Elkin, J. (1999) Informal Programmes to Support Reading and Libraries in Developing Countries, *The New Review of Children's Literature and Librarianship*, **5**, 55–83.

Feldman, S. and Needlman, R. (1999) Take Two Board Books and Call Me in the Morning, *School Library Journal*, **45** (6), 30–3.

Forrest, M. E. S. (1990) Reminiscence Therapy in a Scottish Hospital, *Health Libraries*

Review, **7** (2), 69–72.

Forrest, M. E. S. (1998) Recent Developments in Reading Therapy: a review of the literature, *Health Libraries Review*, **5** (3), 157–64.

Gillies, C. (1988) Reading and Insight. In Clarke, J. M. and Bostle, E. (eds), *Reading Therapy*, London, Library Association Publishing, 36–43.

Gold, J. (1990) *Read for Your Life: literature as a life support system*, Ontario, Canada, Fitzhenry & Whiteside.

The Guardian (2002) Brought to Book, *Guardian Society*, (16 October), 3.

Guerin, C. (2000) *Hospital Libraries and the Public Library System in France: how can they work together?* Jerusalem, 66th IFLA Council & General Conference. Available at www.ifla.org/IV/ifla66/papers/135-143e.htm. [Accessed 18.03.03]

HM Prison Service (2002) *Prison Libraries*. Available at www.hmprisonservice.gov.uk/library/dynpage.asp?Page=539. [Accessed 20.10.02]

Hoy, S. (1984) You're Charging Too Little for the Tea, Me Duck: library clubs for senior citizens in Leicestershire, *Health Libraries Review*, **1** (2), 90–104.

Imagination Time. Available at www.readingagency.org.uk/download_files/ImaginationTime.doc. [Accessed 18.03.03]

Jacobsen, L. et al. (1984) The Children's Library – an important part of the Children's Hospital, *Scandinavian Public Library Quarterly*, **17** (1), 2–4.

Jones, N. (2001) Reading Rights, *Literacy Today*, 27. Available at www.literacytrust.org.uk/Pubs/jones.htm. [Accessed 18.03.03]

Kars, M. and Doud, M. (1999) Ready to Read: a collaborative, community wide emergent literacy program, *Reference Librarian*, (67/68), 85–97.

Kee, R. (1982) A Crowd is Not Company. In Shavit, D. (1999) The Greatest Morale Factor next to the Red Army: books and libraries in American and British prisoners of war camps in Germany during World War 2, *Libraries and Culture*, **34** (2), 113–34.

King, S. (1981) Danse Macabre. In Brewis, W. L. E., Gericke, E. M. and Kruger, J. A. (1994) Reading Needs and Motives of Adult Users of Fiction, *Mousaion*, **12** (2), 3–18.

Kings, T. (2001) Libraries, Partnership and Social Inclusion: 'the Big Book Share' at HMP Nottingham, *Assignation*, **18** (4), 42–5.

Marshall, M. R. (1988) Special Reading Materials for Handicapped Children. In Clarke, J. M. and Bostle, E. (eds), *Reading Therapy*, London, Library Association Publishing, 106–26.

Matthews, D. A. and Lonsdale, R. (1992) Children in Hospital: reading therapy and children in hospital, *Health Libraries Review*, **9** (1), 14–26.

Mathias, B. (2002) *Reading*. Personal communication with the author.

Mchombo, K. (1999) In Elkin, J. (ed.), Informal Programmes to Support Reading and Libraries in Developing Countries, *The New Review of Children's Literature and Librarianship*, **5**, 55–83.

Military Intelligence Service (1945) American Prisoners of War in Germany. In Shavit, D. (1999) The Greatest Morale Factor next to the Red Army: books and libraries in

American and British prisoners of war camps in Germany during World War 2, *Libraries and Culture*, **34** (2), 113–34.

Murphy, B. (2002a) *February Quarterly Report. Bibliotherapy Project*. Available at www.resource.gov.uk/action/dcmswolf/rdp2001.asp. [Accessed 8.4.03]

Murphy, B. (2002b) *June Quarterly Report. Bibliotherapy Project*. Available at www.resource.gov.uk/action/dcmswolf/rdp2001.asp. [Accessed 8.4.03]

National Library for the Blind. Available at www.nlbuk.org. [Accessed 18.03.03]

Polese, C. (1994) Resilient Readers: children's literature in the lives of abuse survivors, *School Library Journal*, **40** (3), 156–7.

RAYS (Reading and You Scheme) and Wolfson evaluation. Available at www.resource.gov.uk/action/dcmswolf/rdp2001.asp. [Accessed 8.4.03]

Resource (2002) *Open to All?*, London, Resource.

Ring, A. (1986) Establishing a State-of-the-Art Library in a Nursing Home; how I did it, *Journal of Educational Media and Library Sciences*, **23** (3), 254–70.

Saunders, H. St G. (1949) The Red Cross and the White: a short history of the Joint War Organisation of the British Red Cross Society and the Order of St John of Jerusalem during the War 1939–1945. In Shavit, D. (ed.) (1999) The Greatest Morale Factor next to the Red Army: books and libraries in American and British prisoners of war camps in Germany during World War 2, *Libraries and Culture*, **34** (2), 113–34.

Schlenther, E. (1988) Miffy and Others in Hospital: library services to a children's ward, *Health Libraries Review*, **5** (2), 138–9.

Schlenther, E. (1992) Reading therapy for children: a bibliography. In Ball, F. (ed.) (1995) Special Needs: meeting the demands of information and imagination, *School Librarian*, **43** (2), 54–5.

Schlenther, E. (1999) Using Reading Therapy with Children, *Health Libraries Review*, **16** (1), 29–37.

Share The Vision (2000) *Library Services for Visually Impaired People: a manual of best practice*, London, Share the Vision and Resource.

Shavit, D. (1999) The Greatest Morale Factor next to the Red Army: books and libraries in American and British prisoners of war camps in Germany during World War 2, *Libraries and Culture*, **34** (2), 113–34.

Simon, L. (1984) Library Services to Patients in Psychiatric Hospitals, *Scandinavian Public Library Quarterly*, **17** (1), 22–3.

Singkhamanan, S. (1999) In Elkin, J. (1999) Informal Programmes to Support Reading and Libraries in Developing Countries, *The New Review of Children's Literature and Librarianship*, **5**, 66–7.

Spiers, D. (1992) Literacy, Education and the Needs of the Disabled Child. In Barker, K. and Lonsdale, R. (eds), *Skills for Life?: the meaning and value of literacy, Proceedings of the Youth Libraries Group Conference, Birmingham, September, 1992*, London, Taylor Graham, 90–2.

Spufford, F. (2002) *The Child that Books Built: a memoir of childhood and reading*, London, Faber.

Stephenson, P. (2001) *Billy*, London, HarperCollins.

Sullivan, L. E. (1998) Reading in American Prisons: structures and strictures, *Libraries and Culture*, **33** (1), 113–19.

Vincent, J. (2002) Personal communication with the author.

Walker, M. E. and Jones, J. (1986) When Children Die: death in current children's literature and its use in a library, *Bulletin of the Medical Library Association*, **74** (1), 16–18.

Westheimer, D. (1992) Sitting It Out: a World War II POW memoir. In Shavit (1999) The Greatest Morale Factor next to the Red Army: books and libraries in American and British prisoners of war camps in Germany during World War 2, *Libraries and Culture*, **34** (2), 113–34.

Who Cares? Trust. Available at www.thewhocarestrust.org.uk. [Accessed 18.03.03]

Who Cares? Trust (1994) *A Book of my Own*, London, Who Cares? Trust.

Who Cares? Trust & the Paul Hamlyn Foundation (2001), *Right to Read*, London, Who Cares? Trust.

Wilkinson, S. (2002) Personal communication with the author

Williams, W. F. (1991) For You the War is Over. In Shavit, D. (1999) The Greatest Morale Factor next to the Red Army: books and libraries in American and British prisoners of war camps in Germany during World War 2, *Libraries and Culture*, **34** (2), 113–34.

7

ICT and reader development

Debbie Denham

Introduction

This chapter investigates the link between ICT and reading; is there a perceived conflict or a mutually supportive relationship between the two? The arguments centre on television as a competitor to reading but it is acknowledged that television can also provide support and promotion for books and reading. The potential of the internet to support and encourage reading and allow for contact between global communities of readers is explored here. The chapter also considers the problems and issues inherent in trying to provide access to fictional material and examines the key concepts and examples of interactive fictions.

It might be useful at this point to define some of the terms used throughout this chapter. Information and Communications Technology (ICT), is '[t]he study of the technology used to handle information and aid communication. The phrase was coined by Stevenson in his 1997 report to the UK government and promoted by the new National Curriculum documents for the UK in 2000' (FOLDOC, n.d.). The term 'digital' relates to information transmitted electronically, usually as a binary code and new media are taken as referring to 'products and services that provide information or entertainment using computers or the Internet, and not by traditional methods, such as television and newspapers' (Cambridge International Dictionary of English, 2002).

ICT and media literacy

There is growing concern that the new electronic age will see the demise of the book and a complete change in the way we read and access information. As Eisenstein (1999) points out, this concern is not new and previous technological advances in the print industry, such as the invention of the printing press and the move from hand presses to steam-driven machinery were, in their turn, greeted with scepticism and alarm (182). The development of the newspaper press in the 19th century was held by many contemporary observers to herald the death of the book (194).

This concern is not then a new one. Much of the media focus is on children, who are perceived as not reading enough and conversely are spending increasing amounts of time engaged with 'new' media, in particular television and electronic games. As early as 1993, Buckingham suggested that over 70% of homes in the UK were equipped to play computer games (Beavis, 1998). Numerous studies have provided statistical data to indicate that children are reading less and have more distractions to take up their leisure time (see, for example, Children's Literature Research Centre, 1996).

Television

The chief 'bogeyman' in encouraging children to forsake reading, and the first that was perceived as a significant challenge, is television. As Robinson (1997, 4) indicates:

> Arguments seeking to draw comparisons between television and reading draw on many exnominated ideas about family, about culture and about learning. The arguments themselves tend to revolve around starkly expressed oppositions to do with high and popular culture, active and passive learning and verbal and visual experiences, with television on the less favoured side of the equation.

So the objections are not only concerned with the time children spend watching television compared to reading but with the perception that television itself is at best passive and at worst damaging and dangerous to young minds. However some commentators have provided alternative perspectives:

> Some people set TV and print literacy in opposition to each other and hold TV responsible for a decline in reading. We have no way of knowing that, if they were not watching, children would be reading. . . . The belief that, if not closely monitored, TV will oust traditional print literacy is not so widely held as it was. (Meek, 1991, 217)

Media literacy

It is inevitable that children are being exposed to an increasing range of media, often choosing themselves to spend more time engaging with these media. Although the argument is about the respective values of these media and the damage, or otherwise, they may do to the child, there is growing recognition that these elements of popular culture are taking an increasingly prominent role in the life of the child. Therefore, many teachers argue that children need to be encouraged to develop new additional literacy skills to allow them to interpret and engage with alternative media.

'Literate' is being constantly redefined in the light of the availability and uptake of new technologies. The increasing complexity in the definition of literacy extends beyond the written word and includes the decoding and understanding of images

(Beavis, 1998). The Australian government has recognized the need for children to be examining a range of popular texts by including the use of electronic games as part of the curriculum. As Beavis notes (246), there is recognition of the need to include new technology texts within the school curriculum to develop literacy and interpretation skills.

Many commentators do not see electronic texts as replacing or ejecting traditional, print-based texts but rather as an opportunity to 'enrich and diversify the students' range of narratives and textual experience, to create continuities between school and out-of-school reading, pleasure, analysis and critique' (Beavis, 1998, 252). Others identify the need for high-grade visual literacy skills as vital: '[t]he ability to decode complex visual narrative precedes, but certainly does not preclude, a similar degree of sophistication and facility with written texts' (Reynolds, 1993, 103).

Promotion of books and reading

The internet has proved to be a powerful promotional tool in the book world. It has been used by libraries, publishers and booksellers to sell and promote their products, as well as promulgating the concept of enjoyment of reading for its own sake. However the use of websites by libraries in the UK has been relatively recent. One of the main advantages of the internet is its 'potential to reach larger numbers of children relatively cheaply and make that contact outside the library environment as well as within' (Denham, 2000, 73). The UK research project A Place for Children (Elkin and Kinnell, 2000) identified only a limited number of initiatives and library authorities which made innovative use of ICT to support reading and promote books. A later follow-up survey discovered that, although it was still evident that the full potential of the internet was not being realized, there had been increased use made of ICT in supporting and developing readers:

> Whereas many web pages are used merely to advertise and promote services offered by the library, others offer a range of information, links to other sites of interest to children and young adults, booklists and even pages encouraging interactive participation, such as writing stories and book reviews. (Mynott et al., 2001, 134)

It is this latter use that is the most exciting in relation to reader development. The *A Place for Children* research identified a number of UK library-based websites, such as Stories from the Web, but noted that generally libraries in the USA were further advanced (Mynott et al., 2001). With a few notable exceptions (Essex, Birmingham, Gloucestershire and North Lincolnshire), children's library websites in the UK tended to focus on providing information on library facilities and opening hours rather than using the full potential of the technology to engage with readers and encourage non-readers. Mynott and Elkin (2000, 185) indicate that:

> The opportunities offered by EC programs such as CHILIAS and VERITY represent a new development in library services throughout Europe. UK participation in these projects, along with the establishment of UK Web sites, such as 'Stories from the Web,' goes some way toward realizing the concept of the virtual library for children in the UK and providing the wide-ranging access to online resources that is currently available in the United States and Canada'.

CHILIAS

CHILIAS was a European project that aimed to develop:

> a new concept for future European children's libraries, providing a stimulating environment for innovative learning and creative use of multimedia and networked technology with links to traditional library services. The project aimed to enhance the competence of children using interactive multimedia and networked information and communication systems, and to improve their information seeking skills in new learning environments.
> (CORDIS, n.d.)

The key elements of the project were:

> four complementary and integrated applications, in a WWW environment, named InfoPlanet, comprising:
>
> - A Virtual Library module
> - Storybuilder – an interactive application for creative input from children
> - Guestbook – a structured discussion and feedback tool for use by children
> - Infoton – an information skills tool. (CORDIS, n.d.).

Mynott and Elkin (2000, 185) go on to suggest that future success is dependent on adequate resourcing levels. The role of the public library in supporting the promotion of books and reading through the new technologies is reiterated:

> the future is bright for a new definition of libraries, providing access to electronic resources via the Internet, while preserving access to more traditional forms of printed material which will continue to have a place in a child's growth and development way into the future.

The People's Network

In the UK the importance of using the new technologies to support and promote the use of traditional print-based material was underlined when the training programme for the People's Network was announced. The government-funded programme to install a network of computers in all public libraries by 2002 was to be supplemented by a training programme to ensure that all library staff were confident and comfortable in the exploitation of a range of technologies. Included in the package of basic skills for all staff, alongside IT, internet searching and CD-ROM and online information skills, was reader development. The report outlined that staff would need to:

> be familiar with the range of reader services and information available digitally. They should feel comfortable using electronic sources, and be able to help others use them effectively. This implies both an awareness of reader-related sites and networks that are currently available and the familiarity and skill required to help others use them.
>
> (Library and Information Commission, 1998)

The report continues by outlining specific knowledge that library staff would be expected to acquire and that the training programme would provide. Staff would need to:

- be aware of reader-related sites on the Internet, including:
  – thematic approaches and guides to further reading,
  – sites on specific genres and authors,
  – online bookstores,
  – publishers' sites,
  – reading groups;
- know about literacy initiatives in education, such as the national literacy strategy and literacy hour;
- know about Bookstart and other early-reading initiatives, and have a working knowledge of sites for children and their reading, such as Stories from the Web;
- know about sites and sources of interest to readers with a range of special needs.

(Library and Information Commission, 1998)

It is heartening to note that reader development was placed here as a key skill which underlined its role as fundamentally important to the continued existence of public libraries. This initiative also made a clear link between reader development and the value of the internet in supporting this element of library provision.

My Home Library

www.myhomelibrary.org/

Last year the UK Children's Laureate, Anne Fine, launched her My Home Library website. Her aim is to encourage children to own their own books, their home library, by acquiring books from all kinds of sources, for example sales and charity shops. She also wants children to take pride in their books, by having personal bookplates. The website provides downloadable bookplates designed by leading international children's book illustrators.

Case study: 'Ask Chris' – Essex Libraries website for readers

www.essexcc.gov.uk/askchris

Adult public library services provide some innovative examples of reader development projects that make use of internet technology. Essex Libraries have taken the initiative with their 'Ask Chris' website which provides reading recommendations from library staff and reading groups. June Turner from Essex Libraries writes:

> Chris is a mixture of the enthusiasms and knowledge of Essex libraries staff and recommendations from readers and reading groups across Essex. So when you Ask Chris to suggest what you might read next, you're tapping into the opinions of hundreds of readers. The name Chris was chosen because we wanted a real name, which could be of either gender and did not have any strong resonance for any particular age, class or background. The website launched in September 2001, developed out of Essex Libraries 'Ask Chris' project, funded by the DCMS/Wolfson Reader Development Programme in 2000/01.
>
> The project sought to answer the question at the heart of reader development, 'What shall I read next?' It recognised that three out of four readers borrowing fiction from public libraries do not know what they are looking for and that library staff do not have the time for in-depth consultations or, in many cases, the expertise to undertake them. The project was intended to benefit the widest possible adult audience while at the same time addressing particular needs of emergent readers, readers with a visual impairment and housebound readers.
>
> The initial focus of the project was on training a team of 'Ask Chris' champions, the development of a fiction knowledge network, 'Ask Chris' promotional events and 'Ask Chris' reader advice sessions. It was always intended that the project would have an ICT strand but it quickly became clear that the web site content would in fact be one of the most important ways of sustaining 'Ask Chris' into the future, as well as of improving overall accessibility. Additional funding was secured from Essex County Council to develop a readers' website that was both dynamic and interactive, and recognised the needs of different users.
>
> We wanted to create a site that was easy to use, involved readers and created a strong sense of sharing reading experiences. The design was kept simple with bold colours providing clear direction within the site and clear signposting of all the interactive features.
>
> The database of reviews behind the site can be searched in a variety of ways, ensuring that the user can exploit reader comments and introduce books to readers from lots of different angles.
>
> *Widening reader choices*
>
> Through using 'Ask Chris', the reader is almost guaranteed to discover something they want to read, recommended by other readers. On the website, unlike library shelves, books can be highlighted simultaneously in as many categories as appropriate. Thus the crime reader will come across conventional crime but also books with a crime element which on the library shelves might be hidden in modern fiction. The Advanced Search facility allows readers to combine two categories, e.g. a humorous crime book or an action-packed book with a sense of history available in Large Print.

Themed selections, which change regularly, provide different ways of engaging readers and highlighting books. The website is linked to the library catalogue ELAN allowing for books to be reserved quickly and delivered to any Essex library. The website and library catalogue are available 24 hours a day so the reader is not constrained by library opening hours. A number of readers have commented on how useful these facilities are:

> Looking at the 'Ask Chris' web site and discovering some great reads, I also discovered ELAN. I have often thought how great it would be to use this at home. It was so quick and easy. I have ordered another book I want to read! (Member of 'Booktalk' Group)

> The 'Ask Chris' website is my favourite. Not only can I find lots of marvellous information about books, but I've found it a perfect site for someone with little computer knowledge to use to learn to access the web. It is very well designed. (Member of Senior Computer Users Group)

The quality of support available to readers at any library is improved. It is no longer dependent on the particular reading tastes of staff concerned:

> I used to dread questions from readers who did not share my tastes in books. With 'Ask Chris', I can recommend love stories and adventure books set in historical times with equal confidence as my own favourite reading. (Librarian)

Widening choice for readers with a visual impairment

The website is the first to consider the needs of readers who need Large Print and audio materials. Readers can search by their preferred format and there is also a theme selection, which highlights books new in Large Print and audio. This section is particularly valuable to housebound volunteers who often struggle providing readers with something different.

Widening choices for emergent readers

Essex Libraries, in partnership with Essex adult education department, developed 'Quick Reads', a way of identifying and promoting mainstream books accessible to emergent readers. 'Quick Reads' is one of the options on the website and students are contributing their reviews to the site. This section is rapidly becoming a national resource, as there is currently nothing else available to engage adult basic skills students as readers:

> Just to let you know how useful I have found the Quick Reads section on 'Ask Chris'. I was also impressed by the obvious range of reviewers – from members of reading groups to people who maybe don't find reading and writing quite so easy. It is good to see everyone being allowed their opinion." (Special Services Adviser, North Yorkshire County Library)

> I like seeing the reviews on the website. I think it's good because people can read what we think and it will help them decide what to choose. (Basic Skills Student)

Sharing reading experiences

We wanted readers to get involved with the site; not only to use it to find their next great read but also to share their reading experiences with others. The great success of the site is the way that this has happened. Reviews added to the site have increased dramatically since the launch providing powerful reader-to-reader comment in a variety of different voices.

Reading groups

Reading groups are, of course, an established way of sharing reading experiences. Essex Libraries now supports over 200 'Booktalk' groups and produces a quarterly newsletter for readers and reading groups. The 'Booktalk' section of the website enhances the service in a variety of ways. There is a searchable directory of reading groups, with short descriptions giving a reading flavour of each group. Current and previous 'Booktalk' newsletters are available electronically. The 'Reading Lives' section encourages further reading journeys of discovery.

Future of the site

The website has demonstrated real benefits to readers and is now very much part of the core service provided by Essex Libraries. As such it will continually develop and seek to engage readers in different ways. Autumn 2002 will see the launch of a children's section of Ask Chris. (Turner, 2002)

One of the main advantages that new media have over traditional print-based materials is their ability to allow increased interactivity. From a simple 'Choose your own adventure story' of the 1980s, to sophisticated online interactive fiction texts, from websites that allow children to comment on and review their reading through online discussions between author and reader to interactive texts which allow the reader to determine the way the story will go, there are numerous opportunities for readers to engage with the text and the author of the text.

Case Study: Stories from the Web

www.storiesfromtheweb.org

The Stories from the Web project provides children with opportunities to explore their reading choices and interact with authors. The website includes a section that allows children to offer continuations of texts started by key children's authors. Doreen Williams from Birmingham Libraries' Centre for the Child describes the project and identifies its key components and benefits to children:

> Stories from the Web is a website designed to encourage young people aged 8–11 years to enjoy finding out about books, authors and publishers. In conjunction with the website which averages around 1800 user sessions daily, some library authorities have delivered special Stories from the Web clubs where young people are guided through a programme of reader development sessions designed to develop literacy skills through the range of activities which accompany the book extracts featured.
>
> *Background and funding*
>
> Librarians were asking themselves how libraries could sustain the interest of young people in the future.

Would personal computers (PCs) detract from libraries and books? It was evident for most libraries that book borrowing figures were in decline; how could libraries compete with new technologies? Libraries needed to embrace new technologies to complement traditional library services whilst retaining and gaining the interest of young people. The UK Office for Library Networking (UKOLN) had created a website based around R. L. Stevenson's *Treasure Island*, recognising that young people enjoyed both reading the story text and undertaking activities based on the story.

During the same period staff in the newly opened Centre for the Child realised that families using the new facility of CD-ROMs were more likely to request to use storybook CD-ROMs than information based products, unless for a specific homework enquiry. The Manager met with staff from UKOLN and they agreed further research would be beneficial. As a result a two year research grant was secured from the Library and Information Commission (now Re:source), with Birmingham, Bristol and Leeds Library Services and UKOLN forming the Managing Partner Steering Group.

The research period commencing 1997 proved a success and subsequently a bid was secured from DCMS/Wolfson for the period July 2000–June 2001. This new funding enabled Stories from the Web to expand to a total of twelve authorities across England. Since July 2001 Birmingham Libraries has supported the website and is considering other sustainable funding models to ensure this successful website will continue as a resource for reader development work.

Development of website

Stories from the Web has continued to utilise funding to develop the website in response to both the success and the growing demand. The most significant development was the website becoming database driven from March 2002; this ensures that the large quantities of work submitted by young people around the world is published on the site the following day. The introduction of password protected areas for each Stories from the Web club member to develop their individual Reader development portfolio has proved a huge success because it enables them to showcase their work to family and friends and continue to develop their portfolio after completing the programme of activity at the library club. The latest development in response to the wide age range submitting work to the site is the new area for 11–14 year olds (launched September, 2002). This area of the site is different in design and content in response to consultation with the 13–14 age range.

How does 'Stories from the Web' help young people's reading skills?

Evaluation is an important element for the Stories from the Web team when considering both the impact and future developments. Young people are given the opportunity through 'Feedback Frenzy' to share their views about the site. In addition questionnaires have been designed for club members, staff and parents relating to the club activities and an online questionnaire was designed during the DCMS/Wolfson funded period. Comments collated from the above are briefly summarised below and clearly show how young people have responded to Stories from the Web:

- young people's confidence grows as a result of attending Stories from the Web and seeing their work published on the site
- parents have commented that teachers have noticed a difference in several of the children in relation to their willingness to look at books and write creatively

- parents and siblings of young people attending clubs who were not traditional library users have become members of libraries as a result of coming to bring their children along for club sessions and finding out about libraries
- success relating to young people with dyslexia has been highlighted, particularly in relation to their confidence
- some adults have commented about spellings and grammar not being corrected, however children enjoy being able to focus on the creative writing aspect and are spurred on by knowing the work they produce will be valued and published in a nonjudgmental way
- club members enjoyed meeting authors and emailing authors at the club sessions
- young people enjoyed meeting other young people away from the school environment.

It appears that young people are encouraged by the nonjudgmental framework provided through the website and that they enjoy attending club sessions in the relaxed atmosphere. It is questionable whether they see it as a 'learning' activity, rather they appear to see it as an opportunity to belong to a club or online community that ensures the publication of their work. Observation of the young people would suggest that the focus is the activity and that through this online activity they are enthused to look for the books or other titles written by authors featured on the site. (Williams, 2002)

Alternative media and increased interest in the text

As suggested above, rather than detracting from reading, the use of alternative media, particularly when it is book related, can result in an increased interest in the original, written text :

> their anxiety is clearly misplaced, for far from discouraging children from reading, television and film adaptations have given birth to a vigorous new publishing activity – the book of the film/programme. Indeed, since research first began into the relationship between adaptations and reading it has been shown that broadcast adaptations stimulate reading of the original and other works by the same author. . . . In the period 1985–1990 UK children's book sales increased by 170 per cent, precisely the period during which domestic sales of VCRs also peaked and the end of children's reading as a leisure activity was gloomily predicted. (Reynolds, 1993, 104)

It is impossible to consider this issue without mentioning the amazing popularity of the Harry Potter books and the revival of interest in *The Lord of the Rings* since the production of the first two films of each set of stories. Harry Potter books have been consistently in the top ten bestseller lists. To date (January 2003) *Harry Potter and the Philosopher's Stone* has been in the top 50 children's bestsellers for a total of 290 weeks. It is questionable whether it would have maintained this phenomenal success without the boost of the two films released in the Novembers of 2001 and 2002. An examination of the book sales for this period demonstrates a resurgence in sales immediately after the distribution of the films.

Reynolds suggests that a previous viewing of a text before coming to the written word allows for the reader to be familiar with the text and therefore have increased confidence when approaching the written word: 'the child . . . is almost invariably being introduced to a work which is capable of providing a rich and satisfying reading experience if s/he decides to seek out the original work on which the adaptation is based' (Reynolds, 1993, 104).

Despite the continued resistance to new media on the part of adults it is evident that children will continue to engage with these texts and, as a number of writers have pointed out, it is the adults who may need to learn how to teach and develop these new literacy skills. There is considerable support for the view that adults could develop these skills in conjunction with the child through joint 'reading and sharing of a variety of popular culture texts' (Bearne, 2000, 145).

Reading communities

In Chapter 1 the importance to the individual of sharing their reading experiences was highlighted. The potential for ICT to provide opportunities for readers to interact with texts, other readers, and with others in the fiction supply chain (from the author onwards) has received increasing recognition. These connections may be made through general sites such as Readerville, where the only criteria is a love of reading *per se* to very specific genre-based and fanzine sites such as Chaletopia, a site dedicated to the Chalet School stories. (Unfortunately this latter website is no longer accessible. This is an indication of the problem of fan-based websites which may be closed because the owner loses interest or because of publisher pressure as experienced by the creators of a number of Harry Potter fan-based sites). As outlined in *The Bookseller* (2001a) Tom Porter, co-founder of Pedalo, a website design company specializing in sites for authors, noted the desire for more information about authors, their lives and thought processes, leading to some forward-thinking authors, such as Jeanette Winterson, enlisting Pedalo to develop sophisticated sites to allow interaction between author and reader.

HarperCollins has been at the forefront of UK book publishers who are prepared to take risks with the new technology. Their Fire and Water site provides links to information about more than 200 authors. The BBC World Service and publishers such as Penguin have also launched their own online book groups to link readers virtually, unrestricted by time or geography.

The use of communications technology such as e-mail and the internet enables virtual reading communities to become established, linking like-minded people around the globe. Projects such as Stories from the Web allow readers to interact with authors through online discussion and by allowing children to engage in writing activities with the creators of texts. Initiatives such as Ask Chris allow readers to interact with each other.

Outside of libraries the promotional power of the internet is increasingly recognized by other players in the world of books. World Book Day 2003 will see the first online reading festival. The first online writer in residence in the UK, Martyn Bedford, has already taken part in the Ilkley Literature Festival (Bookseller, 2000). The organizers recognized the importance of using the potential of the internet to do something different and not merely to replicate the print form electronically. The internet has the potential to do much more than the printed form and it is this interactivity which is explored in later sections on e-books and interactive fiction.

Access to fiction

One of the most enduring problems with fiction, particularly in a library context, has been the difficulties surrounding the cataloguing of fiction and accessibility for users. A number of studies have identified that the A–Z sequence proves both daunting and difficult for readers to negotiate (Sear and Jennings, 1991). It has been suggested that users prefer to make their selections from smaller, browser-type collections. Libraries have traditionally tried to overcome some of these problems by providing genre-specific collections, either shelved separately or notionally indicated by a series of relevant spine labels and shelved in the A–Z sequence. This method provides limited possibilities for categorization, however, and as fiction genres become increasingly complex it is difficult to decide on how to categorize any individual title. Each library authority will approach this problem in a different way. There is no national or international standard for organizing genre-based fiction.

Library borrowers have often found their own strategies to get around this problem. The library returns trolley has long been recognized as a haunt for less confident readers who wish to find their next read, partly because this represents an apparent recommended section because someone has already borrowed the books! This rather hit-and-miss method of selection has provided the basis for new and innovative ways of providing access to fiction on library shelves. The success of focused promotional initiatives undertaken by Branching Out and Well Worth Reading, discussed elsewhere in this book, have demonstrated that readers are responsive to such strategies as they make choosing fiction more satisfying and potentially more successful.

Physical access is not, though, the main problem readers are likely to encounter, as Davies (2002) suggests '[a] key factor is bringing suitable reading to people's attention'. Cataloguing and classification procedures also make it difficult for readers to access books beyond the basic author and title search facility. There have been a number of print-based resources which allow for the easier access of suitable reading material, books such as *The Bloomsbury Good Reading Guide* (McLeish,

1996) and *Who Else Writes Like? A readers' guide to fiction authors* (Huse, 2002). Amazon.com has utilized this idea effectively by including links for potential buyers such as 'people who bought this title also bought . . .', although this may not be the best way of providing support as Davies (2002) notes: 'it may not offer perfection, but its value for some circumstances is convincing.'

However, if we revisit the concept of the returns trolley and the motivations mentioned in Chapter 1, it would appear that this more subjective and personal approach may be what many readers require. Readers employ diverse strategies to aid them in the selection of their reading matter and these methods are frequently based on feelings rather than any objective or scientific criteria. Annie Proulx's choice of a book by the colour of its cover, the choice of a book by mood and the importance of previous reading experiences may all be determiners of future reading choices.

Fiction and information retrieval

Below, academics Pauline Rafferty and Jane Faux (2002) explore traditional and new approaches to help readers access fiction:

> The tendency within 'classic' universal classification schemes created in the 19th century was to facilitate access to fiction from an academic perspective. The Dewey Decimal Classification (DDC), the Library of Congress Classification (LCC) and the Universal Decimal Classification (UDC) contain classes for literature, with the main subdivision in each case being language. Further subdivision is possible based on literary form, historical period or the works of an individual author (Riesthuis, 1997). None of the major classification schemes allow for topical access to works of fiction, which is the starting point of many library users' fiction requests. Fiction analysis and classification historically has been the poor relation, but in recent years this has changed as innovative retrieval systems such as Bookhouse and Book Forager attempt to provide subject access to works of fiction. Since 1997, the British Library has assigned genre headings to works of fiction catalogued for the BNB (British National Bibliography). These genre headings are applied in accordance with the ALA's *Guidelines on subject access to individual works of fiction*. In the USA, the OCLC/LC Fiction Project has enriched catalogue records for works of fiction to allow access by form/genre, characters or groups of characters, geographical setting and topic (Down, 1995). However, despite detailed guidelines for cataloguers, determining the subject or topic of a work of fiction is still open to a degree of subjectivity.
>
> The development of fiction classification schemes grew out of a desire to provide some degree of topical or subject access to works of fiction. Baker and Shepherd (1987) identified three basic principles inherent in early fiction classification schemes that are still used and accepted today:

- 'fiction classification should make it easier for library users to find the types of fictional work they want
- any method of subdivision that serves to guide patrons to the type of book desired should be used
- fiction classification should perform the valuable function of exposing readers to authors they might otherwise overlook.

While the basic principles of designing fiction classification schemes may be widely accepted, the starting point for designing such schemes is not. Clare Beghtol (1994, 91) discussed the 'warrant' for a classification system, defining warrant as:

> the set of rationalizations and justifications that are invoked to govern judgements about what classes and concepts are to appear in the system and how they are to be structured in relation to each other.

Beghtol concluded that the warrant for a fiction classification scheme can be drawn either from the fiction itself or from the requirements of the users of fiction, clearly expressing her own preference for a warrant drawn from the literature. Annelise Pejtersen is another prolific contributor to the discussion surrounding fiction classification and a vocal proponent of the user warrant concept.

Using genre to classify fiction in public libraries

Genre classification schemes are frequently used in public libraries as opposed to one alphabetical sequence of fiction. Genre classification involves the division of all or part of the fiction stock into broad categories e.g. 'crime' or 'romance'. Genre categories are not mutually exclusive and therefore, as Iivonen (1988) explained, 'the genre in fiction is not a class but a type as it is based on the family similarity'.

A novel might fit into two or more categories in any particular genre classification scheme. This leads to problems, as the novel can only be physically allocated to one category. The fact that only one aspect of a novel's content can be highlighted is the major drawback of genre classification schemes.

Several possibilities exist for the shelving of genre categories; different genres may be denoted by spine labels and the books left interfiled within an alphabetical fiction sequence, books of selected genres may be physically separated from the rest of the fiction stock, or indeed all stock may be physically separated into different genre categories. The impact of these various methods of shelving genre categories has been investigated in a number of experiments, but the results are somewhat inconclusive (Baker and Shepherd, 1987; Saarti, 1997 and Cannell and McCluskey, 1996).

The Bookhouse System

Pejtersen began her studies of fiction classification by critiquing the use of genre classification as the sole method of organising fiction. Her view was that fiction retrieval needed a deeper, multi-dimensional treatment because:

- single genre classification or organising fiction by author's name ignores the multidimensional needs of the user
- and the result of using genre classification in particular is that there are a large number of works which remain unclassified.

Pejtersen analysed the content of user–librarian conversations in Danish public libraries, and identified four dimensions in which users subconsciously classify fiction: subject matter; frame; author's intention; and accessibility. During the 1970s she developed the Analysis and Mediation of Publications (AMP) multidimensional indexing system which was used in card catalogues, but could not be used for filing. The books were still shelved alphabetically by author. Pejtersen recognised the potential of separating the classification scheme from the shelving arrangement for fiction, thereby allowing multiple aspects of a novel's content to be classified. This separation is not unlike the approach taken in the virtual environment of internet bookshops, where novels can be simultaneously located in any number of different categories.

The widespread development of computerised cataloguing systems enabled Pejtersen to automate the project through the design and implementation of the GUI-fronted, interactive Bookhouse system. Pejtersen's design brief was to design an OPAC system which would accommodate the addition of supplementary information to the basic book descriptions in existing card catalogues and would provide an interface to the database comprising a uniform series of displays which can be matched to varied levels of user abilities. A framework for subject analysis was developed for the project and a thesaurus of controlled terms and rules for indexing were developed, 'to ensure a consistent and suitable vocabulary, and to reduce, as far as possible, the subjectivity of judgments within categories such as author intentions' (Pejtersen, 1989).

Working from the principle of literary warrant, Beghtol (1994) established four fundamental data categories for fiction: characters; events; spaces; and times. From these fundamental data categories, Beghtol developed the Experimental Fiction Analysis System (EFAS) for use in a computerised library environment. MacLennan (1996) argued that the complexity of EFAS may deter libraries from implementing it. Indeed, no attempts to implement EFAS have been recorded.

whichbook.net and reader development

The Society of Chief Librarians' initiative, Branching Out, has played an important role in developing innovative 'reader development' projects within public libraries in England and Wales during the last three years. One of the Branching Out managed projects was the development of a fiction retrieval system, Book Forager, now re-launched as 'whichbook.net', which runs on Youmeus software developed by Applied Psychology

Research. The philosophy underpinning Book Forager is that as the 'subject approach' to fiction is multi-dimensional, fiction retrieval systems should allow readers to search for fiction using 'affective dimension' searching rather than confining searches to known-item searching or to genre-based searching. The books which make up the project's dataset are read by a team of 150 people drawn from public libraries and literature organisations who have been trained to create entries. The system has been built on the assumption that it is possible to train people to interpret both the fictional texts and the controlled vocabulary of the Book Forager indexing language in a relatively standard way. It has been designed on the principle that meaning resides (almost) entirely within the text and that its representation within the artificial language of the indexing system is fairly straightforward and unproblematic. (Rafferty and Faux, 2002)

Case Study – whichbook.net

ICT has clearly increased significantly the opportunities for classifying and cataloguing fiction and for allowing the reader greater access to fiction. As identified above, one of the most innovative projects in recent years has been the development of whichbook.net. Dr Daniel Brown, Founder and Deputy Chairman, Applied Psychology Research Ltd, outlines the rationale behind the project:

whichbook.net is the result of a creative synergy between different disciplines. In 1997 I had just founded Applied Psychology Research (APR) with John Turner when I met Rachel Van Riel of Opening the Book. Rachel's imaginative approach to promoting literature from the reader's point of view offered exactly the sort of opportunity we were looking for.

APR worked to design new navigation systems that harnessed the power of technology to offer multiple variable choices in an intuitive way. Our first product, later developed into Youmeus™, was called Forager™ and was used to power sites such as lastminute.com.

The conditions necessary for the development of whichbook.net were firstly, the creative partnership between APR and Opening the Book; secondly, the commitment of the Society of Chief Librarians and the involvement of librarians to create the data; and thirdly, the financial support of the Arts Council and the New Opportunities Fund.

At the heart of whichbook.net is Opening the Book's concept of creative reading – empowering readers to analyse their own reading needs and preferences in order to get more out of their reading (Van Riel and Fowler, 1996). APR's powerful software presents reading choices in a way that is playful, responsive and mind-expanding; there are 20 million different permutations possible, all easily accessible from just two screens.

The choices cover the full spectrum of human emotions – do you want a book that is disgusting, funny, optimistic, unusual . . .? You can mix and blend different quantities of these ingredients to suit your mood of the moment. Within seconds whichbook.net finds books that match your requirements. In addition to the emotional effect of the book, the user can specify the length; the age/race/gender/sexuality of the lead character; the plot shape; the country the book is set in.

whichbook.net is now a unique web resource for readers, the most sophisticated book-choosing tool in the world. It enables readers to make choices which are unavailable to them by any other method. The element of play, combined with speed and ease of use, encourages readers to experiment; the range of

> titles that fulfil a specific set of preferences means that readers are always discovering new authors.
>
> In order for information to be useful it must be ordered and filtered according to our needs, tastes and preferences to support the decision to be made at any one time.
>
> Choosing a book to read from the tens of thousands available is an impossibly difficult decision. whichbook.net makes it easy, individual and fun. (Brown, 2002)

whichbook.net focuses on readers rather on library retrieval systems and hence is responding to a fundamental tenet of reader development, that the reader is and should be at the centre of any reader development activity. This compares with much traditional cataloguing and classification which has focused on how to make life easier for the professional librarian rather than examining the reader and their needs.

However, whichbook.net is not without its problems. It relies on a manual process for the categorizing of books on the scales assigned to the various moods. Despite substantial training of the assessors and discussion sessions, it is always likely that there will be disparity between the opinions of different assessors and, therefore, of different readers, as to where a book fits on any one scale. This then is a subjective approach to fiction retrieval rather than a systematic or scientific approach.

whichbook.net is now managed by Openlibraries Ltd, a company created by Opening the Book and the Society of Chief Librarians. Openlibraries has been awarded £350,000 from the New Opportunities Fund to expand whichbook.net over the next two years, by increasing the number of titles on the system and by creating links between whichbook.net and public library catalogues on the web (Branching Out).

E-books and fiction

E-books or electronic books have quickly become an integral part of non-fiction publishing and there are many companies who make non-fiction e-texts available for libraries. The case for e-fiction, however, is much less clear-cut. E-books lend themselves to the academic market where students, lecturers and researchers often want to search large texts for relatively small items of information. There is still a strong resistance to reading on screen when it comes to leisure reading, however. The concern about the impossibility of laying in bed cuddled up with a computer or a laptop has largely been circumvented by the arrival of the PDA (personal digital assistant). However this has not lead to an overnight acceptance of the technology for the reading of fiction.

It is difficult to find a clear-cut definition of what constitutes an e-book although Ormes provides a useful explanation in her *An e-book primer*:

> the term e-book is used specifically to describe a text which requires the use of e-book software or hardware to be read. This software or hardware reproduces the text in a high-quality, easy-to-read digital format which aims to replicate the text quality available in a paper-based book. (Ormes, n.d.)

Garrod (2002) indicates that no single item makes an e-book, rather it 'comprises hardware, software and content'.

There are numerous ways in which e-content can be delivered to readers and the terms e-books and hypertext can encompass many texts from simple transposition of the printed word to screen, through traditional texts solely or simultaneously produced in an electronic format to fully interactive texts designed specifically to use the unique capabilities of the electronic medium.

Libraries face a number of difficulties in making e-books available. Numerous decisions need to be made in relation to hardware, software and the circulation of e-books. The hardware possibilities range from the highly portable palmtops and PDAs to desktop computers on which e-books can be viewed online or downloaded. Ormes notes the difficulties for libraries with this new technology:

> The challenge for libraries is how to integrate this new format of texts into the traditional library service model. E-books are not physical items and so do not fit into existing acquisition or circulation models. However, judging from the millions being spent on the development of the e-book market by mainstream publishers like Simon & Schuster, Random House and Time Warner, e-books are a challenge that libraries cannot afford to ignore.
> (Ormes, n.d.)

Libraries 'lending' these items need to consider how the texts will be 'returned' to the library shelf. As with traditional books, libraries also have to ensure that a single copy of an e-book is only on loan to one person at a time. The traditional structures of library circulation therefore have to be adapted so they can apply to these virtual texts. Ormes indicates how such a system would operate:

> Each e-book will be automatically issued with an encrypted certificate. As well as including information about how long the book is available for loan, the certificate will also prevent it from being copied to another reader. At the end of the loan period this certificate will become invalid and the e-book will automatically delete itself from the library user's e-book reader. The library catalogue will then automatically make a copy of this e-book available for loan again. No overdue notices need to be sent out, no fines need to be collected and the library does not need to be visited. (Ormes, n.d.)

Ormes notes the necessity of libraries providing the equipment to permit these books to be read because of the low penetration of the market in terms of handheld readers. It is to be hoped that in the future libraries will merely lend the text and readers will supply their own handheld reading devices on which to access the books.

There are increasing numbers of e-books available, both freely on the internet and as commercial products which have to be purchased. Early attempts to produce electronic texts include initiatives such as Project Gutenberg which makes out-of-copyright texts available free online (Project Gutenberg). Alternatively, as already noted, many mainstream publishers are producing e-books alongside traditional texts, for example in August 2000, 'Farrar Straus and Giroux became one of the first publishers to produce an e-book for young adults, with the simultaneous e-book and p-book (traditional print book) release of *Joey Pigza Loses Control* by Jack Gantos. Although the publishers noted that press response was enthusiastic, the paying public are proving to be much more conservative' (Maughan, 2001). By January 2001 the five Gantos books available via the Barnes and Noble website had sold fewer than 75 copies each. This lack of enthusiasm was also noted by Dearnley and Collinge in a scheme operated at Market Harborough Library, where trials with different age groups produced a lack of excitement among readers and highlighted a number of managerial, operational and technical problems (Dearnley and Collinge, 2002, 39).

E-publishing is also providing opportunities for new material to become more widely available via the internet. For example Storycircus makes stories available free to parents online with the aim of using 'electronic media to deliver a love of stories to children' (Bookseller, 2001b). Hosts include e-parents.org which features some of the fiction written for Storycircus. It is funded by 'host' sites who are charged for a 'story service'. An alternative model is that of StoryPlus which charges parents a small fee for accessing the online material and provides royalties to authors through Scribum.com which operates as a 'clearing house' for their work (Bookseller, 2001b).

There are numerous opportunities for e-publishing and the future appears to offer increased opportunities of access to a range of fiction and a wider range of material from authors who may find it difficult to get their material published through more traditional routes.

Interactive fiction

The key advantage of electronic fiction is its interactivity. Academic Robert Hidderley (2002) discusses some of the key features and examples of interactive fiction:

> The phrase 'Interactive Fiction' (IF) is being used to describe a genre of products that could be described as fictional but are different to conventional printed novels and stories. Fiction has always included more than just printed texts. For example performances and recitations can both be fictional and need not ever have existed as printed 'hard-copy'. The experience of the consumer of these fictional products is likely to be a different one to that of the consumer of a printed fictional text but it is, nonetheless, the consumption of fiction. Where are the boundaries in a discussion about 'interactive fiction'? Some, like Granade (2000), limit the meaning of IF to computerised interactive games. It would not seem unreasonable, though, to include 'fictional experiences', for example computer games, films and videos as well as text-based fiction, allowing a broad, inclusive, definition of 'fiction' to be taken.

The consumption of a piece of fiction, whether printed, performed or contributed to, is a search for meaning and understanding. If we first consider printed fiction, 'meaning' is generated firstly between the author and their [emerging] work and then between the reader and the author's [finished] work. The balance between the author's role in the creation of printed fiction and the reader's role in consuming that fiction are changing. Readers have more, and different, opportunities to understand fictional products and may become the author to varying degrees in the construction of the text or fictional experience.

Fiction and the struggle for meaning

Graddol (1994a) discusses the nature of text. He expands the meaning of text from a collection of words to include any kind of 'media' item. For example, a poem recited live in front of an audience, or a film, could both be considered as texts. This expansion of the term is related to a discussion of *semiotics*. Graddol (1994a) uses the phrase 'the semiotic materiality of a text' to describe two sides to a text. The *signifier* of a text is its form: printed word, recorded sound, video, film (or website?). The *signified* part of a text is its content or meaning.

Graddol (1994b) reviews language as a theory of communication. He identifies three communication models: structuralism, social and post-modern models. It is the third model, the post-modern, that is of most relevance to this discussion of interactivity and fiction. In the post-modern model, '. . . meaning arises ephemerally and precariously from an intimate interaction with context and the social activities of participants.'

In the post-modern model of language there is no single unproblematic meaning to a text. Rather, readers will respond to a text depending on their ideological states, culture and previous experiences. Further, an individual's interpretation of a text is not fixed but will change as their experiences widen and discussions regarding the text's meaning occur. *Little Red Riding Hood* is generally thought of as a child-oriented fairy story that is told to, and consumed by, small children. However, many interpretations, including warnings about strangers, child abuse or paedophilia, are possible but such interpretations are unlikely to be made by the infant audience.

A fundamental role that readers play in the consumption of fiction is their use of their own imagination. Depending on the author's objectives, the dependence on a reader's imagination may be increased, for example by only describing scenarios in an incomplete or abbreviated fashion. In the case of text-based fiction the reader must use their own imagination and this may lead to different interpretations of the text. How many times has someone said that a television adaptation of a book isn't satisfying because the actor who plays a character is different to how the viewer imagined them? In the cases of film and plays the freedom to imagine is much reduced, the issue of visualisation is solved by the director's choice of actor for the part. Thus the interaction is different and possibly more limited.

Interaction, in the context of fiction, can be considered as a reader's opportunity to *personalise* the experience of consuming the fictional product. All fiction has some opportunities, ranging from empathising with a character in a film to imagining the appearance of a character in a book. However, these interactions with the text are relatively *passive*, they are opportunities provided [or not] by the author/director. These opportunities for interaction may change the experience of the text for an individual but there remains a corpus on which the interaction builds.

Opportunities for reader interaction are expanding, it is now possible to play a more *active* role in the consumption of a 'text'. It is, for example, now possible to choose outcomes of plays, choose narrative structures (Ryman, 1997), create and guide characters within a fictional framework, determine the next scene in a film (Urban Ephemera, 2000) and become a character in a media experience (Online Caroline, 2000).

Structure and choice

The structure of a text is the order in which a reader consumes the text. It may be tempting to think of the structure of fiction being like a fairy story. In *Little Red Riding Hood* the structure is strictly time based, beginning at the start and following a strict 'what happens next' sequence, a linear narrative. However, much fiction is not of such a simple form although there are many examples of strictly time-oriented progressions. An author can choose to alter the structure so that events unfold for the reader but outside a conventional time based sequence. For example, in the crime novel *Playing for the Ashes* (George, 1995), Olivia unfolds details of her life in the past. This is an example of restructuring the reader's exposure to the time-sequenced events.

When a reader of a fictional text (or viewer of a play or film) consumes the product they are under the explicit control of the author. The words that are used, the scenes as they unfold and the narrative structure (the order of the events) is the author's domain and the reader has no choice but to accept it. The reader can, if they choose, subvert this control by, for example, jumping ahead, missing out pages or chapters but this ceases to be a complete or satisfying activity because the product has been designed as a whole, to be read in its entirety from beginning to end. The same principle applies to plays and films but the opportunities for readers [viewers] to subvert the director's control are more limited.

A hypertext, in its simplest form, is a collection of 'chunks' of text. However, unlike a conventional book a hypertext does not have a single sequence. A hypertext may include a more complex structure, than the simple sequence, that allows the reader to choose what 'chunk' of text to read next. Landow (1992) discusses how hypertext challenges all narrative and literary forms based on linearity. For example the plot in a piece of fiction cannot be written in the same way in a hypertext. Landow observes that authors have experimented with hypertext-like forms well before hypertext systems became an electronic reality. One of the essential differences between text and hypertext is the notion of an ending. The consumption of a text, or a hypertext, always has a beginning and a reader knows, in the case of a linear text, if they have stopped before reaching the end or missed out sections of text. The end in a hypertext is defined by the reader's cessation of reading that may or may not be after the entire consumption of the text. Even a beginning in a hypertext may not be fixed. Entry points may be very varied and the idea that there is no starting point or locus from where decisions begin is no more or less difficult than having multiple branches from a particular chunk of text.

Some hypertexts are more sophisticated than simple collections of paragraphs that are linked together in some form of network. The simplest kind give readers limited choices at each stage. *253* (Ryman, 1997) is an example of one such hypertext novel. The author can maintain some control over the readership by limiting the choice of pathways through the collection of text chunks and, in some systems, by making chunks accessible only after other pages have been visited. Likewise the demands on the reader, or necessity to interact, are increased because without their choices the text will not unfold.

The Hyperizons (Shumate, 1997) website provides links and summaries to many fictional hypertexts. The site lists over 27 separate authors and many individual hypertexts. The site also provides an on-line guide to hypertext theory and criticism. Johnson and Oliva (1996) summarise key issues to consider in an analysis of internet, particularly hypertext, texts.

Other forms of fiction

It is generally agreed that IF products began to appear in the early to mid 1970s. There are, generally, two kinds of IF, the graphical and the text-oriented types. Meier (2000) identifies fourteen different types of content that may be present in an interactive fiction product. Aultman (2000) provides an introduction to the kinds of interaction available to readers and characters in an IF product.

The game that is played out between the participants constructs the story, a work of fiction within a fictional environment. The interaction is rich, readers choose characters and their attributes, how those characters interact with the environment and interact with other characters and how the fictional framework (world) evolves.

OnLine Caroline (2000) was an example of an interactive, fictional multimedia environment. The reader interacted with 'Caroline' via email and web page responses. There was a 'web-cam' that allowed the reader to view events in Caroline's flat (although the web-cam actually showed pre-recorded film clips). The reader interacted with the story by providing personal details that were incorporated into the email story and by helping Caroline to make decisions. The environment was quite convincing in that, apart from the serialised/soap-opera like episodes, it could have been a real 'electronic' friendship. *OnLine Caroline* was a 24 episode, fictional, multimedia [soap-opera] experience.

In the past, the author of a text had significant authority over the text. Some forms, particularly oral storytelling, mingle the role of author with that of the actor in determining the contents and structure of the text. Technology, in the form of hypertext and multimedia, has accelerated the opportunities for, and examples of, texts that are 'multi-linear'. Multi-linear texts are much more the product of a reader's choices and imagination than earlier 'linear' texts, thus blurring the distinction between author and reader. Some on-line works encourage readers to participate in writing new parts of the text thus creating a collaborative text.

Does interactive fiction therefore lead to a situation whereby there is no longer a shared meaning of a text? Whilst some people may believe that interactive fiction cannot provide a single, shared experience, IF seems to have developed from earlier [non-computerised] literary efforts. Rather than see IF as a negative development, IF should be viewed as a different genre, with different opportunities and demands. At the heart of this changed experience is the shift from 'authorship and readership' into 'authorship and reader/author-ship'. (Hidderley, 2002)

Conclusion

There are evident tensions between the new technologies and reader development, particularly in the field of children's reading. However it is clear that there are many innovative initiatives which make use of the opportunities provided by the new technologies to engage with readers. One of the key advantages of these new technologies, including the internet and e-books, is their potential for interactivity. This supports the concept of the 'creative reader' as discussed in Chapter 3 and allows for readers to interact with not only the texts but also the authors and creators of texts. It is this concept of interactivity with texts that provides most opportunities for future development.

References and further reading

APR. Available at www.aprsmartlogik.com. [Accessed 17.03.03]

Aultman, J. W. (2000) *A Beginner's Guide to Interactive Fiction*, I-F Archive Edition. Available at www.ifarchive.org/if-archive/starters/Beginner.txt. [Accessed 1.11.01]

Baker, S. L. and Shepherd, G. W. (1987) Fiction Classification Schemes: the principles behind them and their success, *RQ*, **27** (2), 245–51.

BBC World Service/ Available at www.bbc.co.uk/worldservice/programmes/world_book_club.shtml. [Accessed 03.01.03]

Bearne, E. (2000) Past Perfect and Future Conditional: the challenge of new texts. In Hodges, G. C. et al. (eds) *Tales, Tellers and Texts*, London, Cassell, 145–56.

Beavis, C. (1998) Computer Games, Culture and Curriculum. In Snyder, I. (ed.) *Page to Screen*, London, Routledge, 234–55.

Beghtol, C. (1989) Access to Fiction: a problem in classification theory and practice. Part 1, *International Classification*, **16** (3), 134–40.

Beghtol, C. (1990) Access to Fiction: a problem in classification theory and practice. Part 2, *International Classification*. **17** (1), 21–7.

Beghtol, C. (1994) *The Classification of Fiction: the development of a system based on theoretical principles*, London, Scarecrow Press.

Bell, A. (1994) *Telling Stories*. In Graddol, D. and Boyd-Barrett, O. (eds), *Media Texts: authors and readers*, Milton Keynes, The Open University, 100–18.

Bell, L. J. (1980) *The Large Print Book and Its User*, London, Library Association Publishing.

Bookseller (2000) Bedford, M., Hypertexting Miriam, *The Bookseller*, 20 October 2000, 26.

Bookseller (2001a) Rickett, J., Authors of their Own Fortune, *The Bookseller*, 4 May 2001, 14.

Bookseller (2001b) Libraries in Cyberspace, *The Bookseller*, 14 December 2001.

Booktrack. Available at www.booktrack.co.uk/?pid=79. [Accessed 28.01.03]

Branching Out. Available at www.branching-out.net/. [Accessed 28.01.03]

Brown, D. (2002) Personal communication with the author.

Cambridge International Dictionary of English (2002). Available at www.dictionary.cambridge.org/. [Accessed 28.01.03]

Cannell, J. and McCluskey, E. (1996) Genrefication: fiction classification and increased circulation. In Shearer, K. D. (ed.) *Guiding the Reader to the Next Book*, London, Neal-Schuman, 159–65.

Children's Literature Research Centre (1996) *Young People's Reading at the End of the Century*, London, Roehampton Institute.

CORDIS. Available at www.cordis.lu/libraries/en/projects/chilias.html. [Accessed 28.01.03]

Darkzoo (1997) *The Darkzoo Federation – for Active Literature*. Available at www.darkzoo.net. [Accessed 03.04.03]

Davies, E (2002) *What Shall I Read Next?: developing tools for reader support*. Paper presented at 68th IFLA Conference, August, 2002. Available at www.ifla.org/IV/ifla68/papers/121-135e.pdf. [Accessed 03.01.03]

Davis, C. H. (1976) Pragmatic Expansion of an Enumerative Classification Scheme, *Journal of the American Society for Information Science*, **27** (3), 174–5.

Dearnley, J. and Collinge, M. (2002) Outlined at the Speakers Forum. In *E-books and Libraries: proceedings of a seminar. 29 November 2001*, Loughborough, Capital Planning Information and Instant Library.

Denham, D. (2000) Promotion. In Elkin, J. and Kinnell, M. (eds), *A Place for Children: public libraries as a major force in children's reading*, London, Library Association Publishing, 68–95.

Down, N. (1995) Subject Access to Individual Works of Fiction: participating in the OCLC/LC fiction project, *Cataloging and Classification Quarterly*, **20** (2), 61–9.

Eisenstein, E. (1999) The End of the Book? Some perspectives on media change. In Salwak, D. (ed.), *A Passion for Books*, London, Macmillan Press, 181–97.

Elkin, J. and Kinnell, M. (2000) *A Place for Children: public libraries as a major force in children's reading*, London, Library Association Publishing.

FOLDOC [Free online dictionary of computing]. Available at www.wombat.doc.ic.ac.uk/foldoc/. [Accessed 28.01.03]

Garrod, P. (2002) E-books for Public Libraries: opportunity or threat? In *E-books and*

Libraries: proceedings of a seminar, 29 November 2001, Loughborough, Capital Planning Information and Instant Library.

George, E. (1995) *Playing for the Ashes*, London, Bantam.

Graddol, D. (1994a) What is a Text? In Graddol, D. and Boyd-Barrett, O. (eds), *Media Texts: authors and readers*, Milton Keynes, The Open University, 40–50.

Graddol, D. (1994b) Three Models of Language Description. In Graddol, D. and Boyd-Barrett, O. (eds), *Media Texts: authors and readers*, Milton Keynes, The Open University, 1–21.

Graddol, D. and Boyd-Barrett, O. (1994) *Media Texts: authors and readers*, Milton Keynes, The Open University.

Granade, S. (2000) *Interactive Fiction*. Available at www.phy.duke.edu/~sgranade/games.html. [Accessed 27.8.02]

HarperCollins. Available at www.fireandwater.com. [Accessed 03.01.03]

Harrell, G. (1985) The Classification and Organization of Adult Fiction in Large American Public Libraries, *Public Libraries*, **24** (1), 13–14.

Harrell, G. (1996) Use of Fiction Categories in Major American Public Libraries. In Shearer, K. D. (ed.), *Guiding the Reader to the Next Book*, London, Neal-Schuman, 149–57.

Hidderley, R. (2002) Personal communication with the author.

Huse, R. and Huse, J. (2002) *Who Else Writes Like?: A readers' guide to fiction authors*, Loughborough, Library and Information Statistics Unit.

Iivonen, M. (1988) On the Library Classification of Fiction, *Scandinavian Public Library Quarterly*, **21** (1), 12–14.

Ilkley Literature Festival website. Available at www.ilkleyliteraturefestival.org.uk/redesign/page.asp?idno=17. [Accessed 03.01.03]

Jeanette Winterson website. Available at www.jeanettewinterson.com. [Accessed 03.01.03]

Jennings, B. and Sear, L. (1989) Novel Ideas: a browsing area for fiction, *Public Library Journal*, **4** (3), 41–4.

Johnson, J. and Oliva, M. (1996) *Internet Textuality: toward interactive multilinear narrative*. Available at www.tao.ca/~peter/athesis/hypertext/johnson97.html. [Accessed 27.8.02]

King, S. (2000) *The Official Stephen King Web Presence*. Available at www.stephenking.com/. [Accessed 27.8.02]

Landow, G. (1992) Hypertext: the convergence of contemporary critical theory and technology, Baltimore, The Johns Hopkins University Press, 101–61.

Library and Information Commission (1998) *Building the New Library Network*. Available at www.lic.gov.uk/publications/policy reports/building/tg12.html. [Accessed 23.01.03]

McLeish, K. (1991) *The Bloomsbury Good Reading Guide*, London, Bloomsbury.

MacLennan, A. (1996) Fiction Selection – an AI at work?, *New Library World*, **97** (112), 24–32.

Maughan, S. (2001) *A Revolution Waiting To Happen?* Available at www.publishersweekly.com/articles/20010129_94099.asp. [Accessed 23.01.03]

Meek, M. (1991) *On Being Literate*, London, The Bodley Head.

Meier, S. (2000) *Adventureland.* Available at www.lysator.liu.se/adventure/. [Accessed 27.8.02]

My Home Library. Available at www.myhomelibrary.org. [Accessed 28.01.03]

Mynott, G. and Elkin, J. (2000) The Child in the Information Age: new development in resources and services provided for children in public libraries, In Lynden, F.C. and Chapman, E. A. (eds), *Advances in Librarianship*, vol. 24, California and London, Academic Press, 157–88.

Mynott, G. et al. (2001) A Place for Children Revisited: recent developments in the provision of reading support for children by public libraries in the UK, *Journal of Librarianship and Information Science*, **33** (3), 133–44.

OnLine Caroline (2000). Available at www.onlinecaroline.com/. [Accessed 1.11.01]

OpenLibraries Ltd. Available at www.openlibraries.net. [Accessed 23.01.03]

Ormes, S. (n.d.) *An e-Book Primer.* Available at www.ukoln.ac.uk/public/earl/issuepapers/ebook.htm. [Accessed 03.01.03]

Pejtersen, A. M. (1978) Fiction and Library Classification, *Scandinavian Public Library Quarterly*, **11** (1), 5–12.

Pejtersen, A. M. (1989) The 'Bookhouse': an icon based database system for fiction retrieval in public libraries. In Clausen, H. (ed.), *Information and Innovation. Proceedings of the seventh Nordic conference for information and documentation*, Denmark, Arhus University, 165–78.

Pejtersen, A. M. and Austin, J. (1983) Fiction Retrieval: experimental design and evaluation of a search system based on users' value criteria (part 1), *Journal of Documentation*, **39** (4), 230–46.

Pejtersen, A. M. and Austin, J. (1984) Fiction Retrieval: experimental design and evaluation of a search system based on users' value criteria (part 2), *Journal of Documentation*, **40** (1), 25–35.

Penguin Book Groups. Available at www.readers.penguin.co.uk/. [Accessed 03.01.03]

Project Gutenberg. Available at www.textual.net/gutenberg/access/gtnttlnx.htm. [Accessed 23.01.03]

Rafferty, P. and Faux, J. (2002) Personal communication with the author.

Readerville. Available at www.readerville.com. [Accessed 03.01.03]

Reilly, S. N. (1995) *Interactive Fiction Page.* Available at www.cs.cmu.edu/afs/cs.cmu.edu/user/wsr/Web/IF/homepage.html. [Accessed 27/8/02]

Reynolds, K. (1993) Telly Texts: children's books and the media. In Pinsent, P. *The Power of the Page: children's books and their readers*, London, David Fulton, 103–12.

Riesthuis, G. J. A. (1997) Fiction in Need of Transcending Traditional Classification, *Information Services and Use*, **17** (2/3), 133–8.

Robinson, (1997) *Children Reading Print and Television*, London, Routledge.

Ryman, G. (1997) *253: a novel for the internet about London Underground in Seven Cars and a Crash.* Available at www.ryman-novel.com/. [Accessed 27/8/02]

Saarti, J. (1997) Feeding with the Spoon, or the Effects of Shelf Classification of Fiction on the Loaning of Fiction, *Information Services and Use*, **17** (2/3), 159–69.

Saarti, J. (2000) Fiction Indexing by Library Professionals and Users, *Scandinavian Public Library Quarterly*, **33** (4), 6–9.

Sapp, G. (1986) The Levels of Access: subject approaches to fiction, *RQ*, **25** (4), 488–97.

Schofield, J. (2000) The e-Book: and Now a New Chapter Begins, *The Guardian On-Line*, (12 October). Available at www.guardianunlimited.co.uk/Archive/Article/ 0,4273,4075120,00.html. [Accessed 27.8.02]

Scott, P. (1995) Wheels within Wheels: genre fiction in public libraries, *Australasian Public Libraries and Information Services*, **8** (4), 191–4.

Sear, L. and Jennings, B. (1991) Organizing fiction for use. In Kinnell, M. (ed.), *Managing Fiction in Libraries*, London, Library Association Publishing, 1991, 101–19.

Shumate, M. (1997) *Hyperizons*. Available at www.duke.edu/~mshumate/hyperfic.html and www.duke.edu/~mshumate/theory.html. [Accessed 27.8.02]

Sinnreich, A. (1996) *1996 A Bass Odyssey*. Available at www.users.interport.net/~sinnbest/ voyage.htm. [Accessed 1.11.01]

Stories from the Web. Available at www.storiesfromtheweb.org. [Accessed 16.01.03]

Turner, G. (1994) Film Languages. In Graddol, D. and Boyd-Barrett, O. (eds), *Media Texts: authors and readers*, Milton Keynes, The Open University, 119–35.

Turner, J. (2002) Personal communication with the author.

Urban Ephemera (n.d.) *It's Your Movie*. Available at www.urban.ephemera.com/work/britannica/your_movie.htm. [Accessed 17.03.03[]

Van Riel, R. and Fowler, O. (1996) *Opening the Book: finding a good read*, Bradford, Bradford Libraries.

whichbook.net. Available at www.whichbook.net. [Accessed 23.03.03]

Williams, D. (2002) Personal communication with the author.

World Book Day. Available at www.worldbookday.com/. [Accessed 03.01.03]

8

Reading and reader development research: the argument for quality

Briony Train

Introduction

> My challenge to you is that research must transform itself to align with the changes and not follow them. To have any power or influence in today's world, it must work alongside developments, not as a fixed-point intervention. (Kempster, 2002)

This chapter argues that there are in fact cases where research and evaluation in the field of reader development does 'align with the changes', where it is proactive rather than reactive, and where it has a lasting effect on the development of the library and information profession. It also suggests that the evaluation of an initiative is not most effectively conducted as a summative report using quantitative figures hastily collected at the end of the project, but that it should be a part of the overall process, using formative, often qualitative methods in order to investigate the impact over time.

The purpose of the chapter is to demonstrate to what extent the reader development movement has provided both the librarian and the researcher with an opportunity to develop and use many rigorous research methods, to benefit from the strengths of both qualitative and quantitative methods, in order to obtain valuable data concerning the impact of reader-centred initiatives.

> how many of us have often read in the media of research that it has cost much and simply affirmed the bleeding obvious? How many of us have experienced the reading of research proposals or reports and been as clueless as to what it was all about at the end as we were at the start? Who amongst you have reflected to yourself that the research you are engaged in is nice and interesting but will not add to the sum of things – if anything maybe complicate and obfuscate them more? (Kempster, 2002)

The above questions were asked of the UK Library and Information Research Group (LIRG), at its annual lecture in March 2002. Together they raise a key issue of this chapter, that of the role of research and evaluation not only in the life of the academic, but in the life of every library and information professional. The present author is regretfully aware that not all academic research in library and information science is directly relevant to the profession, that in a number of cases it fails not only to answer but even to ask the relevant questions, seeking only, as Kempster suggests, 'to perpetuate its own codes and behaviours'. Can we truthfully state that all research in reader development and reading research is conducted synergistically with the profession? Does it all take into account the changes that take place, the 'seismic changes that need the touchstone and the assaying of good and wholesome research calibre attention' (Kempster, 2002)?

If the researchers themselves do not ask these questions, it is hardly surprising that a degree of scepticism remains within the profession concerning the relevance of research and evaluation in reader development and reading research. The Research Assessment Exercise adds a further pressure to academic departments, requiring them to be 'research driven' in their activities. This may lead to a possible interpretation by external professionals that this work is 'research for research's sake', conducted not to advance the profession but in order to obtain a higher research rating.

In the current project culture, many public library services have been awarded grants with which to develop and trial a new aspect of service provision. The DCMS Wolfson Public Libraries Challenge Fund for reader development, for example, gave services a rare opportunity to use additional resources to create and evaluate new reader-centred initiatives. However, in their evaluation of the overall impact of the first year of funding, Wallis, Moore and Marshall (2002, 10) report that only 'a small number of projects commissioned their own independent evaluations'. This would seem to be evidence that the intervention of researchers and evaluators – often from an alien academic world – is regarded by many to be a waste of time and funding, that resources would be more usefully allocated within the project. Kempster suggests that research and evaluation have 'seemed to thrive more in the academic environment because there is a common language and understanding. . . . This is not the case in public service and in workplace environments.' Research, she argues, 'carries a stigma of taking too long, costing too much, being too difficult and missing the mark of direct relevance' (Kempster, 2002).

A further possible reason for the lack of acceptance of the role of research and evaluation in this area of the library profession is that it can be misinterpreted as a process to find justification for reducing budgets. 'Evaluation, especially on the lips of central government officials, has come to mean finding something to cut' (O'Rourke, 1994, 14).

It is certainly the case that as budgets have been reduced, accountability has become more significant, and library managers have been under pressure to demonstrate that all aspects of their service offer value for money, and at the same time can be proved to be effective and efficient.

It could also be argued that the current project culture offers a barrier to evaluation, as library services wishing to extend the lifespan of an initiative beyond the original funded period may feel that an external evaluator could persuade funding bodies that the project did not merit additional funding. It may even be the case that salaries depend on the success of the initiative, so why willingly introduce a threat to one's own career?

The context of reader development evaluation and research

As was mentioned above, the management of libraries in all sectors has in recent years become more complex, as a result of increased pressure caused by both tightening budgets and the growth of ICT and electronic networking, the latter now providing the user with instant access to that which used to be offered only by the library or information service itself. Nowhere is this pressure more apparent than in the public sector, which under the current Government is now subject to regular scrutiny. Kinnell Evans (2000) summarized this scrutiny as follows:

- External inspections and audits by government agencies such as the Audit Commission, OFSTED [the Office for Standards in Education], the Further and Higher Education funding councils;
- Measures of service effectiveness used to produce 'league tables';
- Market testing of public sector services;
- Quality and value for money initiatives such as Charter Mark and Best Value.

Prior to the implementation of such processes, very little effort had been made to fundamentally appraise the effectiveness and impact of a library or information service. Library administrators and managers were then forced to face the pressures outlined above, and it rapidly became commonplace for all public library authorities to collect data pertaining to the inputs and outputs of their services. Yet many of these data collected failed to provide a more detailed picture of the *outcomes*, of the extent to which library services were meeting their targets. As recently as 1996, Brophy and Coulling stated: 'All too often, performance measures are based on the philosophy of "measuring the measurable". The fondness of librarians for issue statistics over hard measures of in-library use illustrates this tendency' (1996, 157).

Similarly, Usherwood proposed that the evaluation of public library services must be 'much more than a mere measurement', that statistics 'are just a small part of the reality and any meaningful evaluation has to go beyond simplistic quantification' (1996, 68). Surely the 'meaningful evaluation' of a reader development initiative, to which the assessment of the reading experience is of more relevance than a quantitative calculation of people passing through the library doors, would require alternative methods in order to 'measure the *un*measurable'?

The following sections will present the characteristics of quantitative and qualitative research methods, describing ways in which they differ, ways in which each can be most effectively used to evaluate the impact of reader-centred public library services.

Quantitative and qualitative research

Before investigating the application of quantitative and qualitative methods, it would be useful to consider their definitions.

'*Quantitative research* is typically associated with the processes of enumerative induction. One of its main purposes is to discover how many and what kinds of people . . . have a particular characteristic' (Brannen, 1992, 5).

'*Qualitative research* is a process of enquiry that draws data from the context in which events occur, in an attempt to describe these occurrences, as a means of determining the process in which events are embedded and the perspectives of those participating in the events' (Gorman and Clayton, 1997, 23). 'Qualitative research methods are designed to help researchers understand people and the social and cultural contexts within which they live' (Myers, 1997, 2).

The most significant difference between the two methods is the way in which each treats the research data. At the risk of over-simplifying, quantitative research therefore tends to begin with certain questions or hypotheses and then collects data to support or contradict these assumptions. The qualitative researcher usually begins with a definition of very general questions or concepts which may change significantly during the research process.

Combined methodologies and the argument for triangulation

Many sociologists have defined triangulation in terms of using, for example, multiple data sources, researchers, theories or methods (Denzin, 1978; Jick, 1979; Patton, 1990. In Tashakkori and Teddlie, 1998, 42). The most common interpretation of triangulation is the use of multiple methods. This is believed to increase the validity of the data, as it offers the researcher the opportunity to determine to what extent – if any – the results converge. Greene et al. (in Tashakkori and Teddlie 1998, 43) reviewed more than 50 multiple method studies from the 1980s and their summary of the benefits of such methodologies included the following:

1 *Complementarity* – examining overlapping aspects of a phenomenon
2 *Initiation* – discovering paradoxes or fresh perspectives
3 *Development* – using methods sequentially, so that results from an earlier method inform the use of a subsequent method
4 *Expansion* – Mixed methods adding breadth and scope to a project.

The following comment by Boyle (2000, 92) neatly summarizes the above benefits: 'When you break away from one solitary measure of success, you do get closer to the truth.'

A number of combined methodologies that have been used to evaluate reader development initiatives in public libraries will be presented later in this chapter.

Strengths of quantitative methods

> I think that there is a terrible danger in libraries of ignoring the quantitative data that they have . . . it's defeatist and defensive, and I think that there is a lot of quantitative data that they should be proud of. The fact that there are declining issues at the moment, they should address that, but they should also celebrate the number of books that are actually borrowed and read through public libraries every year. (Forrest, 2002)

As Forrest suggests, the most obvious strength of the quantitative evaluation of reader-centred services is that systems are often already in place by which to collect data. Distributing a survey to the general public, for example, may not always be necessary, as the existing computer system has the capability of counting and measuring many aspects of the work of the library.

Not only are systems already in place to collect data, but even analysed data is sometimes ignored by the library manager. An example of this is the data collected for the CIPFA (The Chartered Institute of Public Finance and Accountancy) National Standard User Survey, which allows a large number of public library services to benchmark their services in terms of customer satisfaction. Van Riel (2002) suggests that for many library services, this experience is in some sense a wasted opportunity: 'The CIPFA survey, there's a remarkable amount of data there . . . but how is it being used?'

The issue, therefore, is not that insufficient data are collected to demonstrate the impact of services, rather that existing data may not be used particularly effectively. As Usherwood (1996, 80) confirms: 'Measurement by itself will never improve the public library service. What is required is a strategy that uses the results of measurement to assess levels of service.'

Strengths of qualitative methods

> There is a very real danger that librarians will count that which can be counted but ignore that which is important (Usherwood, 1996, 74)

Riggs' editorial, 'Let Us Stop Apologising for Qualitative Research', underlines the difficulty that many researchers have in convincing their audiences of the value of qualitative research. The primary focus of academic research has long been on quantification and, above all, precision. How does qualitative research fit into this framework? Quantitative researchers have argued that they can find no meaning in a research process that consists of 'evolvement and flexibility' (Riggs, 1998).

One of the main myths that exist regarding the goals of qualitative research is that they are narrow in focus. In fact, the aim of such research is to obtain a depth and richness of data. To demonstrate this, O'Rourke (1994, 15) gives the following example from an assessment she conducted of a creative writing course in Cleveland:

> Questions make or break research. Imagine the kind of answer you get from the question: 'Do you like your writing group?' compared with: 'What is it you like about your writing group?' The first gives you numbers – x people did or didn't like the writing group – the other gives you a feel for the experience and the issues within the group. Numbers count, but not for everything.

A further strength of qualitative research is that the data are collected from events taking place in their natural settings. In this way, argue Miles and Huberman, 'the influences of the local context are not stripped away, but are taken into account' (1994, 10). Promoting qualitative measures, the Comedia report *Borrowed Time* (1993) stated that commonly applied performance indicators could measure the quantitative elements of a service – the issue figures, reservations, etc., 'but in no way can measure the quality of the relationship between a library, its users and the geographical area it serves'.

A final point regarding the strengths of qualitative research is that such methods are often used to evaluate the impact of an activity over a prolonged period. In this way, as Miles and Huberman suggest, 'we can go far beyond "snapshots" of "what?" or "how many?" to just how and why things happen as they do' (1994, 10). The previously criticized 'evolvement and flexibility' (Riggs, 1998) arguably result in a more fluid, responsive approach to changes that take place in the course of the study.

The misinterpretation or misuse of qualitative and quantitative research

> Qualitative and quantitative research methods in librarianship and information science are not simply different ways of doing the same thing. (Riggs, 1998).

As has been illustrated, both qualitative and quantitative research have their strengths, but both can be wrongly applied, leading to inaccurate and wrongly used findings.

Quantitative research

Boyle, acknowledging that numbers are 'an absolutely vital tool for human progress' (2000, 57), proposes that their limitation is that they are relied on too heavily, before their significance has been truly determined. 'All too often, policy decisions are taken on the basis of a single number which actually just symbolizes the question, while the truth scuttles away through our hands as we try to snatch it.'

A further misuse of quantitative research is when researchers, or those interpreting research reports, extrapolate inappropriately. Van Riel (2002) gives two possible examples:

> where an individual comment has been made, that's interesting in itself, but does that necessarily mean that was true for 3,000 people? No, and you can't assert that . . . in this reading group of ten people, five said this . . . you then have a piece of research which said '50% of readers in a survey', and people are assuming that this was a massive survey.

Sadly, such misinterpretations only serve to reinforce existing scepticism concerning the validity of research into and evaluation of reader-centred initiatives.

Qualitative research

The primary misuse of qualitative research is comparable to the above example, as it involves making similarly unfounded generalizations. All too often, we see the same quotations or anecdotes – extracted from research reports – published at the head of documents that promote or advocate the benefits of the project evaluated in the report. As Forrest (2002) comments:

> I'm very sceptical about some of the qualitative approaches which are simply about testimonials. Testimonials can be very powerful, and we can all use that, but you don't need to keep repeating it. In terms of research and techniques, they're not actually going to give you another dimension. We've got the picture, we know what it's like when somebody reads a book who hasn't read for a long time, we know it's powerful . . . but we can't keep on chasing those as evidence.

Qualitative research provides the opportunity to obtain an in-depth response, based on structured or semi-structured interviews conducted with the research subjects. Direct quotations from these subjects can be powerful, and can indeed be used to promote a project or service, but only when used in their context, to give a balanced and well researched viewpoint.

Research influencing policy and practice

> Research can contribute to informed decision making, but the manner in which this is done needs to be reformulated. We are well past the time when it is possible to argue that good research will, because it is good, influence the policy process. That kind of linear relation of research to action simply is not a viable way in which to think about how knowledge can inform decision making. The relation is both more subtle and more tenuous. (Rist, 1994, 546)

Researchers completing a report concerning any public sector issue are often well aware that its destiny is to remain unused on the desk of a senior manager, in an organization in which all other staff are blissfully unaware of the document. In part, the blame undoubtedly lies with the researcher: can it be truthfully said that all research is disseminated as widely as possible? In addition to producing the original research report, other means of dissemination could include, for example, a PDF file of the report to download, summary documents for rapid reference, articles in the refereed and non-refereed professional press, promotion via mailing lists and websites, conferences and workshops.

The main difficulty, however, lies in ensuring that research findings reach staff at all levels of an organization, and to do this requires a cultural change that is beyond the realms of the academic. In her LIRG 2002 lecture, Kempster argued that it was the responsibility of all professionals – not only the senior managers – to make themselves aware of current research:

> So can there be a new alignment of research and delivery? . . . Quite frankly, we are not being very professional about our knowledge – we cannot leave good action centred research to the vagaries of happenchance and whether service leaders can bother to update their skills or translate the language of the research world. It needs effort and change on all sides because the results evidencing the impact matter enormously to us all. (Kempster, 2002)

In order for research findings to become part of future policy or practice, they must be widely promoted, not only in their original format, but also framed in such a way that their organizational benefits are apparent to the senior manager or policy maker. In other words, suggests Usherwood, 'they must influence the organisation and persuade policy makers that change along the indicated lines will be valuable' (2002, 12). Kempster (2002) exemplifies this by referring to the 'translation skills' of a researcher who had evaluated a three-year reader development initiative with 'two versions of what was going on – the in-depth and highly credible research speak and also – critically – the lite version for busy managers asking "So what?"

Case studies

This section presents examples of methodologies used for the evaluation of various reader-centred projects that have taken place in public libraries in recent years.

A cross-study evaluative tool: the DCMS/Wolfson reader development evaluation

The overall impact of all projects conducted during the first year of DCMS/Wolfson reader development funding (2000–1) was evaluated by a team of researchers from the Social Informatics Research Unit at the University of Brighton (Wallis, Moore and Marshall, 2002). The evaluation team felt that it was not possible to conduct a detailed evaluation of each of the 33 projects within the existing budget. A model was therefore developed and distributed to each project manager, the objective of which was to enable 'each of the projects to assess their own progress and achievements' (35). This model used three measures: of achievement, impact and outcome.

Margaret Wallis, Principal Lecturer, outlines some of their key findings and methodologies:

> In order that all the DCMS/Wolfson projects could be evaluated on the same basis a common evaluation model was developed which allowed each of the projects to assess their own progress and achievements. Detailed case studies of ten projects were also carried out exploring, both qualitatively and quantitatively, the work in greater depth. The information given in the project application form provided the basis for the evaluation criteria. The model used three different but related measures: of achievement, impact and outcome. These were deliberately designed as a mixture of quantitative and qualitative measures in order to assess the full richness of reader development projects.
>
> *Achievement measures*
>
> The achievement measures were essentially concerned with whether or not the project carried out the concrete activities that were specified in the proposal. They are quantitative measures and are concerned with assessing the volume of activity undertaken. At their most basic, they provide a means of accountability. Some of these measures refer to initial or preliminary activities that were required to set up the project, such as the appointment of staff or the purchase of equipment.
>
> Other achievement measures are concerned with simple counts of the activities undertaken during the course of the project. Measures of this kind include for example, the number of reading groups established or the number of publications that were produced.

Impact measures

Impact measures assess what happened as a result of the activities undertaken. They are also, mostly, quantitative. They include such things as the number of new members of the library, the rise in the number of fiction books issued, the number of children attending activity sessions. As such, they can also be seen as measures of participation.

Frequently measures of impact are expressed in terms of the degree of change that took place during the project. Thus, some projects were required to measure the extent to which book loans increased, number of hits on a web site or the extent to which people used the fiction collection.

Outcome measures

Measures of outcomes are concerned with the overall changes that occurred as a result of the project. These measures are usually qualitative and are also frequently subjective. They might, for example, assess the extent to which the project has resulted in stronger partnerships between the library and other community groups, the extent to which staff attitudes have changed, or the extent to which participation in activities has developed participants' self-esteem and confidence.

Outcome measures attempt to assess the enduring results of the project. To obtain a full picture of outcomes, it is usually necessary to review the position at the end of the project and to repeat the exercise some months or years later. With these projects, however, it was only possible to assess outcomes at the end of the projects. If evaluation is to feed back into the overall planning process of libraries it is crucial that authorities continue to monitor outcomes in the longer-term.

Monitoring the criteria

To facilitate evaluation of the project a template lists target achievements, impacts and outcomes against the final project evaluation results. In the case of the DCMS/Wolfson project evaluation project managers were also asked to assess the project in terms of difficulties encountered, particular successes and the sustainability of the project in the longer term.

All the project managers submitted final reports, which evaluated the extent to which their project met the original criteria. For some this was the first time they had had to measure and report on the extent to which a project had met its original aims, a useful development in the current climate of Best Value and performance measurement.

The results provided valuable evidence to key stakeholders, locally and nationally, of the scale of the work that took place and the value of reader development projects, both quantitatively and qualitatively. Sadly it became clear that, largely because of the short-term nature of the funding, many projects would struggle to develop sustainability in the longer term. For many projects the work ceased or was considerably scaled down at the close of the project funding. However more positively, a number of projects went on to secure further funding and, for a few, the work begun showed real evidence of being embedded in core library activity. (Wallis, 2002)

Overall, the Brighton methodology was an effective means of assessing the overall impact of the first year of DCMS/Wolfson funding. A series of measures was devised that was straightforward to use, and could be passed to individual project managers to use. This was particularly beneficial as it enabled a more widescale collection of data than would otherwise have been possible with the resources available, thereby potentially increasing the overall viability of the findings.

The weakness of the measures devised was that they failed to effectively include a longer-term perspective. The DCMS/Wolfson reader development programme did not regard the activities it funded as short term, instead it aimed to stimulate a longer-term process that would embed reader development into core public library service provision: 'The programme aims to combine the interest and proactive approach which can be generated by innovative short-term reader development projects with the creation of solid foundations for longer term reading promotion work' (Great Britain, DCMS 2001, 31).

Indeed, Wallis, Moore and Marshall (2002) noted that in devising their evaluative methodology they were particularly interested in 'the extent to which the activities funded under the programme were sustainable' (14). However, they also commented that it had been difficult – given the limitations of the resources available to them – to monitor 'the enduring results of the project': 'to obtain a complete picture in such studies it is usually necessary to review the position at the end of the project and to repeat the exercise some months or years later. With these projects, however, it was only possible to assess outcomes at the end of the projects' (8).

It is undoubtedly a disadvantage of funded projects that their evaluation rarely includes an investigation of the *actual*, rather than merely the perceived, sustainability of the initiative. Yet with a methodology that includes more qualitative measures, measures that are taken on a formative basis – during the entire course of the funded period – it could be argued that more valid evidence of the sustained impact of the project could be collected.

The combined use of qualitative and quantitative data

Mind's Eye

Further illustration of the potential sustainability of reader development initiatives can be found in the few independent evaluations that were conducted for individual projects. The following extract is taken from the evaluation report of the Mind's Eye project, an initiative targeted at all readers, but in particular at adult male readers under 50. The aim of the project was to improve the reading and library experiences of this target group, in relation to narrative non-fiction books.

> There were many examples of staff and reader responses to the Mind's Eye promotion that had been collected relatively easily during the period of the project, for example:
>
> - Staff training evaluation forms
> - Reader response forms
> - Anecdotal evidence from each.
>
> The positive examples (of which there were many) could be used in order to justify to potential funding bodies the value and impact of professionally devised book collections and promotional materials.
>
> In addition, these qualitative data could be used in combination with issue figures and new membership figures in order to support library authorities in reviewing service provision and performance, including the Best Value inspection process.
>
> The Mind's Eye promotion could be regarded as a template for the straightforward collection of both qualitative and quantitative data to be used as ongoing evidence to promote the service provided by each authority.
>
> Further library promotions using similar professionally produced materials could also help to enhance the public perception of the library service. Mind's Eye clearly had a significant impact on both customers and library staff, and has conveyed to many the idea that libraries are dynamic and responsive to readers' needs. If it is not viewed as an isolated project, but has instead helped to permanently change the way library stock is promoted, then cultural change will occur.
>
> A final recommendation would be to contact the five pilot authorities twelve months after they had finished promoting the Mind's Eye collection within their library service, in order to investigate to what extent this cultural change had taken place. (Train, 2001, 24)

As the above extract illustrates, although the funded period of the Mind's Eye project was limited to 12 months, there are ways in which the evaluation of reader development initiatives can be devised in order to increase the likelihood of the initiative being sustained and incorporated into core service provision.

Adult fiction stock quality measurement tool

As part of the Audit Commission Best Value inspection service, the reading promotion agency Opening the Book was commissioned to develop and test a tool to measure the quality of adult fiction stock in a public library service. This was designed to be:

- straightforward to administer and to interpret
- cost-effective

- visibly ‘fair’
- applicable to all sizes of authority
- possible to revise and update
- helpful – not punitive – to library managers.

The tool is based on a list of 570 titles chosen to give a representative sample of the whole range of adult fiction from classics to current popular writing. The list is not intended to be a canon or a blueprint for the ideal collection – its creators would argue that there is no such thing – but to bring together titles which will test the range of a library service’s collection. Titles do not stand on their own as absolutes; they only work when used as a whole. The whole list has a statistical rigour which was tested with 12 public library authorities and a national bookshop chain.

In selecting the 570 titles Opening the Book arranged them into 41 categories. They also identified titles within the 570 that would enable further cross-category analysis. Three cross-category areas were chosen: first novels, Black writing and books with a younger audience appeal.

The list of 570 titles with their main and cross-cutting categories was coded into a spreadsheet which is easy to complete and quickly produces the statistical analysis of the results. The booklist spreadsheet is accompanied by documentation that gives the rationale behind the assessment tool and guidance on the interpretation of the results.

The assessment tool utilizes quantitative techniques to measure quality. The data create a profile for the authority’s collection which shows the relative strengths of the 41 categories and the profile can be compared with those of other authorities. The authorities in the pilot immediately saw the benefits of this quantitative analysis and acted on the information by purchasing more stock in the categories where they were weak.

For many years the library profession has been debating the need to measure the quality of stock. At the same time as this tool was being developed for the Audit Commission, the Department for Culture, Media and Sport (DCMS) issued its draft standards for public libraries which included the aim to develop a quality index for bookstock. The DCMS has welcomed Opening the Book’s assessment tool and is now working with the Audit Commission and the Society of Chief Librarians to ensure that it is kept up to date and made available to all authorities as a self-assessment tool. Collecting data in this way can act as a stimulus for informed debate and decision making, giving library service managers the opportunity to investigate to what extent they provide the most appropriate materials for their community. It is, therefore, an example of how research and evaluation techniques can have a direct impact on professional practice and lead to service improvement.

Measuring longitudinal impact: Branching Out

The second case study shows how formative qualitative methods can be used to obtain an accurate record of the longitudinal impact of an initiative.

Branching Out was a three year initiative (1998–2001) from the Society of Chief Librarians, managed by Opening the Book and supported by the National Lottery through the Arts Council of England. The project involved the participation of 33 local authorities plus the National Library for the Blind. The aims of the project were summarized in the original project application as: 'Instead of simply making books available, library staff will work with groups and individuals both inside and outside the library to pilot new opportunities for people to explore contemporary writing and to participate in their own development as readers' (SCL, 1998, 7).

From the outset, the University of Central England in Birmingham (UCE) was the academic partner, required to evaluate the development and overall impact of the initiative (Train and Elkin, 2001b). The main objectives of the evaluation were:

- to investigate the personal and professional development of the participating librarians
- to investigate the extent to which the work of the project had an impact on colleagues and senior managers both within and beyond participating authorities
- to investigate the extent to which the outcomes of the project affected reader development service provision
- to conduct a longitudinal study (through observation and interview) of two of six projects devised during the second year of the initiative.

Many performance measurements are limited as to what they can evaluate, as the quality or impact of any service on people – staff or customers – is difficult to quantify. As a rule, local authorities undertaking a piece of research or project-based work have not tended to have sufficient time, financial support or general resources with which to evaluate their work apart from collecting basic quantitative data pertaining to, for example, issue statistics or audience figures. In addition, evaluation they have conducted has tended to take place at the end of a project, as an entirely summative piece of work.

However, in order to achieve the objectives listed above, it was clear that such an initiative could not be comprehensively evaluated using only quantitative, short-term measures: the Branching Out initiative was a sufficiently large-scale project to require a longitudinal approach. 'Longitudinal data allow the analysis of duration; permit the measurement of differences or change in a variable from one period to another, that is, the description of patterns of change over time' (Ruspini, 2000).

Table 8.1 *Examples of evaluative methods used throughout the Branching Out initiative*

Evaluative method	Dates used
Observation	
Attendance at and observation of:	
• core training days of years 1–3	Throughout the project
• planning meetings of Open Ticket and Unclassified Year 2 group projects	
• selected training sessions of the above projects	
• selected project consultancy days	
Learning Reviews:	
1 The initial exercise	02.99
2 Agents of change	01.00
3 Project-based work	08.00
4 Best Value, regional networks, personal changes	03.01
5 The overall impact of Branching Out	08.01
Skills audit:	02.99 08.01
Year 2 group projects:	
Evaluation of the impact of participation in Year 2 group projects on participants	Throughout Year 2
Evaluation of the views of Heads of Service:	
Cultural change, advocacy, staff training, future planning	07.00
Overall impact of the project	08.01

Table 8.1 gives examples of the evaluative methods used throughout the Branching Out initiative. Data such as these provided the participating local authorities with a unique opportunity to have ready access to evidence of the impact of those hitherto 'intangible' elements of their work.

Experiential learning: theory and practice

The Branching Out evaluation methodology monitored the impact of participation on the library staff, using various methods based on the concept of experiential learning. As an evaluative method this was particularly appropriate, as the training methodology used in Branching Out was also an experiential model, involving the cycle of learning, action, reflection and testing in practice. The rationale behind experiential methods is that the most effective learning is achieved when grounded in experience.

The application of experiential learning methodologies to the academic evaluation of a practical, profession-based project is not new: in 1938 Dewey underlined the relevance of experiential learning programmes in higher education. Explaining and attempting to resolve the increasing conflict between traditional educational programmes and a more progressive approach to teaching and learning, he wrote: 'I take it that the fundamental unity of the newer philosophy is found in the idea that there is an intimate and necessary relation between the processes of actual experience and education' (Dewey, 1963 (revised edition), 20).

A further leading exponent of experiential learning and the necessary relationship between professional practice and academic knowledge is Donald Schön. In his text *The Reflective Practitioner* (1991), he both describes this relationship and suggests new ways of developing it. The work of Schön has generated a great deal of debate, for example in an attempt to answer the question 'What is the reflective practitioner?', Hatten, Knapp and Salona (1997) describe 'reflection' as: 'the processing of the experience and re-evaluation of perceptions, which then become the basis of transformed or new knowledge, and decisions on further action'.

Learning reviews

As illustrated in Figure 8.1, a major focus of the evaluation of Branching Out was the impact of participation on the participating library staff, and a key method used to investigate this impact was the distribution and analysis of a series of learning reviews. A learning review is a qualitative method of evaluation that gives respondents an opportunity to reflect upon their own development during a given period (Train and Elkin, 2001a).

The structure of the learning reviews was simple: a series of qualitative questions that focused on a specific theme and contained a limited – and therefore non-intimidating – space in which to note responses. During the three years of Branching Out, five such reviews were devised:

- Learning Review One – the initial exercise
- Learning Review Two – agents of change
- Learning Review Three – project-based work
- Learning Review Four – monitoring the impact of Branching Out
- Learning Review Five – the overall impact of Branching Out.

N.B. In the original document space was provided for responses.

Learning Review Five: the overall impact of Branching Out

The aim of the final learning review is to give you the opportunity to reflect on the impact of Branching Out on your personal and professional development, and on your view of the future of the project in your authority, in the following areas:

1. Emotions
2. Your colleagues and senior managers
3. Your authority
4. Sustainability
5. Overall satisfaction
6. Any other comments.

Please answer all questions as fully as you can, in order that the overall evaluation can be as accurate a representation of your views as possible. As always, all responses will be regarded as confidential.

1. Emotions

After 3 years of involvement in Branching Out, how do you feel today about the project coming to an end?

Have your feelings towards Branching Out changed in any way since the beginning of the project? Please explain your answer.

Please indicate here two negative aspects – either personal or professional – of your involvement in Branching Out.

Please indicate here two positive aspects – either personal or professional – of your involvement in Branching Out.

2. Your colleagues and senior managers

During Branching Out, to what extent have you felt supported:

by your colleagues?
by senior management?

Has this level of support remained the same throughout the project:

from your colleagues?
from senior management?

3. Your authority

Could you describe any changes that have taken place within your authority as a result of Branching Out e.g. policy changes, training programmes developed, cultural changes?

To what extent do you feel that you have contributed to these changes?

Fig. 8.1 *Learning Review Five (July 2001)*

4. Sustainability
In what ways would you like the work of Branching Out to be continued within your authority and beyond?
Do you think that this is realistic? Please explain your answer.

5. Overall satisfaction
Finally, how satisfied do you feel with the role you have played in Branching Out?

6. Any other comments
Your oppo rtunity to make a note of any thoughts or concerns you have about the impact of Branching Out on you as an individual.

Fig. 8.1 *continued*

Learning review findings

The findings of the five learning reviews revealed clear evidence of the changing attitudes and developing confidence of the participants. For example, the first review showed that just four months into the project, participants had already experienced significant changes in their reading habits and in their general attitude towards contemporary fiction and reader development work in general. However, they did not yet feel that they had been able to encourage similar changes in their colleagues or service users.

Nine months later, the second review showed that participants were now able to appreciate the opportunity that Branching Out had given them to increase their status within their authority, even in some cases to influence senior management decision-making processes. This had evidently given them a sense of both personal and professional achievement: 'I have made a major contribution to real change . . . and this gives me a sense of achievement', 'It [Branching Out] makes me feel involved at all levels of the department' (Train and Elkin, 2001b).

The overall message of this second review was that participants now felt that improvements were being made in their local authority as a result of the work they had done.

The third review, conducted seven months after the second, revealed that the Branching Out librarians undoubtedly appreciated the value of the training programme in which they were participating and the benefits of the reflective learning process, and were beginning to recognize the added value their work was giving to user services. They were now cascading their reader development work in accordance with the project remit, and a number of participants were beginning to recognize the impact of their work both on their local authority and even beyond: 'Staff awareness is good, and growing as I cascade training throughout the authority', 'at first constantly asking staff to get information was necessary but now the scheme has extended beyond the original libraries the comments are unsolicited and have been very positive' (Train and Elkin, 2001b).

It is apparent that although conducting one learning review would have been useful, it would have been an insufficient means of monitoring the personal and professional development of the Branching Out librarians throughout the three year period of the initiative. Short-term evaluation would not have revealed this invaluable form of data collection, which could be adapted by any library manager in order to justify the value of investing resources in a longer-term project.

Evaluation of Year 2 group projects

In the second year of Branching Out, participants were given the opportunity to work in small project development groups. One such example was Open Ticket, the world literature promotion developed and delivered by Opening the Book. A group of six Branching Out librarians worked in commercial partnership with Book Communications Ltd – a reading promotion agency in the private sector – to design and market the promotion. The evaluation of Open Ticket was devised in order to take into account its growing impact on the many parties involved, and included the following elements:

- Observation:
  - of project planning meetings
  - of training programme development meetings
  - of the training sessions themselves

- Obtaining feedback:
  - from Branching Out trainers: before and after delivering training
  - from trainees
  - from the Opening the Book project management team
  - from senior library managers
  - from project partners, including any future plans.

The evaluation of Open Ticket took place throughout the second year of Branching Out, and using the data collected during this period it became possible to detect changes in skills and confidence levels on the part of the librarians. For example, although each member of the group had delivered some form of training before working on the project, this was his or her first experience of helping to devise and deliver a complete training package to other library staff in their authority and beyond. At their presentation at the Branching Out conference in March 2000, members of the group listed three things that they felt they had learned during their work on the project:

- a range of different learning styles and how to incorporate these into training sessions
- the skills appropriate for designing successful training
- the difference between training and simply presenting information.

From theory to practice

As illustrated above, experiential learning theories advocating individual reflection can be used to support professional learning practice. In addition, professionals can derive personal benefits from experiential group learning, and can adapt experiential theory in order to devise training tools through which to share knowledge acquired.

The strength of the Branching Out reader development initiative as a model of professional learning lay in two areas. Firstly, the project remit was such that it supported the application of a theoretical framework to professional practice, thereby providing guidance to both the trainer and the trainee. Secondly, the learning methodology combined elements that encouraged both group interaction and individual reflection: as in Kolb's learning cycle (Figure 8.2), group members acquire knowledge through experimentation and experience, which is subsequently embedded through individual reflection. Following this process of reflection, the cycle recurs, as participants are encouraged to modify their experience as a result of their observation of or reflection on such an experience.

The effective combination of the ongoing training programme and the evaluation methodologies demonstrated the value of research to practice, and vice versa.

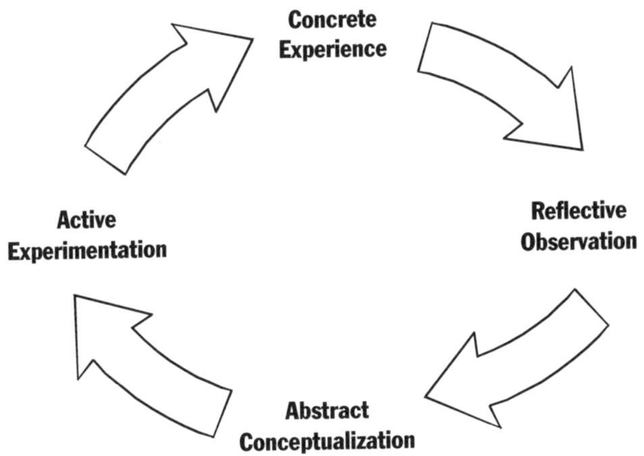

Fig. 8.2 *Kolb's learning cycle, taken from McLoughlin (1999)*

In summary

The evaluation of reader development projects is complex, as there is often no hypothesis to test, no clear solution to search for. The overall objective of the evaluation of Branching Out was to investigate the impact of participation over time on 34 staff from 34 different library services, each with varying levels of experience and status within their organization. In order to investigate such an impact, considerable triangulation of methods is necessary, as so many stakeholders are involved in such a large-scale initiative. This triangulation should not be set in stone from the outset; for a longitudinal project, methods can be usefully adapted as the project progresses.

The methods used to evaluate the Branching Out initiative addressed the less obviously quantifiable aspects of the work of a local authority, such as confidence development, attitudinal changes and skills development in its staff, who in turn provide a higher quality service to the end user. In the model presented above, evaluative methods are not merely used once, but are revisited and adapted according to developments in a constantly changing initiative. 'Traditional' quality measures tend to be static, measuring a single point in time, but the methodology outlined above has arguably enabled librarians to move away from the limitations of previous measures, with the evaluative focus transferred from systems to people.

The social audit

> At a time when so much emphasis is being placed on quality, standards and accountability, it should not come as a surprise that the academic world is spending time devising new ways of assessing the value and impact of organisations. At the same time, those of you responsible for managing and marketing library services are having to demonstrate their value to the public, policy makers and other stakeholders. However, serious difficulties can arise for researchers and practitioners alike if they try to deal with these issues using inappropriate tools. For example, tools used to demonstrate outputs may not be the same as those used to demonstrate outcomes. (Usherwood, 2002)

In the 1990s Usherwood, a former public library manager and now an academic, became aware of the applicability of the social audit method to the public library sector. Previously used in the corporate sector to measure the effect of an organization on society and frequently described as having 'no bottom line' (Boyle, 2000, 142), a social audit goes a stage further than the financial or environmental audit, considering an organization from many perspectives: 'it is no longer the rigid business of looking at the profits and nothing else' (Boyle, 2000, 143).

Boyle describes the potential outcomes of the audit as follows:

1. It can prevent organisations from deluding themselves that their public relations are ideal – but it can be embarrassing when the results become public knowledge.
2. It gives all stakeholders – whatever their position – an opportunity to speak out and be heard. This is a more objective approach than usual market research, which tends to consist largely of closed questions.
3. Rather than measuring standard 'performance', it measures reputation: 'it's about listening and distilling what people say about you' (146–8).

Critics of the social audit may feel that without numbers, a degree of accuracy is lost. Certainly, an audit of this nature will never result in rows of carefully analysed statistics that can be 'mapped' on to those of the previous year – or those of an organization – in order to determine future targets. Yet if organizations approach it with an open mind, and are prepared to act upon the findings, they can be extremely effective. It may not be 'measuring' in the conventional sense, but as Zadek, a well known social auditor, suggests, 'it's helping you count what counts' (in Boyle, 2000, 146).

The social audit and the public library sector

With colleagues from the Department of Information Studies in the University of Sheffield, Usherwood adapted the social audit methodology for use in public library services. The first social audits were undertaken in public library services in Newcastle upon Tyne and Somerset (Linley and Usherwood, 1998). The intention of these and subsequent audits is to provide a framework to enable professionals and policy makers to come to an informed judgement about the value and impact of public library services.

Following the audits of Newcastle and Somerset, Linley and Usherwood reported that the methodology had enabled them 'to identify some of the matches, mismatches and differences' between the social objectives of the services they were auditing, and their findings of the actual outcomes of such services' (1998, 88). They felt that they had devised an entirely qualitative method that would be of great value if repeated by other public librarians and their policy makers:

> we have attempted to evaluate library services in a new way. Rather than relying on outputs, such as the number of books issued, we have examined the outcomes, the impact and value of public libraries. Many of our conclusions are based on qualitative, if you like anecdotal, evidence. This is real world data that has been obtained in a rigorous way. We make no apology for our approach, and if there is one message that we want readers to take away from our report it is that, qualitative data, properly gathered, are valid evidence and . . . should be treated as such by politicians and professionals alike.
>
> (Linley and Usherwood 1998, 85)

The social audit and reader development

The social audits as described above were used to audit the social impact of an entire library service, albeit in a limited geographical area. However, the same methodology can also be applied on a smaller scale to investigate the value and impact of an individual element of the overall service.

'The Vital Link: reader development and basic skills' was an initiative that was funded via an award from the second year of the DCMS/Wolfson Public Libraries Challenge Fund for reader development (2001–2). Over a 12-month period, nine local authorities worked as a consortium, representing four English regions (the East of England, London, the North West, Yorkshire and the Humber). This consortium was managed by a group comprising representatives of the National Literacy Trust, the National Reading Campaign, The Reading Agency and two independent co-ordinators. The evaluation of the initiative was conducted by a team from the University of Sheffield, and combined the qualitative social audit approach with quantitative techniques used by the School of Education in previous evaluations of literacy initiatives.

The application of the social audit method to The Vital Link was intended to enable professionals and policy makers to come to an informed judgement about the value and impact of public libraries and reader development on people who were seeking to attain basic skills.

The 'starting point for any social audit approach is to identify and clarify the values against which the activities of the business or other type of organisation are to be judged' (Zadek and Evans, 1993). In the evaluation of The Vital Link, the starting point was therefore the stated objectives of the project, as cited in the original project proposal. The evaluative approach was then to crosscheck the views and perceptions of selected stakeholders, in order to determine to what extent these objectives had been achieved. The key stakeholders for this project were identified as:

- adult basic skills students
- basic skills tutors and managers
- library staff
- members of the project management group.

Prior to The Vital Link, there was assumed to be an obvious relationship between public libraries and the basic skills sector, but this had not been practicably demonstrated. Use of the social audit methodology facilitated the monitoring and recording of ways in which this relationship could become more tangible, investigating ways in which staff from both sectors could work together with a common aim. Considerable progress was made in beginning to reach the target group, and a significant body of knowledge acquired. The findings of the audit also revealed many examples of ways in which reader development could be used to enhance basic skills education, for example in encouraging self-direction and self-confidence. It was also felt that reader development could become part of the infrastructure of basic skills education (Train, Usherwood and Brooks, 2002).

Reviewing the first of the social audits conducted by the University of Sheffield, the American journal *Marketing Library Services* summarized the potential value of the social audit method to the public library sector as follows: 'if libraries . . . carry out a social audit then . . . they could well end up with the kind of images that marketing people could use to communicate to fund holders, members of the public, the media and so on. . . . It's a very powerful technique' (Lyon, 1998).

The benefits to reader development of a revised evaluative process

Thanks to recent changes in funding availability for public library projects from both regional and national arts and government, local authorities have been able to participate in funded reader development initiatives, and have in many cases been able to appreciate through experience the value of formative evaluation processes.

In the first instance, this value could be evident in securing further funding, but library managers should also be able to recognize the merit of evaluating a programme which is developmental, incremental, focusing on continuous improvement and innovation. Hopefully, participation in projects such as these has also underlined the dangers of more prescriptive measures of quality, which arguably stifle innovation and encourage participants to strive to reach a standard, rather than to exceed it.

Although the evaluation of the impact of an initiative on people is more difficult to undertake than the impact on systems, this altered focus is nonetheless more appropriate to the emerging qualitative, person-centred evaluation that initiatives such as Branching Out and the social audit method have brought to light and developed. These methodologies attempt to evaluate the intangible elements of a library service. To a large extent, these elements are those that the current Government frequently cites as its key concerns, such as life-long learning, social inclusion and access to ICT resources. It therefore follows that if measures are adopted that evaluate the impact of a library service on these areas, the data collected will surely enhance the overall monitoring process of that service.

As the nature of public sector funding changes, and each local authority is required to submit more and more evidence-based documentation as to the quality of the service it provides, it seems only reasonable to suggest that subscription to the 'new', quality-based performance measurements will subsequently enhance the standing of that local authority within the community it supports.

Conclusion

> 'If you can't measure something, you can't understand it; if you can't understand it, you can't control it; if you can't control it, you can't improve it (Harrington 1987, 103)

The current project culture in the field of reader development often discourages evaluation, because of the need to sustain or continue a service or project: if further funding or even salaries depend on the success of an initiative, organizations can understandably be reluctant to subject themselves to potential criticism.

Yet without evaluation and reflection, how can change occur? How can a service develop if its managers are unaware of its strengths and weaknesses, are unaware of ways in which it could be improved? Without an openness to change, services stagnate and eventually become irrelevant to the people they serve. This stagnation could be particularly damaging, given that all public sector organizations are required to adapt their services to the current government agenda. The social inclusion agenda, for example, is one of which all public library services must now be accurately aware: as society evolves, there is a requirement to deliver targeted services to different disenfranchised groups. In society the needs of people, and therefore of library users, are changing, and the measurement of such needs necessitates more than just short-term, quantitative methods.

Where evaluation does occur, the traditional project cycle frequently includes only summative evaluation, a report of perceived change written at the end of the project. The accuracy of the findings contained within such documents can be questionable, as perceived change is not measured change. As Boyle suggests, 'there are times when we simply have to try measuring the unmeasurable – that is the nature of the counting crisis in education, business and politics' (2000, 219). An accurate measurement of the more 'intangible' elements of a service does not necessarily require quantitative methods; the longitudinal and reflective approaches to measurement in the evaluation of the Branching Out initiative and in the development of the social audit methodology can be highly effective and rigorous means of investigating the value and impact of a service or project on a wide range of people.

Quantitative and qualitative methods are equally valid, but not necessarily to measure the same activity: we need to be aware why we are using a particular evaluative method, and equally importantly, how we are going to use the results. As Riggs (1998) observes, 'even though qualitative research is different from quantitative research, both must be evaluated on the same basis; that is, does it make a significant contribution to the knowledge base and/or advance theory?'

The role of library and information science researchers has arguably changed in recent years: with the current focus on evaluation, auditing and monitoring in the public sector, they have an opportunity to contribute to the future of reader development services. They can provide library managers with an unbiased audit of a reader-centred service or services, and it is this neutrality which increases the validity of the exercise, thereby increasing the credibility of the service with other libraries and even with other sectors. With regular adaptation of evaluative methodologies to the current social priorities, academic evaluation and research can be extremely valuable to public library services.

> In the maelstrom of change and pace acceleration that surrounds us today in the library and information world, everyone is seeking touchstones for a future increasingly unpredictable. There is a sense that nothing that has gone before can be a predictor of what is to come – we occupy new and fused territories with increasingly mature customer or client expectations. I was once happy to wait in a queue at a bank to get some money out – now if the ATM experience takes more than a minute I am frustrated. This amnesia of the recent past is the price of progress and is equally true in our environment. New users, new uses of services are exploding and that means a quite different approach to the reflective nature of research. (Kempster, 2002)

References and further reading

Boyle, D. (2000) *The Tyranny of Numbers: why counting can't make us happy*, London, HarperCollins.

Brannen, J. (ed.) (1992) *Mixing Methods: qualitative and quantitative research*, Avebury, Ashgate Publishing Company.

Brophy, P. and Coulling, K. (1996) *Quality Management for Information and Library Management*, Aldershot, Aslib Gower.

Comedia (1993) *Borrowed Time? The future of public libraries in the United Kingdom*, Bournes Green, Comedia.

Dewey, J. (1963) Experience and Education, rev. edn, Kappa Delta Pi lecture series, London, Collier-Macmillan.

Forrest, T. (2001) Who's Afraid of Those Declining Adult Issues?, *Library Association Record*, **103** (3), 168–9.

Forrest, T. (2002) Interview with the author.

Gorman, G. E. and Clayton, P. (1997) *Qualitative Research for the Information Professional: a practical handbook*, London, Library Association Publishing.

Great Britain. Audit Commission (1999) *Best Assured: the role of the Audit Commission in Best Value*, London, The Audit Commission.

Great Britain. Audit Commission (2000) *Seeing is Believing*, London, The Audit Commission.

Great Britain. Audit Commission (2002) *Building Better Library Services: learning from audit, inspection and research*, London, The Audit Commission. Also available at http://ww2.audit-commission.gov.uk/publications/lfair_libraries.shtml. [Accessed 13.03.03]

Great Britain. Department for Culture, Media and Sport (2001) *DCMS/Wolfson Public Libraries*

Challenge Fund Annual Report 1999–2000, London, DCMS. Also available at www.dcms.gov.uk/heritage/wolfson_libraries.html. [Accessed 13.03.03]

Harrington, H. J. (1987) *The Improvement Process*, New York, McGraw-Hill.

Hatten, R., Knapp, D. and Salona, R. (1997) Action Research: comparison with the concepts of 'the reflective practitioner' and 'quality assurance'. In Hughes, I. (ed.), *Action research electronic reader*, Sydney, The University of Sydney. Also available at www.cchs.usyd.edu.au/arow/reader/rdr.htm. [Accessed 13.03.03]

Kempster, G. (2002) *So What? The power of action centred research to change perceptions*, Library and Information Research Group annual lecture, London, 27 March, unpublished.

Kinnell Evans, M. (2000), *Quality Management and Self Assessment Tools for Public Libraries*. In 66th IFLA Council and General Conference, Jerusalem, Israel, 13–18 August 2000. Available at www.ifla.org/IV/ifla66/papers/112-126e.htm. [Accessed 13.03.03]

Linley, R. and Usherwood, B. (1998) *New Measures for the New Library: a social audit of public libraries*, Sheffield, University of Sheffield.

Lyon, J. (1998) Measuring the Unmeasurable Value, *Marketing Library Services*, **12** (8), 4–5.

McLoughlin, C. (1999) The Implications of the Research Literature on Learning Styles for the Design of Instructional Material, *Australian Journal of Educational Technology*, **15** (3), 222–41. Also available at http://cleo.murdoch.edu.au/ajet/ajet15/mcloughlin.html. [Accessed 13.03.03]

Miles, M. B. and Huberman, A. M. (1994) *Qualitative Data Analysis: an expanded sourcebook*, London, Sage Publications.

Myers, M. D. (1997) Qualitative Research in Information Systems, *MIS Quarterly*, **21** (2), June 1997, 241–2. Also available at www.auckland.ac.nz/msis/isworld/. [Accessed 13.03.03]

O'Rourke, R. (1994) *Written on the Margins: creative writing and adult education in Cleveland*, Leeds, University of Leeds.

Riggs, D. E. (1998) Let Us Stop Apologising for Qualitative Research, *College and Research Libraries*, **59** (5), September. Also available at www.ala.org/acrl/srlsep98.html#editorial. [Accessed 13.03.03]

Rist, R. C. (1994) Influencing the Policy Process with Qualitative Research. In Denzin, N. K. and Lincoln, Y. S. (eds), *Handbook of Qualitative Research*, London, Sage Publications.

Ruspini, E. (2000) Longitudinal Research in the Social Sciences, *Social Research Update*, **28** (Spring), University of Surrey. Available at www.soc.surrey.ac.uk/sru/SRU28.html. [Accessed 13.03.03]

Schön, D. A. (1991) *The Reflective Practitioner: how professionals think in action*, London, Kogan Page.

SCL (1998) *Branching Out: project application*, London, Society of Chief Librarians.

Tashakkori, A. and Teddlie, C. (1998) *Mixed Methodology: combining qualitative and quantitative approaches*, London, Sage Publications.

Train, B. (2001) *Mind's Eye Evaluation Report*, Birmingham, University of Central England.

Train, B. and Elkin, J. (2001a) Branching Out: a model for experiential learning in professional practice, *Journal of Librarianship and Information Science*, **33** (2), 68–74.

Train, B. and Elkin, J. (2001b) *Branching Out: overview of evaluation findings*, Birmingham, University of Central England. Available at www.cie.uce.ac.uk/cirt/projects/past/branching.htm. [Accessed 13.03.03]

Train, B., Usherwood, B. and Brooks, G. (2002) *The Vital Link: an evaluation report*, Sheffield, University of Sheffield.

Usherwood, B. (1996) *Rediscovering Public Library Management*, London, Library Association Publishing.

Usherwood, B. (2002) Accounting for Outcomes: demonstrating the impact of public libraries, *Australian Public Libraries and Information Services*, **15** (1), 12

Van Riel, R. (1998), *Creating the Readership for Literature in Translation*, presentation to international conference in 1998 at University of East Anglia, British Centre for Literary Translation, unpublished.

Van Riel, R. (2002) Interview with the author.

Wallis, M. (2002) Personal communication with the author.

Wallis, M., Moore, N. and Marshall, A. (2002) *Reading our Future: evaluation of the DCMS/Wolfson Public Libraries Challenge Fund 2000–2001*, Library and Information Commission Research Report 134, London, Resource: The Council for Museums, Archives and Libraries.

Zadek, S. and Evans, R. (1993) *Auditing the Market: a practical approach to social auditing*, Gateshead, Traidcraft/New Economics Foundation.

9
Overview and summary

This book has attempted to show the benefits of reading for people of all ages, backgrounds and needs. It suggests that these very individual benefits and intimate reactions to reading will survive for the foreseeable future, and that books are unlikely ever to be replaced by electronic or digital alternatives. Technology, though, will enhance access to books otherwise unobtainable, improve an individual's ability to read with special aids and be of valuable assistance in locating reading materials.

Value of reading

Readers talk about being 'lost in a book' – distanced from the world around them, suspending disbelief, totally absorbed in their reading. Readers of all kinds feel that reading has made a difference to their individual lives. Reading can give joy, satisfaction and pleasure throughout life, from babyhood to old age and at varying levels from intellectual satisfaction to a simple vicarious experience. Reading can educate, inform, help to develop language and vocabulary, and enrich the imagination. Reading can be life enhancing, health enhancing, stress relieving and therapeutic. Reading can bring freedom, empowerment and personal development for the human being, maybe particularly in those countries in which individual freedom is severely restricted. The importance of introducing children to language and reading early in life is recognized throughout the world. Early reading brings life-long reading.

In a culturally diverse society, all members of that society, whatever their racial or cultural background should be able to find themselves reflected in books and reading choices. The concept of books as bridges to international understanding is not a new one but is particularly applicable in today's global society. Readers with special needs should similarly have access to literature which celebrates diversity through reading for everyone whatever their needs, whether they are physical, mental or associated with being excluded from society in some way.

Sharing reading

Readers talk about the solitary pleasure of reading but also recognize that reading brings social opportunities, those of belonging to a community of readers, whether formally, informally or virtually and globally. Sharing with friends, colleagues, within the family, have different but equally beneficial outcomes. For parents and children, it may be sharing the same frame of reference and crucial for building and sustaining relationships and providing stability and security.

Reading aloud to children at bedtime has long been a favourite pastime for parents who recognize the mutual benefits of this secure bonding at the end of a busy day. Reading aloud at storytelling and poetry-reading sessions for adults as well as children remains a popular public activity and one that has grown rather than declined in recent years. Indeed, story remains the way in which we communicate our ideas and experiences with others, even within a business and professional context.

Libraries and reading

Throughout this book, the role of libraries has emerged as instrumental in allowing individuals easy and free access to books and reading materials, as well as increasingly playing a role in supporting the reader and reader development. The growth of reader development activities has enhanced public library service provision to all age groups in the UK, and reading as a cultural activity is regarded by many as a potential means of achieving social change. Socially inclusive projects have been initiated and sustained, and in a number of cases such work has become part of core service provision.

Public libraries, in theory if not always in practice, provide a socially inclusive cultural environment for everyone regardless of age, gender, background, ability, ethnic origin or wealth. They can offer a place of sanctuary that is welcoming to all, non-judgemental, non-competitive and non-accrediting, contributing significantly to social inclusion. However, for many so-called 'excluded' groups, with no tradition of using them, libraries can be seen as alien, hostile environments, with little or no relevance to their lives or anyone known to them. This can pose significant challenges for libraries, because clearly they have a responsibility to serve all communities and recognize all elements of society in any work with readers.

For many of the readers identified in this book, particularly those with special needs due to some physical disability or as a result of being institutionalized or housebound, the library takes on a particularly crucial role, in terms of allowing access to reading materials in appropriate formats or at appropriate levels, for example for poor readers. It is here that the professional sensitivities of the prison librarian, hospital librarian or librarian in some other specialist institution come into play and where reader development takes on a different but no less valuable hue.

Reader development

Public and school librarians for many decades have worked with children supporting and helping their reading and reading choices. It is only within the last ten years or so that the growth in reader development in libraries has begun to fully address adult readers' reading needs and reading choices. Over that period, librarians have increasingly become champions of reading, with reader development work being seen as fundamental to cultural and community development.

But a change in library culture was needed for this to happen. Interestingly, the catalyst for change in the UK largely began outside the library profession itself, through independent reading promotion agencies, such as Opening The Book and Well Worth Reading.

Training

The skills required for reader development work are a mixture of professional and personal skills, including self-confidence and respect for individuals – whatever their background or reading needs; communication skills; book knowledge; promotional skills; enthusiasm and commitment. All library staff have a role to play in reader development and can influence its impact in the workplace. Thus appropriate and ongoing training and the ability to cascade training to all staff becomes particularly important. The Branching Out initiative recognized this as a basic requirement. It had considerable impact in terms of improving staff knowledge of contemporary literature, their awareness of reader needs, acquisition of training skills, understanding of sustainable models of partnerships and focused stock selection and promotion, as well as on the use of ICT as a reader development tool.

Outreach work, attempting to reach those who for many reasons do not currently use libraries, presents a particular challenge: what is it appropriate for librarians who lack prior experience in this area to become involved in? Allied to this is the issue of identifying particular training and awareness-raising needs. Librarians are often very keen to support the social inclusion agenda and, indeed, believe they have been doing this for many years. But Vincent (private communication with the author, 2002) raises the issue of librarians getting involved in areas of work without the necessary development of expertise. Library staff working in inappropriate areas without a proper training and support system could potentially aggravate an already difficult situation.

Partnerships

Partnership working is increasingly important to libraries wanting to develop and expand their work. Partnerships, whether with the public or private sector, need to be beneficial to both parties, leading to mutual sharing of expertise and/or resources. Additional funds potentially available from partnership support may help to provide a better-quality and higher-profile service and, through high-quality, professional materials, may raise the profile of libraries in terms of how they might support other local council work. Partnerships require good co-ordination and, ideally, sustainable relationships.

Recent developments in the UK have been dominated by the recent bidding and project culture. Growth in reader development activity has been dominated by such funding opportunities, in particular the DCMS/Wolfson Public Libraries Challenge Fund, which in 2000–1 and 2001–2, concentrated in part on funding reader development projects, to the tune of £4 million.

There are undoubtedly huge benefits from extra funding: to jump start new ideas and new initiatives; to allow for experimentation and opportunities to trial new ways of working and new methods of service delivery before introducing them to the service as a whole. Under normal circumstances, financial constraints in authorities allow little opportunity for experimentation.

Evaluation

Effective and independent evaluation of the quality and impact of individual projects and how good practice can be carried forward and shared is an area that is growing in respectability and credibility, with reference to project development, sustainability and effective management. Quantitative and qualitative methods of evaluation are equally valid, but not necessarily to measure the same activity. It is necessary to be clear why a particular evaluative method is being used, and equally importantly, how the results are to be used.

The role of library and information science researchers has arguably changed in recent years: with the current focus on evaluation, auditing and monitoring in the public sector, they have an opportunity to inform the development of public library services. The researchers can provide library managers with an unbiased audit of a service or services. Neutrality increases the validity of the exercise, thereby increasing the credibility of the service with other libraries and even with other sectors.

Advocacy

It is in the area of long-term sustainability, promotion, sharing of expertise, economies of scale and speaking with a common voice that advocacy agencies play an increasingly significant role. Advocacy for libraries is important if the unique role of libraries in the nation's reading is to be effectively highlighted and brought to the attention of decision makers and policy makers. The place of reading in the current Government's agenda is part of this advocacy but needs promoting actively if it is not to be undervalued. Reading contributes to social inclusion, citizenship, life-long learning, educational standards, lifeskills, creativity, community cohesion, and economic growth.

The future of reader development

Reader development work with adults is still relatively new and therefore potentially vulnerable. Concerns have been expressed about its sustainability once major funding opportunities, such as DCMS/Wolfson Reader Development challenge funding have ceased. However, there is a marked confidence in the area. The concentration and refocusing of public libraries' attention on the vital relationship with the culture of reading and an engagement with contemporary literature has provided something of a re-awakening and re-energizing which promises a dynamic future for the public library system.

The Audit Commission's Best Value inspection now requires library services to focus on reader development. The process of producing library plans for DCMS has also been essential in raising the profile of reader development. Reader development has thus become more embedded in the guidelines and the resulting plans. Reader development in libraries has also become a much higher-profile activity, with its value and impact recognized by other agencies, in both the public sector and the commercial world.

ICT and reading

The internet has proved to be a powerful promotional tool, used by libraries, publishers and booksellers to sell and promote products, and has the potential to support and encourage reading and reader development and facilitate contact between global reading communities and reading groups.

Significant amounts of UK government funding have been invested through the New Opportunities Fund (NOF) in establishing the People's Network, in developing digital content and in training librarians to use technology effectively to both retrieve information and support reading. This has had the benefit of raising considerably the profile of public libraries in the digital age.

International co-operation and communication and the sharing of professional experience and expertise globally is also aided by using digital communication as a means of freeing the individual from the limitations of geography. Virtual reading communities and reading groups aided by technology can be genuinely global. The full potential of the internet has yet to be fully explored but this opens up all kinds of exciting and imaginative opportunities for the future.

The future of reading

Who can predict what the future may hold? What a sad world it would be, though, without books and the myriad of reading opportunities they offer to people of all kinds and of all ages. Readers can be empowered to enjoy, to share and expand their reading. Pre-readers can be caught during babyhood to ensure they become readers for life. Readers should be confident and sufficiently relaxed to be emotionally moved, excited or frightened by whatever they are reading, genuinely absorbed in the story. Technology can support and enhance reading and reading opportunities but never be a total substitute.

BOOK

An unattributed message posted on many listservs recently caused many a wry smile amongst technophobes and technophiles alike:

> Introducing the new Bio-Optic Knowledge device, trade-named – **BOOK**.
>
> - **BOOK** is a revolutionary break-through in technology: no wires, no electric circuits, no batteries, nothing to be connected or switched on. It's so easy to use, even a child can operate it. Compact and portable, it can be used anywhere – even sitting in an armchair by the fire – yet it is powerful enough to hold as much information as a CD-ROM disc.
> - **BOOK** is constructed of sequentially numbered sheets of paper (recyclable), each capable of holding thousands of bits of information. The pages are locked together with a custom-fit device called a binder which keeps the sheets in their correct sequence.
> - Opaque Paper Technology (OPT) allows manufacturers to use both sides of the sheet, doubling the information density and cutting costs. Experts are divided on the prospects for further increases in information density; for now, **BOOK**s with more information simply use more pages. Each sheet is scanned optically, registering information directly into your brain. A flick of the finger takes you to the next sheet.
> - **BOOK** may be taken up at any time and used merely by opening it.
> - **BOOK** never crashes or requires rebooting, though, like other devices, it can become damaged if coffee is spilled on it or it becomes unusable if dropped too many times on a hard surface. The 'browse' feature allows you to move instantly to any sheet, and move forward or backward as you wish. Many come with an 'index' feature, which pin-points the exact location of any selected information for instant retrieval.
> - An optional 'bookmark' accessory allows you to open **BOOK** to the exact place you left it in a previous session – even if the **BOOK** has been closed. Bookmarks fit universal design standards; thus a single bookmark can be used in **BOOK**s by various manufacturers. Conversely, numerous bookmarks can be used in a single **BOOK** if

the user wants to store numerous views at once. The number is limited only by the number of pages in the **BOOK**.

- You can also make personal notes next to **BOOK** text entries with optional programming tools, Portable Erasable Nib Cryptic Intercommunication Language Styli (PENCILS).
- Portable, durable, and affordable, **BOOK** is being hailed as a precursor of a new entertainment wave. **BOOK**'s appeal seems so certain that thousands of content creators have committed to the platform and investors are reportedly flocking to invest.

Index